CRIME
in America

CRIME
in America

By Estes Kefauver

Chairman of the Senate Crime Investigating Committee
(May 10, 1950–May 1, 1951)

Edited and with an Introduction by SIDNEY SHALETT

GREENWOOD PRESS, PUBLISHERS
NEW YORK   1968

The Library of Congress cataloged this book as follows:

Kefauver, Estes, 1903–1963.
    Crime in America. Edited and with an introd. by Sidney
    Shalett. ₁1st ed.₎ New York, Greenwood Press, 1968 ₍ᶜ1951₎
      xvi, 333 p. illus., ports. 22 cm.

      "Based upon the testimony taken at the hearings and upon the
    reports of the committee to the Senate, prior to May 1, 1951."

      1. Crime and criminals—U. S.   I. U. S. Congress. Senate.
    Special Committee to Investigate Organized Crime in Interstate
    Commerce. Investigation of crime in interstate commerce. II. Title.

HV6775.K4 1968   364'.9'73   68–8062

Library of Congress   ₍3₎

Reprinted in 1968 by Greenwood Press, Inc.,
51 Riverside Avenue, Westport, Conn. 06880

Library of Congress catalog card number 68-8062
ISBN 0-8371-0126-3

Printed in the United States of America

10 9 8 7 6 5 4 3

To my father, ROBERT COOKE KEFAUVER, whose long and honorable life has been my inspiration; and to the people of America, who, I hope, will be sufficiently aroused to help us, through public opinion and legislative action, to strangle crime in America, this volume is dedicated.

ESTES KEFAUVER

AUTHOR'S NOTE

This account of *Crime in America* is based upon the testimony taken at the hearings and upon the reports of the committee to the Senate, prior to May 1, 1951.

E.K.

CONTENTS

Estes Kefauver

By SIDNEY SHALETT

IN THE spring of 1951 the American people were
a little sick of politicians. Some of the con-
temporary exhibitions of what passed for political morality didn't sit well against the gnawing heartache
of the Korean war and the awful feeling that here we go again.
Rising taxes and the return of economic restrictions the people
could take, though they didn't like it. But when they saw their
children being drilled from kindergarten up to lie down on the
dirt and cover their heads with their hands as protection
against the atom bomb that the Russians were supposed to
drop on us, the people were heartsore and angry—and, Amer-
icanlike, they started looking around for a whipping boy.
Rightly or wrongly, the politicians filled the bill.

That same spring—and it was a typically American sort of
paradox—a man who must be listed, by vocation, at least, as a
politician became a national symbol to the people of everything
a politician wasn't. That man was Estes Kefauver, United
States senator from Tennessee, and chairman, from May 10,
1950, to May 1, 1951, of the Special Committee to Investigate
Crime in Interstate Commerce—popularly known as the

Kefauver Committee. The tall, broad-shouldered Tennessean with the firm jaw, the honest, searching eyes behind the old-fashioned glasses, the soft-spoken, courteous, fair, but firm manner, became the conscience of America. As Senator Tobey, his Republican colleague, put it in an eloquent tribute at one of the final hearings, "This man, Estes Kefauver, had in his heart a need of decency in America." The people heard him, saw him (thanks to the youthful television industry), and liked him.

His message was nothing that was particularly new to Americans: our cynical breed always had known (a) that there were a lot of criminals; (b) that there were a lot of politicians who were no better than criminals; and (c) that the criminals and politicians all too often operated hand in hand to the great detriment of John Q. Public. But Kefauver patiently dug out facts about the stinking mess, and he told the story to the public in a way that made all but the most cynical want to get out and do something about it. The phenomenal thing is that, in many communities, the citizens, through newly formed Crime Commissions inspired by the Kefauver Committee, are doing something about it.

It was no surprise to those of us who have known Estes Kefauver since he was a young lawyer in Chattanooga, Tennessee, and who have watched him in Congress, that he conducted himself so effectively as chairman of the Senate Crime Investigating Committee. Kefauver always has been a mixture of inborn gentleness and gentlemanliness laced with iron. He never rants or raves when locked in dispute with some opponent, but he has an inexorable habit of achieving what he fights for. An independent Southern Democrat with no patience for Dixiecratism, he was best known politically before the crime hearings for donning a coonskin cap—a remarkable act for him, for he definitely is not an extroverted showman —and going out to win his Senate seat over the vicious, almost fanatical opposition of Boss Crump's then powerful Tennessee machine. As a Democrat, he didn't particularly enjoy turning the merciless spotlight on some of the conditions he found in Chicago, Kansas City, etc., but he did it anyhow.

Kefauver's handling of the crime hearings was a very special feat. To a lesser man, such an assignment could have been political suicide. The temptation to become a publicity-grabber, a table-thumper, a modern Torquemada was great. Indeed, some of Kefauver's colleagues in the Senate predicted—and rather hoped—that he would cut his own throat in the precarious process of becoming the nation's Number One crime buster. Some Democrats were suspicious of him because he always has been something of a political maverick who places personal ideals and independence above blind party allegiance. Some Republicans, on the other hand, hollered that the Tennessee Democrat surely would "whitewash" the sins of his own party. (Before he was through, a newspaper highly critical of the Administration, in tribute to the thoroughly honest job Kefauver did, ran a headline saying: "WHITEWASH" BRUSH WITH TAR ON IT?)

Kefauver avoided the pitfalls forecast for him. He conducted hearings with the dignity of an old-school Supreme Court justice. In his contacts with the press and other public information media during the twelve months that the spotlight was constantly upon him, his demeanor remained modest, courteous, and intelligent. His technique for getting facts out of reluctant hoodlums of the "I Refuse to Answer" school was highly effective; the Tennessee coon hunter just kept on asking questions, quietly but firmly, until the hoodlums usually became mesmerized and began answering in spite of everything, including the lessons carefully taught them by expensive mouthpieces. Never did he browbeat witnesses, but the hoodlums came to fear Kefauver with an almost psychotic dread. In fact "Kefauveritis," that mysterious ailment that struck crooks and politicians just before they were about to be subpoenaed, became a widely discussed national malady. It manifested itself in unexpected heart attacks, laryngitis, nervous breakdowns, appendicitis, and/or acute desire for privacy;

the most pronounced symptom on the part of the victims was an irresistible compulsion to travel—far away from Kefauver.

Physically, Kefauver performed a job as committee chairman that would have shattered the physique of a lesser man; in the early days of the committee he conducted most of the hearings singlehanded. All in all, he traveled 52,380 miles on committee business and conducted hearings on ninety-two separate days, many of which included night sessions. Fortunately Kefauver is an old University of Tennessee football tackle, whose gridiron nickname was "Old Ironsides," so he bore up pretty well.

Estes Kefauver always has been counted as an intelligent, constructive, definitely non-demagogic member of Congress, in both the House and the Senate. What many persons do not know is that he is a remarkable person as well as a remarkable senator. Even at the height of his fame Kefauver never showed any signs of becoming one of those well-known Washington types about whom they coined the cliché, "He can strut sitting down." A little incident occurred just before he relinquished chairmanship of the Kefauver Committee that perfectly illustrates his non-stuffiness. It happened on a busy day when, after a full schedule of committee meetings and floor debate, the senator had to rush to a dinner for the Tennessee D.A.R. Black tie was required, so to save time Mrs. Kefauver brought his dinner clothes to the office. She forgot his shoes, and the senator happened to be wearing tan shoes that day. There wasn't time for another trip home so, wondering what the ladies were going to think about him sartorially, he started down the elevator in the Senate Office Building. He brightened up when he saw that the elevator boy, a tall lad with big feet, was wearing black shoes. "Buddy," said the Tennessean, "what size shoes you wear?" "Twelves, Senator," said the elevator boy, who happened to be new on the job. "Would you mind swapping shoes with me for the evening?" asked the senator, who also wears twelves. "Man!" exclaimed the elevator boy, bending over to unlace his footgear. "Only two weeks in Washington and I'm already stepping into a senator's shoes!"

Whenever his Senate duties give him time for it, which is all too seldom, he hugely enjoys family life with his lovely and witty wife, Nancy, and their four attractive and energetic children. Almost any Sunday, if they can catch him in town, the kids have no trouble inveigling him into their more active games. It is an awesome sight of a Sunday morning in the Kefauver neighborhood to see the 6-foot 3-inch senator being pulled on roller skates by Linda, Diane, and David (Gail Estes is still too little). One Sunday during the peak of excitement over Costello and O'Dwyer, Linda even got him on a pogo stick.

Kefauver's capture of the public imagination was spectacular. The pleasant face, the kindly, courteous manner took hold. Radio and TV programs beseeched him for appearances; every columnist printed items, analyses, or anecdotes about him. His fan mail was monumental and for the most part highly favorable. "I was deeply moved by the quietly eloquent, almost Lincolnesque quality of your words," wrote a New Orleans housewife. The mighty Senator Tom Connally of Texas, after he had slipped up and made the famous remark over the radio that Senator Kefauver seemed to be "off chasing crapshooters," wrote that "it was merely an attempt at facetiousness" with "no discourtesy" or "lack of appreciation" intended. A lady from Oakland reported: "My husband started to repair a screen door at the noon recess, but was so interested in the broadcast, he did not finish the job yet. We watched the whole day." From St. Louis came a wire: "I am a small time racketeer. . . . Don't know nothing but think you are a swell guy." A "lifelong Republican" from San Francisco wrote that he had decided "I'd like the privilege and pleasure of voting for you for the next President of the United States."

There were a lot of those Kefauver-for-President letters, by the way. In Tennessee, Kefauver-for-President clubs already have been formed. Though the senator himself says he wants no part of it and is not seeking the presidency, anything can happen. Political lightning definitely has struck the man from

Tennessee. It may not come in '52, but Kefauver is only forty-eight. The Crime Committee job which he did so magnificently will not be his last public service. The American people, who already have demonstrated how much they like him, a e not likely to forget him.

CRIME
in America

CHAPTER 1

BIRTH OF THE CRIME COMMITTEE

THE Senate Crime Investigating Committee came into being because of an idea and an ideal. Ordinarily, unless prodded by some unusual circumstances, Americans don't think much about the existence and influence of organized crime; they know vaguely that it is there, and they let it go at that. For some years, however—since the days when I was a young lawyer interested in good government in Tennessee—I had been troubled by the unpleasant realization that there was a tie-up between crime and politics. This realization disturbed and offended me, but I believed, as Woodrow Wilson once wrote, that "very few men are unequal to a danger which they see and understand." Later, as a member of the House of Representatives, I was named chairman of a judiciary subcommittee to investigate the conduct of a crooked federal district judge in Pennsylvania. In the process of gathering the evidence that subsequently resulted in the retirement of this man who disgraced his robes, the full import of what rottenness in public life can do to our country came home to me. From then on the subject never was far from my mind.

The idea stayed with me when I became a member of the United States Senate in January 1949. More and more I was concerned with the phenomenon of politico-criminal corruption and what it was doing to the country. Early in 1950 an accumulation of events highlighted the desperate need for learning the real facts about crime in America. The American Municipal Association, alarmed by the effects of interstate crime operations on local governments, had passed a resolution calling for federal consideration of the problem. Newspapers—and the free press is one of our democracy's most potent weapons—were making startling disclosures about the power of modern crimesters, the white-collar successors to the Al Capones of an earlier era. The Conference on Organized Crime, called by Attorney General J. Howard McGrath in February 1950, focused additional attention on the cancer of organized crime.

Some six weeks before the Attorney General's conference I had felt the time had come to put Woodrow Wilson's words to the test and demonstrate that there is nothing the American people cannot overcome if they know the facts. So I took the issue to the floor of the United States Senate by introducing a bill calling for a full-scale Senate investigation of crime in interstate commerce. After a long and difficult fight the Senate Crime Committee—formally known as the Special Committee to Investigate Organized Crime in Interstate Commerce—was born. I became chairman on May 10, 1950, and served in that capacity until May 1, 1951.

As chairman, I was extremely fortunate in having the backing of four able colleagues. These were Senator Herbert R. O'Conor, Democrat, of Maryland, whose legal training and experience helped bring clarity to the shaping of many important decisions and to whom I turned over chairmanship of the committee when I felt the time had come for me to step down; Senator Lester C. Hunt, Democrat, of Wyoming, whose great gift for common sense and arriving at sound decisions contributed much stability to our deliberations; Senator Alexander Wiley, Republican, of Wisconsin, whose shrewd questioning trapped a number of hoodlums who thought they could flout the committee with contemptuous or perjured responses; and that remarkable moral battler, Senator Charles W. Tobey, Republican, of New Hampshire, who actually unnerved many hardened thugs and corrupt public officials by his indignant castigations of their misdeeds.

Serving on the Crime Committee was a tremendous emotional experience for all of us. For me, it became more than merely a committee appointment: it became a way of life. For twelve months, in committee hearings which often ran from morning until late at night; in staff meetings where we charted our next investigations; in the evenings at home when I pored over transcripts and memoranda; on trains and planes traveling to the hearings, the work of the committee rarely was out of my mind. Almost everything conceivable happened to me: in San Francisco someone stole my hat in the federal courthouse; in Los Angeles a youngster grabbed me in the courthouse corridor as I walked past a telephone booth and asked me to say a word to "Mom"; back in Washington my mail brought me a post card from Alcatraz, inscribed simply, "Wish you were here." The worst thing that happened was that I became a stranger to my three older children, ages nine, five, and three, and didn't get much of a chance to become acquainted with our baby, who was born while the crime hearings were in progress. The older children used to call me "that man on television," and the maid, who had to wipe away the finger marks, told me they loved to pat my face on the cold glass TV screen.

Only an extremely able staff in my senatorial office made it possible for me to keep up with my other duties as a United States senator, and I must admit I neglected my home state of Tennessee in a manner not to my liking. I am proud, however, that thousands of the people at home made it clear to me, through personal letters and telephone calls, that they regarded the work I was doing as of sufficient urgency to justify the temporary neglect.

The emotional uplift came in the way that people everywhere voiced their approval of what we were trying to do.

It made me feel small and humble—but proud of the task
I had been given to do. In the beginning public reaction was
slow. Our early sessions were closed hearings, at which we
carefully developed the evidence to be followed up later in
public hearings. We were feeling our way cautiously, for we
were blazing a trail that no Senate committee ever before had
followed. On occasions in the past Senate committees had
probed specialized aspects of criminal activities, but ours was
the first congressional committee in the history of the country
with a mandate to conduct an all-encompassing investigation
of organized interstate crime.

The public at first was not sure what we were up to; politicians of both parties were ready to take a swing at us. "Is
this to be an investigation or a cover-up?" Minority Leader
Wherry, the Voice of the GOP on the Senate floor, demanded
during debate about our creation. Even Republican Committee Member Wiley, in the earlier days of our existence, while
he was engaged himself in a bitterly partisan fight for re-
election, sometimes sniped at us before he found out what we
really were going to do; after he became convinced that the
committee had no partisan ax to grind, however, we had no
sturdier defender.

There even was a certain amount of ridicule attached to
service on the Kefauver Committee. As my good friend and
colleague, the inimitable Senator Tom Connally of Texas, remarked at a joint meeting of the Senate Foreign Relations and
Armed Services committees one morning when I did not answer the roll call because I was presiding at a crime hearing,
"He's off chasing crapshooters." Realizing that the proceedings
were on the air and his remarks were being broadcast, the
senator hastily added: "That's off the record!" Knowing how
the senator from Texas enjoys a quip, I didn't take his remark
to heart; later Senator Connally wrote me handsomely that his
remark "was merely an attempt at facetiousness." "Let me say,"
he noted, "that I intended no discourtesy to you or . . . any
lack of appreciation of the work you were engaged in. In fact,
I have followed with great interest the revelations developed

by the committee, and I want to take this occasion to congratulate you and the other members of your committee on the splendid public service you have rendered."

As I look back on the struggle to set up the committee I sometimes wonder that we were ever able to bring it into existence. In the first place there was a certain amount of powerful opposition—particularly with an election year coming up—to the idea of having a crime investigation at all. With the aid of some of my colleagues on both sides of the aisle, I kept pressing for a crime investigation. The idea received powerful editorial support from the newspapers of America, and soon it caught hold to such an extent that the opponents could not halt it. The opposition, however, engaged in "strategic withdrawal" rather than unconditional surrender; they decided that if they couldn't lick us they would at least control us. Partisan politics entered frankly into this phase. There was maneuvering on both sides of the aisle to see who would control the committee. My original resolution proposed that the investigation be conducted by a subcommittee of the standing Judiciary Committee, of which I was a member. My resolution thereupon had to be studied and reported out by the Judiciary Committee, headed by Senator Pat McCarran, and in this fine-tooth-comb process every word and every comma was weighed and reweighed.

Then a tussle developed as to whether the Judiciary Committee or the Interstate and Foreign Commerce Committee, also an eager contender for the job, should receive jurisdiction. The Democratic Policy Committee of the Senate finally recommended that a special committee composed of members of both standing committees be created. I introduced a new resolution in line with the Policy Committee's decision, but when it reached the floor Senator Ferguson of Michigan and former Senator Donnell of Missouri, both Republicans, who wanted places on the committee, led a fight to defeat the compromise move and turn over the investigation to the Judiciary Committee. A deadlock developed, with the vote split almost evenly on party lines, and it finally took Vice-President Barkley's vote to break the tie and establish the investigating group as a special committee.

Even after getting our hearings under way the committee had other problems to thresh out with the Senate. As soon as we served subpoenas on certain hoodlums many of their partners in crime, whose testimony was vital, went into hiding—some even fleeing the country. We felt it was urgently necessary for us to be able to go directly to the full Senate and obtain immediate warrants of arrest for subpoena-dodgers. A debate developed over this in the lame-duck session of the Eighty-first Congress, and we found ourselves saddled with a time-wasting procedure which required us to go through the formality of requesting the Senate sergeant-at-arms to search for the missing witnesses before the arrest warrants were issued. The estimable Senate sergeant-at-arms, of course, is a parliamentary officer rather than a policeman and simply has no facilities of his own for tracking down fugitive gangsters. The sensible and, in the committee's viewpoint, proper procedure would have been for the Senate to issue warrants immediately, thus enabling the sergeant-at-arms to call on all federal law enforcement facilities, including the FBI, to assist him in locating the criminals. It was our experience later that when warrants finally were issued, thus putting the fugitive hoodlums on notice that the FBI would come for them if necessary, they usually surrendered meekly and without further ado.

Rather than prolong the controversy, however, the committee decided to go along with this roundabout procedure and did not attempt to reverse it, even in the Eighty-second Congress. Eventually we got everybody we were after but the delay helped some of the fugitives to evade service for months. I raise this point not in a spirit of acrimony but in the hope that Senate investigating committees in the future will not be handicapped with such an unrealistic and hobbling procedure.

Another area of operations in which I hope an example can be set that will benefit the work of future congressional committees is the handling of citations for contempt of Congress against witnesses who arrogantly refuse to answer legitimate questions. Our committee had more than its share of such contemptuous witnesses—so many, in fact, that the stock reply of the evasive hoodlum or dishonest public official, "I refuse to answer on the ground that it may tend to incriminate or degrade me," became a national byword. This old refrain became so boring to us that Senator Tobey, the committee's chief gadfly to insolent mobsters, said to one such character, gambler Harry Russell, "Why don't you have a little sign painted and hold it up and save your voice?" Unfortunately—and I use the phrase advisedly, for the gambler certainly was contemptuous to a degree not protected by constitutional safeguards—Russell was the first of the witnesses cited by us for contempt to come to trial, and he was acquitted by a directed verdict from a District of Columbia judge. The present laws are very definite on self-incrimination. A witness has the right to refuse to answer any question or questions that may incriminate him in connection with a federal offense, but he has no right to decline to answer self-incriminating questions involving a state offense. Though no one on the committee wishes to quarrel with the courts, it was our considered opinion that our record showed that Russell refused to answer legitimate questions that by no stretch of the imagination could incriminate him of anything. Undoubtedly hoodlums throughout the country were encouraged to defy us by the fact that the first of their crew to stand trial got off scot-free. Some witnesses carried their contemptuous defiance to the point of refusing to tell us anything beyond their names. Before it was over we found it necessary to cite thirty-two others for contempt. In my opinion, if the Senate Crime Committee is not backed up by the courts on the contempt issue a precedent will be set that will encourage hoodlums to defy not only congressional committees but the courts as well.[1]

Two of the most delicate points of procedure in organizing

---

[1]The committee would have had less trouble, of course, if witnesses could have been granted immunity from prosecution on the basis of their testimony. One of our recommendations to the Senate, which I shall discuss in a later chapter, was to this effect.

a committee such as ours are the questions of adopting rules of procedure and of selecting a competent staff with which to carry them out. These two points, obviously, are closely linked.

On the question of procedure, we followed a technique that may be a little unusual on Capitol Hill. Before choosing any-one for the staff, we had several committee meetings at which I stated my position to my fellow members. I told them I felt we had a great challenge to prove that we really were going to carry out our promise of a sincere, thorough, and non-partisan investigation. Already critics were playing the anvil chorus—some on the floor of the Senate and some in the pub-lic press—to the tune that our investigation would be a "white-wash." My colleagues all agreed with me that the way to confound these critics was for us to forget that we were Demo-crats or Republicans, to select a non-partisan staff, and to inves-tigate without regard as to whom we might benefit or hurt. I told my colleagues firmly that I never did believe in com-mittees being divided into majority and minority factions; that if we were to do any good at all we had to work as a team. I told them that I had no favorite lawyers or investigators from my home state of Tennessee to place on the committee— as a matter of fact only one minor spot on the staff ever was filled by a Tennessean—and that I would like to see all per-sonnel chosen without regard for patronage or politics. Com-petence rather than influence was to be the yardstick for choos-ing the staff. The committee, I believe, faithfully utilized that yardstick.

Selection of a lawyer to fill the critical spot of chief counsel was not easy, for our standards were exacting and we had several extremely talented and well-qualified men under con-sideration. I think the committee was highly fortunate in finally selecting the youthful but experienced Rudolph Halley. Mr. Halley had served with distinction on the legal staff of the Truman Committee, headed by the then Senator Harry Truman, which probed fearlessly and diligently into war con-tract scandals during World War II; later he became chief counsel for the same committee under Senator Mead. Halley cut himself loose from a successful and profitable law practice in New York City and Washington for a year to devote himself to our investigation. As the months went by, I increasingly appreciated and admired our tenacious and courageous chief counsel. His perception, his powers of withering sarcasm in examination, and his deadpan technique of examining witnesses proved the undoing of some of the so-called "elite" of America's hoodlumdom and the dismay of their diligent and expensive legal advisers.[2]

One of the great aids to our committee—and I wish to voice my appreciation of it here—was the work of an Interstate and Foreign Commerce subcommittee, headed by Senator Ernest W. McFarland. Senator McFarland's group, whose membership included the chairman of the parent committee, Senator Johnson of Colorado, Senator Capehart of Indiana, and two men who, fortunately for us, were to become members of the Crime Committee, Senators Hunt and Tobey, amassed a valuable pool of information on the transmission of gambling information.

[2]The entire staff of the Crime Committee deserves tribute. On the legal staff in the Washington office, Mr. Halley was assisted by George S. Robinson, borrowed from the United States Air Force legal staff; Downey Rice, formerly of the FBI; John L. Burling; Alfred M. Klein, a lawyer and former newspaperman who handled press matters for the committee; Joseph L. Nellis, whose work in preparation of the New York hearings was so outstanding that he was promoted from assistant to associate counsel; E. Ernest Goldstein and Carmel Ebb. Special counsel working in New York included Boris Kostelanetz, Thomas L. Karsten, Louis E. Yavner, Reuben Lazarus, David Shivitz, James D. Walsh, and Arnold L. Fein. Max H. Goldschein assisted us in Kansas City; Ben E. Caldwell in Detroit. Special thanks are due to former Judge Morris Ploscowe, of New York City, executive director of the American Bar Association's Commission on Organized Crime, headed by former Secretary of War Robert Patterson; Judge Ploscowe worked with Counsel Halley and the staff in preparation of the over-all report submitted to the Senate on May 1, 1951.

The investigative staff originally was headed by Harold Robinson, who had worked with Halley on the Truman Committee and at the time we secured his services was chief investigator of the California Crime Commission; Robinson since has returned to California as Deputy Assistant to the Attorney General of the state. The staff included: Henry P. (Pat) Kiley, one of our senior investigators, now with the International Claims Commission; George H. Martin, an outstanding Pennsylvania newspaperman;

Another extremely valuable weapon in the committee's arsenal—perhaps the most deadly we had—was the Executive Order given us by President Truman, authorizing us to examine income tax files in our search for information on the operations of the crimesters and their politician allies. The President's action was an enormous boost to the Crime Committee's effectiveness; without it, our investigation would have been greatly handicapped. The Treasury Department also co-operated to the fullest extent in opening up the income tax files. In addition to turning over to us several thousand tax returns, the Internal Revenue Bureau voluntarily assisted us with hundreds of dossiers which its intelligence agents had collected laboriously on the activities of known racketeers, hoodlums, and gamblers.

As the public hearings became more frequent and as we opened our proceedings to a greater audience via television, the significance of what the Crime Committee was attempting to do caught on. It became apparent we weren't just "chasing crapshooters," and public fervor mounted. In the next-to-final series of public hearings in New York City, when an estimated 20,000,000 to 30,000,000 people in the large cities of the nation were able to hear and see our proceedings via television, the

---

John N. McCormick, whose experience as a race-track investigator was invaluable to us; George White, borrowed from the Narcotics Bureau; Ralph W. Mills, who since has become operating director of the Hillsborough County Crime Commission in Tampa, Florida; William D. Amis, George Ames, John F. Elich, William C. Garrett, John J. Murphy, Howard R. Rand, Thomas E. Myers, Patrick C. Murray, George Fickeissen, Edward T. Burns, H. R. Van Brunt, Herbert A. Blomquist, John E. Kenny, Martin F. Fay, Lawrence C. Goddard, Philip King, Harold B. Bretnall, Dennis O'Shea, William Ruymann, Lieutenant George Butler, borrowed from the Dallas Police Department, and Inspectors Thomas J. Cahill and Francis J. Ahern, borrowed from the San Francisco Police Department. I wish to express special thanks to these police departments which loaned us the services of these valuable officers. Volunteer services were performed by Charles Kress and John Winberry.

Our office in Washington was competently run by Melba J. Coutsonikas, administrative assistant to the committee and secretary to Mr. Halley. Agnes Wolf assisted in research; and statistical, clerical, and other duties were performed by Joyce Mack, Paul Newland, Carl Melton, John Hirten, Jr., Julia Arnold, Mary Mitchell, Vyonne McDonnell, Lillian Sears, Mary Longland, Edith Knight, Freda Lustick, Elsie Hileman, Anne Tynan, and others.—E.K.

pressure to make the Crime Committee a permanent and continuing body reached the proportions of a national crusade. Approximately 60,000 letters and telegrams—and countless telephone calls—were received by the committee and its individual members, mostly urging that we continue.

It would take a calloused man not to be moved by these letters. Not all were favorable; not all agreed with what we were doing or, in some instances, with our methods, but, to me, they truly expressed the voice of the people. Let me quote from a sampling of the correspondence:

". . . [Your] vigor and diligence in the prosecution of this investigation should serve as a guide and an example to honest American citizens and their elective representatives. As parasitic growth perishes in sunlight, so corruption and crime will vanish in the dawn of publicity and exposure. . . ." "I pray that our citizenry will be aroused sufficiently to wipe out evils which tend to destroy the fine principles that have been so vital in the making of our great nation. . . ." "For hour after hour we watched in fascinated distaste the specimens of subhuman scum that squirmed in the glare of their notoriety. I am a political nonentity, only a very small voice in this land where the great masses of people forever remain inarticulate and much too often forgetful, but there must be millions of ordinary citizens like me who are immensely grateful for the work that you are doing and who are silently and fervently hoping that a great measure of good will result from your efforts. . . ." "Slimy, crawling creatures found under rocks cannot stand the bright lights and scurry for cover. . . ." "I believe you are awakening the law-respecting citizens of this country from the depths of moral decay to which we have sunk. . . ." "American parents now can have faith in a future of promise for their children. Thank you very much."

Our first hearing was conducted in Miami, Florida, on May 26, 1950. Between that date and the time my term as chairman ended, I traveled approximately 52,380 miles from coast to coast. Hearings were conducted in Miami, Tampa, New Orleans, Kansas City, Cleveland, St. Louis, Detroit, Los Angeles, San Francisco, Las Vegas, Philadelphia, Washington, Chicago, and New York. These hearings brought in evidence of widespread criminal activities in other cities and states, and our investigators diligently pursued these leads. We questioned witnesses from nearly every state in the Union. I heard literally millions of words of shocking and at times incredible testimony from nearly 800 witnesses, and I read additional hundreds of thousands of words in corroborating memoranda.

Through it all I listened with mounting indignation and revulsion to the shocking story of our national disgrace. When it was over we had established the following major conclusions:

1. *A nationwide crime syndicate does exist in the United States of America, despite the protestations of a strangely assorted company of criminals, self-serving politicians, plain blind fools, and others who may be honestly misguided, that there is no such combine.* This nationwide syndicate is a loosely organized but cohesive coalition of autonomous crime "locals" which work together for mutual profit. Its activities are controlled by a foul and cynical partnership of mobsters, venal politicians, and conscienceless business and professional men—including accountants and lawyers—who travel under the false mask of "respectability."

The national crime syndicate as it exists today is an elusive and furtive but nonetheless tangible thing. Its organization and machinations are not always easy to pinpoint, for obviously it does not operate with the precise and open methods of, say, a large corporation, whose stockholders and operations are matters of record. However, by patient digging and by putting together little pieces of a huge and widely scattered puzzle, the picture emerges.

In the earlier and more violent days of rumrunning and hijacking the big city gangs thrived on murder and other crimes of violence. As the years went by and the mobsters grew suaver and more experienced they realized that killings were not only bad business but bad public relations, that "in union there is strength." Gradually they got together; they toned down on the violence and, astounding as it seems, began reaching more or less peaceful agreements on divisions of territory and "spheres of influence."

Thus crime became big business. Hoodlums—that is, the smart ones who lead the new-style gangs—started cleaning their fingernails, polishing up their language, and aping the manners and sartorial trappings of captains of industry. While "muscle" —the willingness to bomb and kill without scruple—still remains an indispensable business accessory of the mobs, "brain" has supplanted "muscle" as the dominant factor in mob leadership. The new aristocrats of the criminal world are not the rough-spoken, apelike killers of the twenties. They have been replaced by the impeccably tailored, double-talking Frank Costellos and others of his ilk. These new "administrators" of hoodlumdom are the kind of hypocrites who wail and squirm and figuratively bleed at every pore when you expose them for what they are—enemies of society. "We're businessmen!" they protest. "We live quietly, pay our income taxes, and give the public only what it wants." Actually, however, because they are so smooth, because they have learned so well from certain lawyers, tax accountants, and so-called "clean" businessmen who are affiliated with them, the new-style crimesters are more dangerous than the Capones and Dutch Schultzes of the earlier, rawer era.

Today the two hubs of the axis on which the national crime syndicate revolves are New York and Chicago. So far as we have been able to determine there is no absolute boss of the syndicate—that is, no single person who can give a flat order and have it carried out anywhere in the country. It doesn't operate quite like that; however, there are a handful of hoodlums whose influence—particularly since they work in close harmony —is all-powerful. The "most influential underworld leader in America," according to Virgil Peterson, operating director of the Chicago Crime Commission, is that wily string-puller of the mob world, Francesco Castiglia, alias Frank Costello. Costello doesn't have to issue "orders" or enforce his views with bombs or machine guns; when he talks, underworld characters—and even some not directly in the underworld—listen.

The hard core of the national crime syndicate is built on this axis between the faction led by Costello, Joe Adonis, and Meyer Lansky on the East Coast and the Chicago mob, still known as the Capone Syndicate in "respect" to its late leader. From these mobs insidious lines shoot out across state boundaries to every important crime center in the country. The links, of course, are by personal association, joint investments, and mutual understanding between the mob leaders, rather than by constitution and bylaws. There is no need for the mob to call conventions; its members meet automatically at Miami Beach or Hot Springs, depending on the season. As Commissioner Harry Anslinger of the Federal Narcotics Bureau testified, "The members of this combine are very well acquainted with everybody else throughout the country. The fellows in New York, Florida, California, all know each other. . . . It is interlaced and intertwined." Thus a New York hoodlum of good standing in the national crime syndicate has no difficulty in arranging for a colleague in Kansas City, Chicago, or on the West Coast to do him a little favor, such as collecting a gambling debt, rubbing out a competitor, and so forth. The favor, of course, is returned as the occasion arises.

2. *Behind the local mobs which make up the national crime syndicate is a shadowy, international criminal organization known as the Mafia, so fantastic that most Americans find it hard to believe it really exists.* The Mafia, which has its origin and its headquarters in Sicily, is dominant in numerous fields of illegal activity—principally narcotics—and it enforces its code with death to those who resist or betray it. In the big business era on which crime now is entered there often is need for an arbiter when disputes arise within "the family." The Mafia often serves as that arbiter.

3. *Although dishonest politicians and officeholders are a small minority compared with the hundreds of thousands of devoted, honest public servants, political corruption in the United States seems to have sunk to a new low.* The committee members repeatedly were sickened by repetitious evidence of

official dishonesty. Everywhere we went we found the disillusioning facts: there were some constables, policemen, and detectives who took their $10 bribes to protect gamblers and other malefactors; sheriffs and bigger fry who cut themselves in percentagewise on the profits of the criminals they protected. We also found that really big money—$100,000 in one instance—flowed from sources close to the mob elements into the campaign coffers of state governors. The "dishonor roll" of criminals and politicians compiled by the Senate Crime Committee was a sordid and sickening document. It is no wonder that hoodlums and "sharp" businessmen have come to think they can buy anybody.

4. *While law enforcement primarily is a local responsibility, and everywhere we uncovered a monotonous picture of corrupt or passive local officials, much of the responsibility for what is going on rests squarely upon federal enforcement agencies.* The Internal Revenue Bureau, for instance, has been too lax in its scrutiny of income tax returns submitted by known hoodlums and gamblers. In one of its interim reports the committee noted: "It is apparent that many, if not all, of the returns submitted for the gamblers and gangsters are fraudulent, and . . . the federal government is being defrauded of many millions of dollars, perhaps running into hundreds of millions, of tax revenues by the mobsters engaged in organized criminal activities." In California we even found instances of outright grafting and racketeering by Internal Revenue agents mixed up with shady underworld characters; our exposures were followed up by dismissals and indictments of most of the officials accused of crookedness. It would be an injustice, however, to condemn the entire bureau because of the activities of a few dishonest employees. The bureau is made up largely of career men who are trying to do a good job; the recent establishment of a Special Frauds section to ferret out tax evasion by known racketeers is a commendable action.

The Immigration and Naturalization Service likewise has done an inadequate job of denaturalizing and deporting foreign-born criminals who make a mockery of the laws of the land.

Congress must share the blame for this because of its failure to provide stiffer, more specific legislation. In widely separated parts of the country the committee found repeated instances of big-time criminals, perpetrators of crimes ranging from murder downward, who had entered the country illegally and obtained citizenship papers on perjured applications, remaining thereafter in this country to thumb their noses at the law. The Department of Justice, which has supervision over the Immigration and Naturalization Service, could do a better job if Congress gave it stiffer and more enforceable laws to use against these undesirable criminals. The committee therefore went on record as favoring passage of a pending bill to give the Attorney General greater authority in denaturalization and deportation procedures.

The Federal Bureau of Investigation is a highly skilled and praiseworthy organization, one of the world's really great crime-detection bodies. One criticism of the FBI which we did hear from some law enforcement officers, however, was that the bureau tends to be overly secretive with information it collects on criminals—in other words, that exchange of information with the FBI is something of a "one-way street." This, I believe, is a shortcoming not attributable solely to the FBI; improvement of the flow of co-ordinated exchange of information on criminals is needed on all federal, state, and local levels. In my opinion this weakness can be corrected by establishment of a federal crime commission, one of the committee's recommendations which I shall discuss in a later chapter.

5. *Infiltration of legitimate business by known hoodlums has progressed to an alarming extent in the United States.* The committee uncovered several hundred instances where known hoodlums, many of them employing the "muscle" methods of their trade, had infiltrated more than seventy types of legitimate businesses.

How to cope with this situation is a difficult problem. In so far as infiltration of businesses of public or quasi-public nature is concerned—such as utilities, transit companies, and businesses whose interstate operations bring them under control of federal agencies—there are certain safeguards which could be set up that I shall outline in a later chapter. How to keep the hoodlums out of purely local legitimate businesses, however, is more perplexing. Obviously we cannot and do not want to ordain that the man with a criminal record must be banned forever from legitimate enterprise. Indeed, it is the very opposite that we are trying to attain. When a wrongdoer has paid for his mistake and honestly wants to reform he deserves every possible break from the community. What I am objecting to and what I want to expose, however, is infiltration by the criminal who claims he has reformed and gets a strangle hold on legitimate businesses (usually by gangster methods, as you will find if you dig deep enough), and who continues to engage secretly in crime while using the legitimate business as a front for his illegal activities. There are some corrective measures the federal government can enforce, particularly in the liquor and interstate trucking fields, but most phases of the problem, I suspect, can be handled best on local levels. Conscientious local officials, by diligent but fair use of licensing powers in some instances, and by aggressive police action in others, certainly should be able to keep the crooks of their communities from taking over legitimate enterprises and operating them to the detriment of the public.

All the points listed above are frightening disclosures. I have not lost faith in the ability of the people of America, when aroused, to see danger signs which confront them and to spike such dangers. Nevertheless, it is a fearful thing to contemplate how close America has come to the saturation point of criminal and political corruption which may destroy our strength as a nation. It does not take particularly keen perception—only a study of history—to see how once mighty nations of other continents, after the infection of criminal and political corruption sets in, have sunk to the point where democracy and national strength are utterly lost. I asked myself—and it is a good question for every citizen to ask: did the citizens and the legislative bodies of those ruined countries realize what was happening? Couldn't they sense that the mess of politico-criminal corruption would so pollute their countries, morally and economically, that their homelands inevitably must degenerate into ruined, impotent, third- and fourth-class powers?

The big question—and I put it bluntly—is this: has criminal and political corruption, which the Senate Crime Committee's findings have shown us is rampant, reached the point where America, too, must follow the downward path of others? I say that we are dangerously close to that ruination point—if not right on it. However, though the hour is late, it is not yet too late. We can lick organized crime. We can correct the evils plaguing our country if the good citizens will open their eyes to our danger. We can lick it if we recognize the alliance of criminals and their "respectable" front men for what they are— hoodlums and despoilers rather than glamorous figures or heroes—and go after them with the same determination and ruthlessness that they employ in milking and perverting our society for their own gains.

CHAPTER 2

THE MAFIA AND LUCKY LUCIANO

THE Mafia, as I pointed out in the preceding chapter, is the shadowy international organization that lurks behind much of America's organized criminal activity. It is an organization about which none of its members, on fear of death, will talk. In fact some of the witnesses called before us, who we had good reason to believe could tell us about the Mafia, sought to dismiss it as a sort of fairy tale or legend that children hear in Sicily where the Mafia originated. The Mafia, however, is no fairy tale. It is ominously real, and it has scarred the face of America with almost every conceivable type of criminal violence, including murder, traffic in narcotics, smuggling, extortion, white slavery, kidnaping, and labor racketeering.

Our greatest help in tracking down the trail of the Mafia came from the Federal Bureau of Narcotics, the United States Treasury Department's anti-narcotics enforcement arm. Because of the Mafia's dominance in the dope trade, the Narcotics Bureau has become the leading authority on this sinister organization. We received invaluable testimony from Commissioner Harry Anslinger of the Narcotics Bureau, some of

which still must be kept secret in the interests of the ever continuing war against the narcotics traffic. While it was heartening to learn that the federal government has a bureau which
is alive to the danger presented by this criminal organization,
it was discouraging to find that the Federal Bureau of Narcotics is sadly undermanned. I strongly favor increased appropriations to give this bureau more manpower with which
to carry on the fight against the Mafia-dominated narcotics
traffic.

Through the assistance of narcotics agents whose services
were made available to us by Commissioner Anslinger, and by
chipping away pieces of information through relentless questioning of unwilling witnesses, we were able to construct a
revealing picture of the Mafia. The secret society came into
being in Sicily during the early part of the nineteenth century.
Decent Sicilians, who of course are in a vast majority over the
lawless elements of their country, despise the Mafia but for
the most part fear it and are able to do little to suppress it.
Originally *La Mafia* was a protective organization of the peas-
ant classes formed to resist oppression by the great land barons,
but it quickly got out of hand. The *Mafiosi,* as its members are
called, launched a reign of terror—murder, rape, robbery, extortion, and kidnaping—throughout their province. The shortsighted landowners, in the interests of self-preservation, made
deals with the Mafiosi to manage and protect their estates,
and the Mafiosi in turn became crueler tyrants over the peasants
than the gentry ever had been.

La Mafia even has its secret—and of course unwritten—
code, which is called *Omerta,* a derivation of the Italian word
for "man." The code is simple and brutal—death to those who
resist or inform on the Mafia, or who appeal to the legal authorities or assist the law in acting against the Mafia in any way.
Usually a member of the offender's family is killed as an
additional warning. Needless to say, Mafiosi and law-abiding
Sicilians alike live in mortal fear of Omerta.

As an example of Mafia terrorism, Narcotics Agent Claude
A. Follmer, testifying before the committee in Kansas City,

told us the grim story of how, in 1919, the Mafia murdered an eleven-year-old boy named Carramusa in Kansas City, a hot-bed of Mafia activities. Follmer testified:

"The murderer of the Carramusa child was caught red-handed by outraged bystanders and was almost beaten to death before being arrested by the police. He was identified as Paul Cantanzaro, but he was never convicted, as the host of witnesses were methodically terrorized. Even Louis Olivero, the police detective who arrested Cantanzaro, was himself later murdered by the Mafia."

Ironically, the murdered boy's brother Carl became involved with the Mafia some twenty-two years later and was picked up as a member of a narcotics ring. He turned witness for the government in violation of the Mafia code, and his testimony played a large part in breaking up the gang. At the trial, Follmer related, the same Paul Cantanzaro "sat up in the front row of the courtroom while Carl Carramusa testified" and "with subtle threatening gestures . . . attempted to intimidate the witness until it was found necessary to eject him from the courtroom."

Carramusa tried to escape the vengeance of the Mafia by going into hiding, changing his name, and starting a new life with his wife and family in Chicago. It was no use. "Three years later," Follmer testified, ". . . Carramusa's head was blown off by a shotgun blast just as his family was about to join him in his automobile en route to a wedding anniversary party."

The Mafia today actually is a secret international govern-ment-within-a-government. It has an international head in Italy —believed by United States authorities to be Charles (Lucky) Luciano. This notorious white slaver and dope trafficker was sent up in 1936 by Thomas E. Dewey, then a young special prosecutor in New York, for thirty to sixty years on a charge of compulsory prostitution. Ten years later Lucky Luciano was paroled by Mr. Dewey, then governor, and deported. The Mafia also has its Grand Council and its national and district heads in the countries in which it operates, including the

United States. In this country Mafia members have cunningly infiltrated some legitimate businesses—such as olive oil, cheese, candy, fruit, and coffee importing agencies—as fronts for their nefarious activities.

Agent Follmer was asked by Counsel Halley at an executive hearing for information about Mafia activities in Kansas City. The agent replied:

"The best information that we have is that there are possibly twenty-five or thirty members here in Kansas City. The more important ones are fellows like Tony Gizzo, Joe and Frank De Luca, Pete and Joseph Di Giovanni, and Jim Balestrere."

The questioning continued:

Q. Who do you think is the head man? Is there such a thing as a head man?
A. Balestrere is supposed to be the head man.
Q. Who would be the leading ones under him . . . ?
A. Gizzo and [Tano] Lococo, and the Di Giovannis.

Balestrere, Gizzo, and Lococo, together with the late Charlie Binaggio, slain political-gang leader of Kansas City, and Binaggio's murdered henchman, Charlie Gargotta, were known in Kansas City as "the Five Iron Men," according to a statement read into the record by Max H. Goldschein, a Special Assistant United States Attorney General, who gave our committee great assistance. More will be written about these characters and others of the Kansas City gang in a later chapter.

Follmer testified that he had kept watch on the activities of Binaggio and, in line of duty, had become friendly with the gangster. Halley asked him if Binaggio had been a Mafia member. "It is rather difficult to say," the agent replied, "but I heard he was." Later Follmer testified that, when he would ask Binaggio about the Mafia, "he [Binaggio] always laughed and said there was not any such thing—never heard of it."

The questioning continued:

HALLEY: How does the Mafia operate? . . .
FOLLMER: My understanding is that they have no written

rules or bylaws, but . . . once you are a member you can't withdraw. You are always a lifetime member. Their code is that if you double-cross another member of the organization there is only one penalty . . . death. . . .

If they loan each other money they don't take notes or bother about that sort of thing. They just know that if they fail to make good on their obligations to one another they will be killed.

Follmer went on to explain that there is an "inner circle" and an "outer circle" of the Mafia. The inner circle is composed of men who are rewarded for "special duty they have performed in the past" or "through their standing prior to their coming into the organization." They get the cream of the rackets. The outer circle "is just the run-of-the-mill type, the ones who do the heavy work and the rough things. . . ."

"Who makes these decisions, the inner circle itself?" he was asked.

"Yes," the agent replied. "They are supposed to have an international head in Palermo, and through him the various heads in other countries are designated. Through . . . [the head in New York] state heads or city heads in the United States are appointed."

There is "some contention," Follmer said, as to the identity of the New York head of the Mafia. He testified that "it has always been my understanding that either Vincent Mangano or Joseph Profaci" heads up the New York organization. The committee's official report to the Senate noted, in fact, that Profaci was considered by the experts to be one of the top leaders of the Mafia." Mangano is a Brooklyn police character, said by New York police to be active in waterfront rackets. The committee had planned to question him in New York, but our hearing time was consumed by other developments. His brother, Philip Mangano, also active on the waterfront and publicly identified as prominent in the Mafia, was questioned by the committee in executive session. One month after our New York hearings were completed Philip Mangano was found dead in a Brooklyn swamp, shot three times in the head. Police feared his killing might be the first of a new series of crime syndicate murders.

Profaci, a Sicilian by birth, is a prosperous Brooklyn merchant, head of the Mama Mia Importing Company, which deals in olive oil, and an affiliate, the Sunshine Edible Oil Company. Both Profaci and Mangano were among a number of men of Sicilian and Italian extraction arrested at a mysterious meeting in 1928. When we questioned Profaci in executive session he told us the only conviction on his record is a plea of guilty he entered several years ago to a charge of selling adulterated olive oil.

At our public hearing in Kansas City, Agent Follmer told how the Narcotics Bureau in the early forties broke up a vicious Mafia-backed Kansas City narcotics ring. "The story behind these indictments," he related, "began in 1929 when narcotics officers learned that a man known only as Nicoline, later identified as [Nicolo] Impostato, arrived in Kansas City from Chicago and became the strong-arm man for John Lazia, underworld czar. Lazia was later assassinated.

"In New York City in 1937 narcotics agents arrested Nicola Gentile in connection with a nationwide narcotics syndicate involving eighty-eight persons throughout the United States and Europe. Gentile was found to be a traveling delegate for the Mafia, and an address book in his possession was a veritable Who's Who of Mafia narcotics traffickers. The names of Impostato and other members of the Kansas City syndicate were duly listed. Gentile later jumped a heavy bond and fled to his native Sicily, where he is now an intimate of the notorious Lucky Luciano.

"Shortly after his arrival in Kansas City," Follmer continued, "Impostato, according to reliable information, became second in command under Joseph De Luca, who was then in charge of the narcotics branch of the Mafia organization. . . . All of these persons were members of the Mafia, or Black Hand, and were financed in the narcotics traffic as a group by the Mafia.

This Mafia subsidiary placed the illicit drug traffic on a businesslike basis and hired a legal adviser, supervisor, general manager, traveling representative, a bookkeeper, and an extensive retail sales force. They soon developed contacts with major sources of the narcotics drugs at various ports and in a short while were supplying not only the Kansas City area but addicts in the states of Texas, Oklahoma, Iowa, Nebraska, Arkansas, Kansas, and Illinois.

"At St. Louis, Missouri, a branch office of this organization operated under the direction of John Vitale, who was in turn under the domination of Thomas Buffa and Tony Lopiparo, chiefs of the St. Louis Mafia."

(In St. Louis, some months later, the committee summoned gangster Lopiparo, alias Lopip, to ask him about his presence with a group of Sicilian criminals in Tia Juana, Mexico, about the time Binaggio and Gargotta were murdered in Kansas City. Lopiparo at first was a sullen, snarling witness. He crouched in the witness chair and refused even to admit he had been in Tia Juana. When I asked him on what legal ground he could justify his refusal, he snapped back: "Haven't I got a Constitution?" He escaped citation for contempt, however, by changing his mind and answering our questions.)

"In 1942," Follmer went on, "it was determined that one of the sources of supply for the Kansas City group was a Mafia organization in Tampa, Florida, which in turn received smuggled drugs from Marseille, France, via Havana, Cuba. . . . It was also indicated that Sebastino Nani, one-time Brooklyn Mafia hoodlum, now established in California, had furnished several large shipments of drugs to the Kansas City syndicate from New York."

The fear in which Mafia thugs hold their secret code was highlighted by one passage of Follmer's testimony. During the Kansas City investigation in 1943, he related, he and other agents planted a listening device in a Kansas City hotel room occupied by Joseph Antinori (identified by Follmer as an important Mafia narcotics principal in Tampa) and Tony Lopiparo. Joe and Tony both had been questioned by agents and were assuring each other they hadn't spilled anything. The following ensued:

TONY: If anybody had been talking, I sure would like to know who it is.

JOE: You know you don't have to worry about me. Whatever I know I am going to keep to myself. It don't do you any good to talk and have to face three or four tough —— — —— on the outside when you come out!

TONY: Somebody must have put the finger on me, and I have a hunch who it was.

At this point Joe hastily reassured Tony: "They even asked me about the Mafia, as if"—he broke off for a short, ugly laugh—"I would say anything about that!"

After more conversation Lopiparo, who, incidentally, was later acquitted in this case, addressed Joe as follows:

TONY: You just wait until the time comes and we will come out okay. You know these government charges are pretty tough, but there is ways of getting around them, too. Money talks. We will stay to the finish and see who all snitched.

JOE: Yeah. I guess we will find out all right when the time comes.

TONY: Never give confidence in nobody, not even Jesus Christ, and then you won't go wrong—understand?

Joe and Tony may have been smart boys at that—at least by Mafia standards. In connection with the same investigation two alleged Mafiosi forgot the code of Omerta and testified for the government. One was the aforementioned Carl Carramusa, now dead. The other was Lopiparo's associate, Tom Buffa. Buffa testified for the government only in a collateral matter involving perjury on the part of a fellow member's paramour. On his return to St. Louis an attempt was made to assassinate him. He escaped and fled to California. In 1946, at Lodi, California, Buffa was slain by shotgun blasts.

Everywhere it went the committee found evidence to support the belief that the underworld cognoscenti found it healthier not to talk about the Mafia. We questioned a number of witnesses, including some who had been named in testimony as prominent Mafiosi. Bear in mind that the Mafia is as well known by reputation to Sicilians and Italians in general as Jesse James is to Americans. This is the sort of verbal fencing we encountered:

KANSAS CITY—Tony Gizzo in the witness chair in executive session:

Q. Do you now belong to the Mafia?

GIZZO: What is the Mafia? I don't even know what the Mafia is.

Elsewhere, however, Gizzo had slipped up:

Q. Do you know Balestrere [Jim Balestrere, the reputed Mafia head in Kansas City]?

GIZZO: Yes, sir. . . .

Q. He is rather widely known as a prominent man in the Mafia, isn't he?

A. That is what you hear.

Q. What do *you* hear?

A. The same thing that you just said there.

In the public hearings later Gizzo was questioned again about his admission that rumor linked Balestrere with the Mafia. Gizzo, ordinarily a cool customer, got all flustered. He said he didn't remember giving these answers. At another point he expostulated: "I wish to hell I know what the Mafia is!"

WASHINGTON—Salvatore Moretti, an extremely contemptuous New Jersey gambler and racketeer, testifying:

COUNSEL HALLEY: Do you know what the Mafia is?

MORETTI: What?

Q. The Mafia? M-a-f-i-a?

A. I am sorry, I don't know what you are talking about. . . .

Q. You never heard that word before in your life?
A. No, sir; I did not.

At this point Halley incredulously asked Moretti, "Do you read?" Moretti sneeringly replied: "Nah—as I says before, I don't read very much on account of my eyes."

CHICAGO—Jack Dragna, notorious Los Angeles police character, a Sicilian by birth, was asked if he had heard of the Mafia. Only what he read in the newspapers, Dragna replied. "Did you ever hear of it in your home?" Counsel asked him. "Oh no," said Dragna. Not even as a youngster in Sicily, he insisted, had he heard the Mafia or Black Hand mentioned.

Philip D'Andrea, also subpoenaed from California to testify in Chicago, was somewhat more co-operative on the surface—possibly because he was under supervision of parole officers after having been released from the penitentiary in an extortion case. Still, he managed not to say anything particularly revealing. D'Andrea, a onetime pistol-carrying bodyguard for Al Capone, admitted he had "heard" of the Mafia since he was a child, but said he "knew nothing" of its current activities. He related, however, that he had been president of an Italian organization known as the Italo-American National Union—otherwise known as the Unione Siciliano—which he described as a "mutual benefit" insurance organization. Numerous gangsters of Sicilian or Italian origin carried policies in this "union," he testified. Some investigators have charged that the Mafia infiltrated—or attempted to infiltrate—this insurance organization as a cover for its activities, but D'Andrea insisted this was not so. Associate Counsel George Robinson asked him:

Q. Would you say it would be unusual for any man of your age who was born in Sicily to say he knew nothing about the Mafia?

D'ANDREA: Yes, I would think so. If he was born in Sicily I would think so. Because, as I say, years ago it was a byword in every family. People were scared to death of having a little home for fear somebody would come over and blow it up, or for fear they would receive a letter. That was the condition here about twenty years ago that I recall.

Q. What would you say were some of the other concepts or principles of the Mafia that you recall from your childhood, having heard talked about in the family?

A. One of the concepts was that it would be a good idea to keep your mouth closed. . . .

Q. Is . . . [the Mafia] a subject that is discussed among Italian families?

A. Oh, God, no; no, sir! It is not discussed out of the home. . . .

And so it went. None of these vaunted tough boys wanted to admit any knowledge of the Mafia. But the Mafia is there all right. In Tampa the committee heard testimony concerning fourteen unsolved murders and six attempted assassinations in the past two decades, most of which had the earmarks of Mafia crimes. The local police chief in Tampa, when asked if he believed in the existence of a Mafia syndicate, told Associate Counsel Downey Rice, "I absolutely do—yes." Earlier Rice had put into the record a statement concerning the murder in 1937 of one Joe Vaglica, alias Vaglichio, who was killed "at his sandwich stand by four shotgun blasts fired from a passing car." "There were no arrests," Rice stated, "but investigating officers believed that at the time Vaglica was a killer in the pay of the Mafia for jobs in New York, Chicago, Detroit, and Cleveland. . . ." Vaglica, Rice noted, was one of twenty-three gangsters from various parts of the country arrested in Cleveland, Ohio, on December 6, 1928, when, as Virgil Peterson of the Chicago Crime Commission testified, "a raid was conducted on a hotel room in which an alleged meeting of the Mafia Grand Council was taking place."

At our executive hearings in California we heard more about Mafia brutality from Police Inspectors Frank Ahern and Thomas Cahill. These officers were so expert on the subject that we borrowed them from the San Francisco Police Department to assist our committee in our nationwide investigation.

From them we heard of the murder of Abraham Davidian, a material witness in a narcotics case against Joe Sica, California gangster named in our second interim report as "a reputed member of the Mafia." Davidian was shot and killed in his mother's home while the case was pending.

Nick De John, a racketeer who operated in Chicago and San Francisco, was garroted under mysterious circumstances after a rendezvous in the Poodle Dog Restaurant, known in San Francisco as a hangout for the mob. As we put the story together from the evidence gathered all over the country, Mafia leaders from various parts of the United States had a habit of turning up for meetings just before the occurrence of brutal crimes—in Pueblo, Colorado; in Cleveland, Ohio; in a certain San Francisco tavern; in a New Orleans roadhouse; even in a shady restaurant in Tia Juana, Mexico.

Inspectors Ahern and Cahill told us of booking one Leonard Calamia in connection with a Mafia murder, and how he finally broke and "started singing." "He gave us a nice statement," Ahern said; he even named some names and drew a map showing the location of Mafia headquarters in San Francisco. Calamia was acquitted of the murder charge in court, Inspector Ahern went on, but his future is not bright. When asked if Calamia was likely to "suffer the consequence of his singing," Ahern somberly replied: "He probably will."

The two San Francisco inspectors also told about working on another suspect to tell them something about the Mafia. "He got down on his knees and said he would do anything but tell," Ahern related. "He doesn't mind facing anybody, but he would be walking along the street someday and somebody would step out of a dark doorway . . . They all get it."

This is the sort of outlaw government-within-a-government which, we learned, exists in the United States.

When the committee said in its second interim report that Lucky Luciano, now in exile in Italy after his deportation from the United States, was operating as the international arbiter of criminal activities, an associate of Luciano's in Italy protested that once again poor Mr. Luciano was being maligned.

THE COMMITTEE. (*Left to right*) Senators Charles W. Tobey, Lester C. Hunt, Estes Kefauver, Alexander Wiley, Herbert R. O'Conor

SENATOR ESTES KEFAUVER

SENATOR CHARLES W. TOBEY

RUDOLPH HALLEY, Chief Counsel

Joe Adonis

Joseph Di Giovanni

James Licavoli

Arthur B. (Mickey) McBride

James J. Carroll

"—AND NOTHING BUT THE TRUTH . . ."

Al Capone signs his bond for $50,000 when indicted for income tax evasion

PAST MASTERS

Lucky Luciano reads about his release from a Roman prison

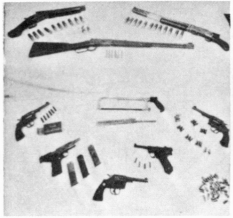

Acme

Tools of the trade

Acme

Automobile of William Drury, former police lieutenant, believed killed to prevent his testifying

Acme

Vault of slain James M. Ragen, guarded by police to prevent any attempt to steal the body

Acme

The late Nick De John, Chicago gambler, found stuffed in a trunk

Acme

Abner (Longie) Zwillman, of
Newark, concerned with bootlegging

BASHFUL ABOUT TALKING

Acme

Morris Kleinman, Cleveland gambler

From what the committee gathered in the way of evidence against Luciano, we do not think so. There was too much solid evidence showing that Luciano, though exiled, still maintained his contacts with overlords of United States crime.

Luciano—born Salvatore Lucania—was one of the fabulous gang figures of the lurid twenties and early thirties. He lived in kingly fashion in one of New York's finest hotels, and he traveled constantly to America's finest resorts, accompanied by ornamental women. His illegal activities allegedly included prostitution, alcohol, narcotics, bookmaking, and even a hand in the infamous Murder, Inc. Then Dewey sent him to jail.

During World War II there was a lot of hocus-pocus about allegedly valuable services that Luciano, then a convict, was supposed to have furnished the military authorities in connection with plans for the invasion of his native Sicily. We dug into this and obtained a number of conflicting stories. This is one of the points about which the committee would have questioned Governor Dewey, who commuted Luciano's sentence, if the governor had not declined our invitation to come to New York City to testify before the committee.

One story which we heard from Moses Polakoff, attorney for Meyer Lansky, was that Naval Intelligence had sought out Luciano's aid and had asked Polakoff to be the intermediary. Polakoff, who had represented Luciano when he was sent up, said he in turn enlisted the help of Lansky, an old associate of Lucky's, and that some fifteen or twenty visits were arranged at which Luciano gave certain information. "The theory behind it," Polakoff said, "was that the government had the Germans pretty well spotted, but they were afraid that if any sabotage might be done it would be done through Italians, who weren't well spotted." He was referring to sabotage along the New York waterfront. From a retired naval commander, who had a hand in the Luciano affair, we received inconclusive testimony as to the substance and value of the information obtained from Luciano.

On the other hand, Federal Narcotics Agent George White, who served our committee as an investigator for several months, testified of having been approached in Luciano's behalf by a narcotics smuggler named August Del Grazio. Del Grazio claimed he "was acting on behalf of two attorneys . . . and . . . Frank Costello who was spearheading the movement to get Luciano out of the penitentiary," White said.

"He [Del Grazio] said Luciano had many potent connections in the Italian underworld and Luciano was one of the principal members of the Mafia," White testified. The proffered deal, he went on, was that Luciano would use his Mafia position to arrange contacts for undercover American agents "and that therefore Sicily would be a much softer target than it might otherwise be."

Luciano's price, as passed on by Del Grazio, was that the military authorities should arrange for his parole, and that he then would go to Sicily to make the arrangements. White said he told the emissary that no such deal could be promised, and that he personally heard no more of it after that.

Anyhow, in 1946, after the meetings described by Polakoff had occurred, Luciano finally was paroled and deported to Italy. Meyer Lansky, Frank Costello, and a man named Michael Lascari, who had grown up with Luciano's family and who now is a partner in a tobacco vending company with Abner (Longie) Zwillman, New Jersey racketeer, went to Ellis Island to see him off. Frank Costello on the witness stand insisted there was no significance to this farewell and that he was just curious. Costello and others denied knowing anything about a party aboard the ship that carried Luciano away from these shores. The guards assigned to Luciano at the time also had denied in a previous investigation that there had been such a party. From a reputable witness, whose name was withheld to protect his personal safety, we received convincing evidence that there had been such a party, at which Luciano's guards were contemptuously ordered to stand aside, while baskets of food and wine were carted aboard the ship for Luciano and his gangster friends. Expensively dressed men carrying obviously phony cards certifying that they were "stevedores" were allowed to pass picket lines set up on the dock by waterfront thugs, who chased away newspaper reporters and photographers and threatened them with violence if they did not leave the dock.

More facets of the Luciano story were turned up by the committee. Meyer Lansky's relationship with Luciano aroused our curiosity. Virgil Peterson, the Chicago crime expert, had testified earlier that Lansky, Luciano, and the slain gangster Bugsy Siegel at one time "had comprised the enforcement branch of the Costello organization" and that their particular little group "was known as the Bug and Meyer mob of executioners." In addition to seeing off Luciano at Ellis Island, Lansky, after much prodding, recalled that maybe he had seen him a couple of times in Havana, when Luciano was taking temporary refuge there. "I couldn't recall what I talked about," Lansky told us. ". . . Purely social. What else could I talk to him about?"

Lansky also told us—it was another of those curious "coincidences" that always seemed to be happening to the characters we questioned—how he found himself in Italy once "by accident"—the touring agency, he explained, booked him on the wrong boat—and while he was there Lucky happened to call him up.

"I said," Lansky testified, " 'How the hell did you know where I am staying?' He says, 'Well, I got it from the paper.' " We asked Lansky what they talked about then. "He [Luciano] told me how he was being crucified," Lansky related, "and I told him, I says, 'You have nothing to kick about; look at the way I am being crucified.' "

Costello, too, once just happened to bump into Lucky in the lobby of a Havana hotel, and Lucky rode to the airport with him. "What did you talk about?" Counsel Halley asked. "Oh," Costello replied, "just his health and what not, and that is about all."

Mike Lascari was a little franker. He admitted visiting Luciano in Italy after the gangster's deportation and taking him $2500 in American money. "I just thought he might need it," Lascari explained.

Lansky's attorney, Moses Polakoff, also had represented Luciano in the trial that led to the white slaver's conviction. "When I undertook his defense I believed he was innocent," Polakoff said in reply to a remark by Senator Tobey. Now, the lawyer added, "sometimes I accept the decision of the court that he was guilty." To which Senator Tobey replied:

"There are some men who by their conduct in their life become a stench in the nostrils of decent American citizens, and in my judgment Lucky Luciano stands at the head of the list."

CHAPTER 3

THE WIRE SERVICE:

PUBLIC ENEMY NUMBER ONE

THE nationwide crime syndicate, as I pointed out in the opening chapter, became "big business" during the prohibition era. When the "noble experiment" ended, the gangs had to look for a new and equally lucrative racket. Organized prostitution had already been made difficult by passage of the Mann (White Slave) Act. Narcotics was profitable but definitely limited as an operation of universal appeal. Searching for a new field that would rival bootlegging as a moneymaker, the mobs turned to illegal gambling, which now, according to the experts, has become a $17,000,000,000 to $25,000,000,000 annual racket in the United States. A huge slice of this is being extracted by the organized criminal syndicates.

"Gambling," said Betting Commissioner James J. Carroll, an unwilling and television-shy witness in the final days of our hearings, "is a biological necessity for certain types . . . the quality that gives substance to their daydreams." No varieties of this "biological necessity" were overlooked by the mobs. Slot machines, punchboards, cards, dice, roulette, wagers on sporting events, and the "numbers" racket were exploited to the hilt. But the big killing came when the mobs successfully penetrated and organized the field (f illegal bookmaking on horse races. Thereby a vast and corrupting new industry—the gang-dominated wire service—was born.

The colossus of the racing news industry in the United States today is an organization known as Continental Press Service, which enjoys a virtual monopoly in the field. Continental Press, operating under a carefully contrived cloak of legality, is a powerful and indispensable ally of the underworld. On the basis of voluminous testimony on the record before the Senate Crime Committee, it is my considered judgment—and the committee said as much in its reports to the Senate—that Continental Press, while professing to be independent and law-abiding, actually is a tool of the Chicago-Capone Syndicate. In my opinion, because the wire service keeps alive the illegal gambling empire which in turn bankrolls a variety of other criminal activities in America, Continental Press is America's Public Enemy Number One.

There is no doubt as to the vastness of the operations of Continental Press. Wayne Coy, chairman of the Federal Communications Commission, testified before us that Continental Press and its so-called distributors lease 23,000 miles of telegraph circuits from the Western Union Telegraph Company, which, he said, derives an annual income from this business of nearly $1,000,000. American Telephone and Telegraph Company and its associated companies, Chairman Coy testified, also "derive substantial revenues from the transmission of racing information by intrastate and interstate message toll telephone service as well as by local service." Continental Press itself admitted to a gross income in 1949 of $2,366,648.99 through sale of its "news."

The history of Continental Press, as it exists today, began in 1939 when the late M. L. (Moe) Annenberg, racing news publisher, about to be sentenced to federal prison for income tax fraud, voluntarily disbanded his own lucrative Nation-Wide News Service. Up till then Annenberg's outfit, working closely with bookies throughout the nation, had been the Number One purveyor of racing information. When Annenberg walked out on the wire service, one of his old lieutenants, Arthur B. (Mickey) McBride, of Cleveland, Ohio, stepped in. McBride, by his own admission, was a friend, onetime employer, and business associate of numerous notorious Cleveland hoodlums. He had become a multimillionaire, with extensive real estate holdings and various properties which included a taxi fleet and a professional football club, the Cleveland Browns. In Miami he also owned Radio Station WMIE, whose commentators conveniently would lambaste the anti-gambling forces in Miami Beach. It was a distinct disappointment that an FCC examiner—even after the disclosures about McBride and his activities had been made public—proposed to relicense his radio station.

From McBride and his bald and seemingly disingenuous brother-in-law, Tom Kelly, of Chicago, both of whom were unhappy witnesses before the Senate Crime Committee, we obtained a remarkable story of the beginnings of Continental Press. It all started very innocently, almost accidentally, as they told it to us. (That was one of the things the committee learned all throughout its investigation of the half-world of gambling and crime we explored: things always happened either accidentally or by "pure coincidence.")

McBride insisted he started Continental on a modest bankroll of $20,000 purely out of sentiment and good will to provide a job for his brother-in-law, Kelly, who had been thrown out of work when Nation-Wide folded. He testified he paid Annenberg nothing for his assets or good will. "I didn't buy anything from Nation-Wide, not so much as a toothpick. . . . I started a new business," McBride said. His original $20,000 investment, which Continental Press, of course, has repaid many hundredfold, was earned back for him in a matter of a few months.

Kelly actually credited Mickey McBride's seventy-six-year-old mother with the idea of starting the new wire service. He told us how he had been visiting with the elderly lady and had told her of his worries for the future now that Annenberg was planning to give up the business. He was so depressed, the voluble Kelly told us, that he thought he "would go over and jump in the river." Mrs. McBride remarked that it was "too bad that the boys working for Mr. Annenberg can't get this organization together and hold it together for themselves." As he left she predicted, "Everything will turn out all right." Next thing he knew he was having a conversation with Mickey himself at the elder Mrs. McBride's house and the Cleveland operator was asking him "how much it would take to start this business up if Annenberg gave it up." Soon McBride had set up Continental Press as successor to the old Nation-Wide organization, and Tom Kelly now is general manager of the whole operation.

The new wire service, on advice of legal counsel, set up elaborate precautions to avoid one of the mistakes that had helped bring on trouble for its predecessor. Instead of selling "news" direct to bookies, as Nation-Wide had done, Continental set up regional "distributors" to whom it sold its service. These distributors, twenty-four in number, were supposed to be in the "publishing" business; they published racing guides and "scratch" sheets, indispensable to horse players. Continental gathered the racing news through an elaborate nation-wide system and telegraphed this information to its distributors. Often the methods of gathering information were of dubious legality. McBride himself admitted that Continental got the news out of the race tracks "by either going in and paying a concession price or taking it out otherwise." The "otherwise" included use of spies with high-powered telescopes and "wigwag" men.

The distributors, in turn, passed on the news for a price to thousands of illegal bookies all over the country. Continental was not supposed to know anything about that. McBride, an impatient witness in Cleveland, conceded, under questioning by Counsel Halley and Associate Counsel Nellis, that "no doubt they sold it to other people." "I," he irrelevantly remarked, "never have been in a bookmaking joint in twenty-five years." Counsel, however, continued to press him, and finally Mickey wearily acknowledged the obvious fact that "certainly" Continental's news "eventually got to bookmakers."

We further established, through evidence painfully gathered from resisting witnesses, some of whom had to be cited for contempt, that a good number of Continental's so-called distributors were merely dummies for the big wire service. The list of persons with whom Continental and its dummies do business, the records show, reads like a Who's Who of gangdom.

As examples of dummy operations fostered by Continental under the guise of distributorships, we isolated instances where parties, supposedly operating as independent distributors, actually kept only small salaries or percentages of profits for themselves and remitted thousands of dollars annually—the bulk of their profits—to Continental Press headquarters. The most obvious dummy was the *Illinois Sports News* in Chicago, run by none other than Tom Kelly's brother George. Tom's son, Thomas Kelly, Jr., also was a partner in the business. Tom told us—and George confirmed it—of the cozy arrangement "I have with my brother and my son." "The arrangement . . . is that they send in the rate every week that they can afford," Tom said. "My deal with George Kelly is [for him] to pay whatever he can afford to pay every week and send in as much as he possibly can to Continental." That "whatever he can afford," George Kelly amplified, varied from $2000 to $10,000 a week, but averaged out at about $250,000 a year. Brother George amiably agreed with Counsel Halley that the setup was "a sort of friendly family affair."

From Mickey McBride, who appeared at the Cleveland hearings in a suit of race-track plaid, hand-painted suspenders, and a bow tie, we elicited by tortuous questioning the equally tortuous story of how Continental's ownership shifted back and forth between the McBrides and the Ragen family. Mickey himself never wanted to run Continental, so in the beginning he went to an old colleague of Annenberg days, the late James M. Ragen, Sr., and asked him if he would take over. McBride admitted that in those days he lacked full confidence in "Uncle Tom" Kelly. Ragen, Sr., was having trouble with his federal income taxes at the time and didn't think he should go into the racing wire business just then. So McBride made a deal with James Ragen, Jr., also experienced in the business, to help Tom Kelly run the show. In 1942 McBride said he sold out to young Ragen. The following year, Ragen, Sr., took over and began putting pressure on Mickey McBride to return to the business. The story McBride told us was that Ragen just wanted the McBride name in the business. Mickey compromised by buying one third of Continental Press back at a price of $50,000 as an investment for his son Eddie, then nineteen years old and about to go into the Army. Eddie "will never have to do a thing; just take one third of the profits," Ragen, Sr., promised the elder McBride. Mickey assured us he talked it all over with Eddie before buying him a piece of the business, and that it was "all right" with Eddie.

Ragen's difficulties with the Capone Syndicate actually went back a number of years, but in 1946 he ran head-on into trouble. The Chicago-Capone mob had been eying Continental Press, and in the opinion of the committee's investigators its leaders came up with the conclusion that if they could seize control of the wire service it not only would provide them with a Golconda of profits but would be a source of jobs for literally thousands of hoodlums. By exploiting Continental's possibilities to the limit, the Capone mob reasoned, it could establish a virtual monopoly over illegal bookmaking throughout the whole United States. This maneuver, if it had been successful, would have given the Chicago mob a strangle hold not only on bookmaking but on many other interlinked forms of criminal activities and would have added tremendous power to the nationwide crime syndicate.

The only trouble was that Ragen, Sr., was a tough, irascible Irishman who wouldn't play the game. He refused to be "muscled." He also was resourceful; as Tom Kelly told us, "Ragen was a fellow that, if he was in charge of General Motors, he would have made more damned cars than they ever made in their life, because he always had one person working against the other."

As the committee reconstructed the story, the mob's initial approach to Ragen was in the form of a conciliatory but thoroughly dishonest proposition, advanced by three leading syndicate members, Jake (Greasy Thumb) Guzik, Tony (The Enforcer) Accardo, and Murray (The Camel) Humphreys. There was no intent to "muscle" him out, the mob sweetly insisted; all it wanted to do was to cut itself in and help build up the business. Ragen would remain as a "partner" and continue to take a big share of the profits, which presumably would be enhanced by the mob's participation.

As Ragen saw the picture, however, he had the feeling that once the mob had moved in and had gained sufficient experience in the wire service business to dispense with his "know-how," he would be found some morning dead in an alley. He also had the conviction that the Federal Bureau of Investigation never would permit such an organization as the Capone mob to gain control of the interstate racing wire service, and that the upshot would be disaster for the whole setup. So Ragen decided to defy the Caponeites.

Though stubborn, Ragen was not foolish. Realizing it was not a healthy thing he was doing, he tried to protect himself by holding conversations with Chicago FBI agents. He told them what was going on and of his fears for his personal safety. After one incident in which he was chased by a car manned presumably by some of the mob's enforcers, Ragen provided himself with bodyguards. He also took the canny—though, as it proved, futile—step of writing himself what he hoped would be an "insurance policy." He prepared an affidavit of some ninety-odd pages and took it to the State's Attorney. In it he told the whole story of the mob's attempt to take over his business. He predicted that he (Ragen) was a likely candidate for a gang ride, and named Guzik, Accardo, and Humphreys as the parties who might arrange the ride.

As part of the incredible scenario, according to Ragen's affidavit, the Capone interests used a man named Dan Serritella as their emissary to Ragen. Serritella had served in the Illinois legislature as a senator for twelve years, during part of which period he also was engaged in the business of publishing a scratch sheet. Serritella had been a friend and business associate of Ragen's, and at the same time was in cahoots with Ragen's enemy, Greasy Thumb Guzik. Serritella told us how Guzik had advanced him $15,000 to $20,000 to start up one scratch sheet venture in which they shared the profits fifty-fifty. Another time Greasy Thumb loaned him $8700 for some purpose which Serritella "couldn't remember." "I am not ashamed of Guzik," the ex-senator defiantly told us. "He is the fellow that helped me politically. . . . I wish there was a lot more like him."

The ex-senator was an erratic and excitable witness, who told us he had been "in and out of the sanitarium" some seven or eight times for "nervous breakdowns." At one point, when pressed for details of the Guzik deal, he exploded: "You are trying to give me the whole book. . . . Jesus, holy God, Jeez! I am beat before I start. . . . You have taken advantage of my good nature!" Though he admitted having talked with Ragen about the matter on several occasions, Serritella specifically denied acting as errand boy for Guzik & Co. Ragen, however, insisted in his affidavit that Serritella did, in fact, bring him the messages from the Capone mob.

The ingenuous "Uncle Tom" Kelly, in one of his several appearances before the committee, sought to indicate his disbelief that Ragen actually had left a statement with the State's Attorney. At this point Associate Counsel George Robinson produced a copy of the affidavit and enlightened Kelly:

"Here, specifically, is what he said: he [Ragen] said . . . Serritella told Ragen that the Capone organization would like to take in the business and give Ragen $100,000 in cash and a part of the business if Ragen would help them get it. . . . Serritella told Ragen . . . that if his people had it they would make $10,000,000 a year on it . . . and that it would make at least a thousand more jobs for his men. Ragen then said he got the flash that he, Ragen, would be in the picture only so long as he taught them the business and after that he would be found in an alley."

At the outset the Capone mob countered Ragen's opposition by starting a rival wire service called Trans-American Publishing and News Service to compete with Ragen's Continental Press. Through its superior gang connections Trans-American made deep inroads into Continental's business; in Chicago opposition to Continental was sparked by the mob's wire outlet, a mysterious outfit known as "R. & H." R. & H., which at one time purchased Continental's racing news, serviced some eighty-eight to one hundred bookies—the number fluctuated—who were known to Ragen as "the Capone books." One of the most clear-cut instances of how the Capone mob muscled in on Continental's business under the Trans-American operation occurred in gangster-dominated Kansas City. A rather timorous Kansas City operator named Simon Partnoy had been content for years to function as the ostensible "independent" distributor for Continental under the somewhat misleading name of Harmony Publishing Company. Continental got the big profits, and Partnoy kept a salary of about $125 a week for himself. When Trans-American came into the picture a Chicago man named Patrick J. Burns, "president" of Trans-American, sort of drifted to Kansas City looking for business. He just happened to wander into a tavern called the College Inn, run by Edward Osadchey, alias Eddie Spitz. Spitz was an associate of the then living Charles Binaggio, Charlie Gargotta, and other leaders of the Kansas City gang. Burns, as Osadchey told us, "happened" to mention that he was looking for someone to open up an office and take over the franchise for the new Trans-American racing news service. The upshot was that Osadchey, Gargotta, and two other Kansas City hoodlums with interstate connections, Tano Lococo and Morris (Snags) Klein, acquired this franchise. They then "called" on the inoffensive Mr. Partnoy, who had been going along happily all these years as a "distributor" for Continental. Mr. Partnoy decided he would sell his business to Osadchey, Gargotta & Co. for the sum of $7500—to be paid out of future profits!—and would remain on as a salaried employee. No "muscle" here, though—everyone connected with the deal assured us of that under oath.

A less stubborn man than Ragen might have let the Capone mob take over the nationwide bookie racket. Possibly, if he had, he would have been alive today. But Ragen kept on fighting, until on June 24, 1946, just as he had predicted, he was ambushed and mowed down with shotgun blasts on a Chicago street. He later died in the hospital. Ragen's murder is one of Chicago's many unsolved gang slayings, just as is the more recent murder of former Police Lieutenant William Drury, who had said a great deal publicly about the Ragen murder and activities of the Capone syndicate. Drury was shot to death the evening before he was to have talked to an investigator about appearing as a witness before the committee.

After Ragen's murder there was a period of nearly a year in which the two services fought each other intensively and neither made any money. Tom Kelly told us that Trans-American "damned near had us licked . . . to tell you the God's honest truth, we were expecting to go out of business." Then suddenly, in May 1947, Mickey McBride came back into the picture. He bought Continental back from the Ragen interests. The price was $370,000, payable over a period of ten years, and the business was to be the sole and exclusive property of young Eddie.

With the Ragens gone, Trans-American folded the very next month, and peace was restored. All the bitterness apparently was forgotten and many of the old Trans-American-Capone crowd came right in with Continental. In Kansas City, for instance, Osadchey & Co., who had taken the lucrative Harmony contract away from Continental, fell right into line with the new McBride outfit; similar *rapprochements* occurred all over the country.

Mickey McBride and all the Continental crowd vigorously and emphatically deny the existence of any deals, connections, or understandings whatsoever with the Capone-Chicago Syndicate, but evidence before the committee indicates otherwise.

The rawest bit of such evidence was the case of the syndicate-dominated R. & H. outfit in Chicago. Although it had been the driving force in attempting to run Continental out of business, R. & H. was able to obtain news from the McBride outfit through George Kelly's *Illinois News* and with Brother Tom Kelly's approval. Both Kellys admitted that the R. & H. outfit even fixed its own rate for such service at $750 a week, which, by comparison with amounts charged other non-mob outfits for similar service, was a ridiculously low figure. George Kelly also admitted that, although R. & H. ostensibly was run by three fellows known as Hymie (Loud Mouth) Levin, Ray Jones, and Phil Katz, it was his understanding that the arch-Caponester, Greasy Thumb Guzik, actually had a hand in its operation.

Among other queer birds of the underworld who flocked to the Continental setup after Ragen's murder was Jack Dragna, the influential Los Angeles mobster. Dragna, who had friendly connections with the Chicago-Capone Syndicate and originally was a Trans-American man, turned up operating as Universal News Service and selling "news" to George Kelly's Illinois Sports outfit for $500 a week, a healthy sum for the service he allegedly supplied. George Kelly's explanation of the Dragna contract was in keeping with the *Alice in Wonderland* tone of the whole business: he didn't even know he had a contract with Dragna, though he made it himself, he testified. It came about one day, he explained, when he got a phone call from Los Angeles from some unknown party who said it was the *Universal Sports News* calling and wanted to sell him some racing news service for $500 a week. Kelly agreeably made the contract and said he thought no more about it until a couple of years later when the papers came out with what Kelly called "adverse publicity" about Dragna working for Illinois. "Naturally," he told us, "everybody at the plant is interested in asking who Dragna is and nobody seems to know the answer." Finally they thought to look on the back of the checks paid Universal to see who endorsed them "and we find Dragna's name on there." So, Kelly said, they fired him.

The charitable Illinois agency even found a job for Pat Burns, the ex-Continental employee who had gone over to the rival Trans-American outfit as "president" and spent his time on the road taking away customers from Continental. Not only was Burns put on the Illinois payroll at $250 a week, but Burns's son and daughter, who also had worked for Trans-American, were taken on at, respectively, $200 and $125. "You didn't give a thought to the fact that Pat Burns had been running a business that had as its objective putting your brother out of business?" we asked him. "No, I didn't," answered Kelly.

Mickey McBride today says he has no connection with Continental Press. He insists that the "sole owner" is his son, Edward J. McBride. Eddie was twenty-three years old at the time his father bought him one hundred per cent ownership of the wire service, and that deal, Mickey said, came about in this way: "I talked it over with Eddie . . . and I said, 'Eddie, what do you think of it?' And he said, 'Well, I will be getting out of school. I will have to have someplace to go. . . . I will take a shot at it if you think that would be all right.'"

Edward McBride, at the time we questioned him, was a twenty-six-year-old law student at the University of Miami. He told us that, although he had "control" of the huge business, he didn't exercise it and that everything was run by Uncle Tom Kelly. "You are a complete figurehead and dummy, is that right?" Counsel Halley asked him. "I guess you would put it that way if you wanted to," young McBride answered. Anyway, it was nice "work" for the youngster, for, as Uncle Tom testified, Eddie received a net income, before taxes, of $692,207.64 out of Continental's 1949 gross income of nearly $2,500,000.

It is the committee's contention, which the elder McBride tenaciously disputed, that the real brains of the Continental Press operation was and is, not Uncle Tom Kelly, not young Eddie McBride, but Mickey McBride himself. "All the deals with the juniors look to me like fronts for a lot of transactions between the seniors, isn't that right?" Counsel Halley challenged. "Well," Mickey retorted, "they might look like that to you, but the seniors—I am one senior, I never got a penny out of it, so therefore I couldn't be in the business." But Halley persisted and finally won McBride's agreement to the facts that "the seniors did all the talking" and that young Eddie, at least, "didn't open his mouth at any time."

"Mr. McBride," Halley asked in another telling exchange, "why were you willing to put your son into a business which was in such friction with unidentifiable characters that the head of it had just been assassinated? Why were you willing to risk your son's life in that business? ... Weren't you afraid that your boy would be bumped off?"

McBride bristled and replied: "Well, Mr. Halley, that business has been in existence for over sixty years and one man got killed, *you say,* in it. I know a hundred lawyers that got killed in the last forty years. ... My boy might get hit by a brick from this building and bumped off. Life is a game of chance."

It was Counsel Halley's contention, which he set forth as part of the Cleveland record, that Arthur (Mickey) McBride's claim of being disassociated with Continental Press is a sham. In Chicago, while probing the McBride-Kelly family setup of Continental and its affiliates, Halley charged that "the whole thing from Ed McBride down . . . is just a small, little, close-knit group that is designed and operates to take the responsibility away from the man who owns the whole works." And in Cleveland the chief counsel asserted:

"I am taking the position, which I am going to ask the committee to take in its report, that all of this business with Ragen, Jr., and McBride, Jr., and all these corporations are a lot of phonies, and that Continental is and was Arthur McBride."

The committee, in a report to the Senate, concluded:

"From the preponderance of evidence before the committee a conclusion is warranted that the Continental Press Service is controlled not by Edward McBride or Thomas Kelly but by the gangsters who constitute the Capone Syndicate.

". . . The committee believes that the façade of legality

which was set up by Continental's counsel with such great particularity must be rejected. It must also reject the insulation erected between McBride and the ultimate customers of Continental's service, the bookmakers, and, having rejected both of these factors, the inference becomes inescapable that Arthur B. McBride created a machine in which Edward McBride, through his agents, operates a racing wire service which is an intricate part of a nationwide system employing discrimination in service and price against the various persons seeking to purchase a commodity.

"The conclusion is also inescapable that through agents and subagents McBride's organization steals news from race tracks and supplies this news through direct and indirect channels to bookmakers operating in violation of the law throughout the country. . . .

"It also becomes inescapable, once the fiction of the divorce of Continental Press and McBride from the various distributors of Continental's news service, particularly in Chicago, has been rubbed out, that Arthur McBride is deliberately making a gift to the Mafia-affiliated Capone mob in Chicago of about $4000 a week, which represents the difference in price paid by the Capone-controlled R. & H. service and the price paid by their competitors in the same city. In Kansas City the Mafia group operating the wire service receives largess of several hundred dollars a week on the same comparative basis. It is also clear that in many other cities the Capone affiliates and the Mafia are now in control of the distribution of racing wire news with a resultant source of enormous profits and power over bookmaking."

We thoroughly explored in Cleveland, of course, Arthur McBride's personal and business relationships with a number of the most influential members of the Cleveland mob, who in turn, partly through Mafia associations, were on friendly terms with members of the Chicago syndicate. The committee wanted, if possible, to learn, as Halley put it, "whether or not the reason Ragen needed McBride in Continental Press was to get some friends who could talk to the Capone mob." McBride himself insisted, "I don't know anybody in the Capone gang." But the record indicated he seemed to have some unexplained ability to keep the powder-keg business from exploding.

What is the answer to the challenge of gambling in general and, specifically, to the menace of the wire service, the new Public Enemy Number One? In regard to the former, I do not think that the evils attendant on Mr. Carroll's "biological necessity" can be solved by legalizing gambling in America, as some sources have suggested. In the first place it is doubtful that legalized gambling would discourage those who seek the extra flavor, or dubious "thrill," of patronizing the illegal operations that would go right on. In the second place, as has been demonstrated by the committee's study of Nevada, the one state in America that has legalized gambling, the results are discouraging: the criminal element infiltrates the legalized setup; violence is common, and the state—as has been proven in Nevada—does not even derive the full amount of revenue it expects through taxation on gambling.

As for eliminating the evil of illegal betting on horse races, some observers have suggested that the only way to stop it was to "shoot all the horses." This facetious suggestion, of course, is as silly as it is undesirable. In my opinion the way to cope with the problem—and it would be the most important anti-crime legislation that Congress could pass—would be a bill placing a legal strait jacket on Continental Press and on any other race news wire services that might spring up.

I fully recognize that this will not be an easy legislative undertaking—either to pass or to enforce. The surest way to strike at the heart of Continental Press, I believe, is by enacting legislation that would make it unlawful for any person, partnership, or corporation to engage primarily in the business of interstate dissemination of information concerning horse racing and dog racing by means of telegraph, telephone, or radio without an annually renewable license from the Federal Communications Commission. The FCC would be authorized to withhold such license unless the applicant established satisfactorily that such information was not to be distributed primarily to facilitate the violation of state laws. The act should be broad enough to make it impossible for Continental Press or any organization like it to evade the law through distributors, whether legitimate or dummies.

In the past legitimate news services, such as the Associated Press, United Press, and International News Service, have objected to such regulation, contending it would pose a threat to freedom of the press. The legitimate news services, of course, carry racing news for use by daily newspapers. In my opinion this objection can be met by calling a spade a spade and defining Continental Press as purely a transmitter of information of interest to gamblers, which it is.

In our exploration of the possibility of curbing the race wire service by placing it under FCC regulation, we encountered vigorous opposition from Chairman Coy of the Federal Communications Commission. He argued that this plan, whereby the FCC would be charged with responsibility for determining that distributors were not sending out racing information primarily for use by gamblers and, if such was the case, refusing a license to such distributors, was impractical and unenforceable. He urged instead consideration by the committee of an FCC-favored bill, which simply would make it a crime for anyone to transmit over interstate communications facilities any kind of information on bets, betting odds, and so forth. Chairman Coy also would shift from the FCC to the Justice Department the responsibility for prosecuting such violations. Senator O'Conor and I voiced our disagreement with Mr. Coy's unwillingness to have the FCC assume the burden of enforcing and administering the law which the committee recommended. I personally took the position that the FCC "should welcome the opportunity of rendering a public service and not try to avoid it."

Whatever type of law is passed will require vigilant and ironfisted enforcement, for Continental Press and the hoodlums who fatten on its operations are not the type to surrender easily. Warren Olney, former counsel for a Special Crime Study Commission in California, told us how his state passed a law banning use of communications facilities for unlawful purposes, which had the effect of knocking out the use in California of Continental's leased wire. After a while the authorities found a couple of horse parlors operating just as if they had the old service. The gamblers had tapped Continental's wire, which still ran *through* the state, and were stealing the information. "In doing so," Olney said, "they short-circuited the signal system for Santa Fe trains," an act which might have resulted in a tragic accident. Even more recently Attorney General Ervin of the state of Florida, which is attempting to clamp down on Continental Press by imposing a twenty-minute delay on transmission of racing results, publicly announced he had "almost conclusive proof" that Continental Press is stealing news from the wires of the Associated Press and other legitimate agencies.

Mr. Olney also told us that in 1942, when California feared air attack by the Japanese, a vital telegraph circuit which served an Air Force field was knocked out by a plane crash. Continental Press managed to get its wire service for the gamblers resumed in something like fifteen minutes. It took the Fourth Army, responsible for the defense of the entire West Coast, something like three hours.

Possibly one of the most valuable jobs done by the Senate Crime Investigating Committee was to awaken the public thoroughly to the great harm that can be done by the cumulative effect of the seemingly innocent little two-dollar bet. A bet of two dollars—even the fifty-cent bets which some bookmakers will take from housewives—can build up into a whale of a bankroll for the underworld when multiplied by many millions.

An electrifying example of how much good can be done by suppressing the illegal bookmakers was called to my attention by Senator Smathers, of Florida. He advised me that as a result of the Crime Committee hearings in Miami bookmakers had been practically driven out of business. The result was that would-be betters were patronizing the legal pari-mutuel machines at the race tracks. Thus the state of Florida was receiving the revenue through a betting tax, to which it was entitled, and with which it supports its worth-while old-age pension and school programs.

The fight to keep bookmakers, the scavengers of crime in America, out of business, and to put a crimp in the pocketbooks of the overlords of the underworld who control them, never should let up. Whatever occurs, I personally intend to fight for legislation which, once and for all, will end the menace of Public Enemy Number One—the wire service.

CHAPTER 4

CHICAGO: THE HERITAGE OF
AL CAPONE

THE Senate Crime Committee visited the city of Chicago on three separate occasions, amassing a record of 1416 printed pages on what we found there and elsewhere in Illinois. If we had gone no farther than Chicago in our quest for evidence of interstate crime and the links between organized crime and politics, we could have written a complete report-in-miniature on the picture of nationwide criminal and political corruption. For practically every example of rottenness which we found anywhere in the United States was duplicated, in some form or other, in the capital of the Capone mob.

Chicago, it is true, bears an unfortunate reputation, and some of the criticism that the city has to take because of its reputation is unjust. There are good citizens in Chicago who devote themselves fearlessly, even to the point of risking their personal safety, to trying to stamp out the vestiges of Al Capone's heritage to America's second city. The Chicago Crime Commission, in particular, has battled ceaselessly and effectively against the hoodlums, and Mayor Martin Kennelly in his recent administrations has made some headway against the criminal element. But the old gang was too powerfully entrenched—and the local tradition of political corruption too firmly ingrained—to be wiped out even in a decade. So Chicago, unfortunately, still remains the stronghold of certain cliques of corrupt policemen and officeholders and of local legislators who openly consort with gangsters.

It also remains the jungle of criminals who walk in the footsteps of Al Capone: men such as Greasy Thumb Guzik, Tony Accardo, alias Joe Batters; Murray (The Camel) Humphreys, Anthony (Tough Tony) Capezio, and Al Capone's cousin, Rocco Fischetti. Also not to be overlooked in the Chicago-Capone Syndicate hierarchy are lesser fry such as Ralph (Bottles) Capone and Matt Capone, brothers of the late infamous Scarface Al; Sam (Golf Bag) Hunt, who got his nickname because he once was arrested near the scene of a gang shooting with a shotgun concealed in a golf bag; Frank (Chew-Tobacco) Ryan; and many others with equally colorful names and reputations.

In his testimony before us in Washington, Virgil Peterson, operating director of the Chicago Crime Commission and a former FBI agent, traced the history of the Chicago mob from the days of Big Jim Colosimo in the period just before the roaring twenties. Colosimo "had risen to power and influence through the operation of a string of brothels to become the vice lord of the First Ward and had married one of the most prosperous madams of the district," Peterson related. On May 11, 1920, Big Jim was bumped off; Peterson noted that there had always been suspicion that the bodyguard imported by Colosimo from New York, Johnny Torrio, had engineered the killing. In any event Torrio, then a much-feared gangster, succeeded Colosimo as lord of Chicago's underworld.

Torrio in turn imported as his bodyguard a cold-blooded little killer from New York's Five Point Gang, a then obscure, scar-faced hoodlum of twenty-three named Al Capone. For four years Torrio enjoyed a bloody reign in Chicago, waxing rich on the profits of prostitution, gambling, beer, and booze.

But in 1924, after Torrio was the victim of an ambush which almost cost his life, he lost his nerve and abdicated in favor of Capone.

With Greasy Thumb Guzik as his paymaster and business adviser, and such stalwarts as Frank Nitti, Paul (The Waiter) De Lucia, alias Ricca, Louis (Little New York) Campagna, and the Fischetti brothers as his principal lieutenants, Capone was able to rule effectively over the Chicago underworld. The shocking St. Valentine's Day massacre of February 14, 1929, aimed at extermination of the leaders of the rival Bugs Moran gang, was an example of how Capone dealt with opposition. In 1931, however, Capone, who had operated with impunity in so far as ordinary laws were concerned, was cut down by Uncle Sam on an income tax evasion charge and was sent to prison. Frank Nitti succeeded him as leader of the mob, but in 1943, facing prosecution on an extortion charge, Nitti was found dead under circumstances that indicated he had committed suicide. Since then the mob—known to this day as the Capone Syndicate—has been run pretty much by a "corporation," in which Guzik and Accardo wield great influence. Paul Ricca was also a top-ranking member of the syndicate. In 1943, however, Ricca was sent to the penitentiary with other members of the mob and affiliated gangsters on the West and East coasts in connection with an attempted plot to extort $1,000,000 from the movie industry. Since his parole in 1947, Ricca has kept in the background, but the Chicago Crime Commission still considers him influential in the syndicate.

Although the Capone Syndicate and other mobs throughout the country have changed their techniques and, in the process of getting rich on the wire service, "policy wheels," and similar "quiet" rackets, have soft-pedaled bloodshed and violence as much as possible, they still do not hesitate to employ murder, kidnaping, and beatings when necessary. The undertone of violence is still there. A brutal example was the murder in September 1950—still unsolved as this was written—of former Police Lieutenant Drury before he could appear as a witness before our committee. Whether Drury was killed because it was discovered he was to be a witness before us, or whether he simply had been talking too much in general about the Chicago underworld, is a question that may never be solved. In this connection, one of the witnesses questioned by the committee was an enemy of Drury's, Robert (Big Bob) McCullough.

McCullough's career presented the significant anomaly of a hoodlum who, after beginning his career by working for Al Capone as a beer truck guard and in other capacities, graduated to the post of "chief of police" at the Miami Beach Kennel Club and Sportsman's Park Race Track at Cicero, two tracks which the committee was told had been linked closely with members of the Capone Syndicate. "He [Capone] was a nice fellow and he treated me nice," Big Bob told us.

The erstwhile hoodlum went on to admit he had made public threats against Drury. He said he was sore because the late police officer had labeled him a "notorious torpedo man" on a radio crime exposé and had broadcast the fact that McCullough was working as a track policeman. "That was a terrible thing," Big Bob told us. "I used to walk into my hotel and people wouldn't even look at me any more. They thought I wasn't living right. Here is a man made that kind of a statement that I was a torpedo man for the Capone mob and ought to be thrown off the track." (At the time he testified before us McCullough, in fact, had lost his job as police chief at Sportsman's Park.)

So McCullough went to a friend who knew Drury and blustered: "You can tell him [Drury] for me the first time I see him I am going to use my fists on him. It is either me or him. If you can make a date with him anywhere at all, I will meet him." However, McCullough assured us, he had nothing to do with Drury's murder.

A wave of suspensions and resignations by higher-ups in the Police Department followed our investigation of great wealth accumulated by a number of Chicago police captains. One of those to resign was the police commissioner himself, John C. Prendergast. This was no reflection on his personal honesty; as Counsel Halley assured Commissioner Prendergast, "You have the reputation of being a completely honest and hard-hitting law enforcement officer." But when Halley asked the commissioner to identify for the committee police officers who obviously had "other means of support than their salary," the commissioner answered, "I can honestly tell you I don't know. I don't know their private lives. I don't know where five of them live."

One police captain who testified before us in executive session was Thomas Harrison, once suspended for failure to suppress bookmaking and gambling operations in his district. "How is it," Associate Counsel George Robinson asked him, "that the Crime Commission reports about eighty-four places that are violating the law in your district? What has been done about that?" Captain Harrison replied: "They never reported them to me, Mr. Robinson." Among other transactions, Captain Harrison, whose salary was $5200 a year, told us of buying an $18,500 house; and of purchasing various stocks between 1933 and 1948 for which he paid out approximately $57,000.

Harrison admitted to us that on one occasion he had borrowed $10,000 from a reputed gambler and $2500 from one John J. Lynch, at that time a power in the racing wire service. Then in 1937, Harrison went on, Lynch "gave me a $30,000 gift" because "I was his friend and a sort of bodyguard for him." Harrison disclosed that Lynch not only gave him the $30,000 but paid the tax on the gift. "He gave me this money in an envelope," Harrison testified. "I said, 'Now, Jack, it seems like quite a bit of money. What am I supposed to do about this? Am I going to file on it?' He said, 'No; I will file on this money. This is a gift from me.'"

At this point I, as chairman of the hearing, remarked (I hope with the proper degree of dryness): "He was a nice fellow."

The most highly publicized case involving a police officer was that of Captain Daniel A. Gilbert, referred to by Chicago newspapers as "the richest cop in the world." At the time Captain Gilbert was serving as chief investigator for the State's

Attorney's office of Cook County, Illinois, and also was the Democratic candidate for sheriff. It has become something of a *cause célèbre* that the Kefauver Committee, of which I, a Democrat, was the chairman, was supposed to have been responsible for the defeat of United States Senator Scott Lucas, then the Senate Majority Leader, because of its inquiry into Captain Gilbert's finances. The exposé was supposed to have made the Cook County voters so angry at the local Democratic machine which hand-picked Captain Gilbert as a candidate that the party failed to poll its customary large majority in Chicago, causing Senator Lucas to go down in defeat.

Actually the truth of the matter is that the committee did not subpoena Captain Gilbert but issued an invitation to him to appear as a witness because there had been considerable public discussion locally about his finances. At first the captain advised us he preferred not to testify; then he appeared voluntarily one day and sent in word, while we were examining another witness, that he wanted to answer any questions we might have because "I felt as though I would be doing my duty to come here." If Senator Lucas, whom I personally like and who was a capable Majority Leader, was hurt by this episode it is regrettable. On the other hand, the Democratic organization in Chicago may be strengthened in the long run by the lesson learned through the vigorous demonstration of the current temper of public opinion. One of the aftermaths of the campaign, incidentally, was the resignation in Chicago of Jack Arvey as leader of the Cook County Democratic organization.

Captain Gilbert had been investigator for the State's Attorney's office for eighteen years and, at the time he appeared before us, was in charge of seventy-six police officers who worked on special investigations for State's Attorney John S. Boyle. Mr. Boyle described Captain Gilbert as "probably the most efficient . . . and one of the hardest-working police officers I have ever known." He admitted, however, that Gilbert also had the reputation of being a gambler and of playing the market heavily. Gilbert, a well-dressed and breezy figure, told us he estimated his net worth was approximately $360,000, and that dividends on stocks and bonds he currently held were bringing him in about $42,000 a year.

The next question for Captain Gilbert, obviously, was how he became so affluent. As I remarked to him, "People don't understand how you got hold of all that money." Whereupon the captain began explaining to us all the details of his badge-to-riches story. There was a little "honest gambling" on the side, but mostly it was done through investments in stocks and bonds, with the market tips furnished by the type of good fellows in which Chicago seems to abound.

In 1921, the captain related, he received his first important stock market tip from a friendly political leader to whom he had been assigned "as chauffeur and kind of bodyguard." It seems that the politician was concerned about the future education of Gilbert's son, so he advised him to buy 100 shares of a certain stock, then selling for around $18. If 100 was good, 200 was better, Gilbert reasoned, so he dug up about $400 and purchased 200 shares on margin. He kept pyramiding his holdings, and by the time the stock reached 45 he had 1000 shares. He branched out into other stocks and also, with the helpful advice of another good fellow, began trading in the grain market.

By 1929 he was worth $98,000; then the crash came and he lost all but $15,000. He began again and gradually built his holdings up to the $360,000 mark.

At approximately this point our perspicacious chief counsel inquired with elaborate politeness: "May I ask a question? ... When do you find time to take care of your law enforcement duties?"

Captain Gilbert's income tax returns also showed annual winnings on wagers. "I bet on the football games and I bet on prize fights," Captain Gilbert said, "but mostly it would all be elections." I asked him:

Q. How big election bets do you make?
A. In 1936 I think I won around $10,000 or $12,000. . . .

Q. You just like to bet?

A. I have been a gambler at heart.

Q. What do you think about a sheriff being a gambler?

A. On football games or on elections, I don't feel it is any violation of my oath of office on them because I take straw ballots, and if a fellow bets against me I am willing to bet. I have won every election bet since 1921.

In the last presidential election, Captain Gilbert went on, he picked up around $1500 by taking odds of 7 to 1 on President Truman's re-election. This amazingly ingenuous police captain, chief investigator, and would-be sheriff went on to tell us the name and address of the betting commissioner with whom he placed his football bets. I gently asked him, "Is that legal?" "Well," said Gilbert, "I would say it was legal if a fellow wants to make a bet on an election. There is nothing illegal about it. No violation of the law."

A final philosophical gem came from Captain Gilbert after Counsel asked him if it would not be natural for the public to lose confidence in a police officer who amassed such great wealth. Gilbert replied rather sorrowfully:

"The failure of human nature is that we are prone to believe evil about our fellow man, and especially about a peace officer."

It was about two weeks after this that the voters of Cook County registered their disapproval of Captain Gilbert—he told us, incidentally, that he campaigned in his own Cadillac so that people wouldn't say he "was campaigning in the county's car"—by defeating him at the polls.

In Chicago, too, we gathered evidence of a disturbing phenomenon that we found repeated in other large cities of the country. I refer to the active participation—amounting almost to subsidization—in gang affairs by a certain element of lawyers, accountants, and tax consultants. As Judge Samuel Leibowitz, of Brooklyn, an outstanding jurist, remarked in his testimony at our final hearings many months later, "There are criminal lawyers and lawyer criminals." Judge Leibowitz said it was one thing for a criminal lawyer to defend his client honestly and squarely and to see that he got his day in court according to our laws and our Constitution, but it was "another thing to be in the hire of some gang to advise the gang how to operate, and to be at the beck and call of the gangster or act as his right-hand man." Nationwide disclosures on this particular problem were so disturbing that the Senate Committee felt it would be desirable for local bar associations everywhere to take a new look at how the canon of ethics supposedly governing conduct of members of the bar was being heeded. On the federal level, we felt it would be wise to tighten up the regulations regarding standards for admission of attorneys permitted to practice before federal courts and other United States judicial bodies.

One of the fascinating stories into which the committee delved in Chicago was the net of strange circumstances surrounding the parole from the federal penitentiary at Leavenworth of three Capone Syndicate gangsters, Paul Ricca, Louis Campagna, and Charles (Cherry Nose) Gioe, alias Joye. Ricca, as the most important of the three mobsters, was the central figure of the episode.

The three of them, along with a pack of other Chicago, New York, and West Coast mobsters, were sent to the penitentiary in 1943 to serve ten-year sentences on conviction of conspiracy to extort huge sums from the movie industry by threatening to call a strike of a gangster-controlled union. This was the case in which George Browne, president of the International Association of Theatrical Stage Employees, and the notorious Willie Bioff were the central figures. All the time that Ricca & Co. were in prison strenuous efforts, including the employment of expensive legal talent, were exerted to have their sentences commuted.

After Ricca, Campagna, and Gioe had served only about one third of their sentences the efforts to secure their paroles were successful.[1] At the time Ricca and Campagna went to prison,

[1]The committee noted in its report to the Senate: "The three mobsters were released on parole after serving a minimum period of imprisonment although they were known to be vicious gangsters. A prominent member

however, they also were in trouble with the federal government on charges of income tax evasion. The Internal Revenue Bureau entered huge deficiency claims against them—$370,-583.02 in the case of Campagna and $141,631.72 against Ricca. The claims had to be settled before the gangsters could be paroled. At this point the mob stepped in, and there ensued a series of events aimed, first, at settling the cases, and, second, at raising the money necessary to pay off the government. It was as strange as anything that ever came from the pages of a dime novel.

The attorney at law who was called in to settle the tax case for Ricca and Campagna was Eugene Bernstein. Many years ago Bernstein had been with the Internal Revenue Bureau. When he obtained his law license and left the bureau he specialized in tax cases. Over the course of years he accumulated a list of clients that read like the Blue Book of the Capone Syndicate: Guzik, Accardo, Humphreys, Ralph Capone, the R. & H. Syndicate, and numerous others. Bernstein had never done any work for Ricca or Campagna, but one day the wives of the two gangsters came to him and asked him to take over the matter of settling the tax claims against their husbands so that they could be released from the penitentiary. He said he had no idea why they came to him, unless it was that he had "handled a couple of other cases and bit by bit your reputation starts to grow."

Bernstein made a trip to confer with his new clients in the Atlanta Federal Penitentiary, where they were then incarcerated, but both clammed up on him. "They were vague, evasive," he said. "They gave me no information." So he called Mrs. Campagna and "told her if I couldn't get any help I would have to step out of the case." He made a second trip to Atlanta and attempted, with Mrs. Campagna's aid, to get

---

of the Missouri bar presented their parole applications to the parole board, which granted the parole against the recommendations of the prosecuting attorney and of the judge who had presided at their trial. In the opinion of this committee, this early release from imprisonment of three dangerous mobsters is a shocking abuse of parole powers."

the information he would need to effect a settlement with the government. The imprisoned mobsters still wouldn't—or couldn't—give him the facts he needed about their net worth, and again, Bernstein said, he was about to withdraw from the case.

Then, Bernstein continued, Tony Accardo entered the picture. He "just walked in one day" at Bernstein's office and announced, "I would like to help you on this if I can," the lawyer said. Counsel Halley asked:

Q. Who first told you Accardo was coming to your office?
BERNSTEIN: Nobody did. . . .
HALLEY: It just doesn't sound like something I can visualize.
. . . Who walks in but a notorious gangster, and he tells you, "I am the man," and you accept that without checking back?
BERNSTEIN: I never knew Mr. Accardo to be a notorious gangster, sir, at that time, nor do I know him to be a gangster now.

Then began a series of visits by Bernstein and Accardo to Leavenworth—Ricca and Campagna had been transferred by then—to confer anew with the gangsters, under Accardo's management. There were ten or twelve trips—perhaps more—in all, Bernstein said.

Q. (By *Associate Counsel Robinson.*) What was discussed on the way down to Leavenworth?
BERNSTEIN: Nothing, sir.
Q. You didn't talk about anything?
A. No. Mr. Accardo read and I read going down. I generally read tax bulletins. . . .

At Leavenworth, Bernstein signed the prison register for admission. He "assumed" Accardo also signed. It later came out that the gangster had signed a false name on the penitentiary register; he posed as Joseph Bulger, a Chicago attorney and onetime president of the Italo-American Union, who had conferred with the wives of Ricca and Campagna in an earlier phase of the case. Accardo and Bernstein later were indicted by a federal grand jury on a statute which made it a crime to deprive a government agency or official of exercising proper judgment. Both, however, were acquitted by a jury.

With Accardo present, things went much better between Bernstein and his suspicious clients. With the information obtained with Accardo's help he was able to effect a settlement with the government. Campagna's case was settled for $90,371.49, Ricca's for $36,146.50, and accumulated interest brought the total settlement for the two cases to approximately $190,000. This was approximately $322,000 less than the total of the original deficiency claims.

With the settlement effected, the next question was how to raise the money with which to pay it. Bernstein went back to the penitentiary to talk with his clients about it. Again they were stubborn. "They both took the position they didn't owe the money and wouldn't pay it, and nobody could make them pay it," the attorney told us. "They were rather adamant in that position."

Bernstein returned to Chicago to think this one over. There was a period of either thirty or sixty days, as he remembered it, in which to pay the settlement. Almost immediately, he said, strangers started walking into his office and leaving packages of bills, usually wrapped in paper, in amounts varying between $10,000 and $20,000. When the first batch of bills came in, Bernstein told us in what seemed to be a masterpiece of understatement, he was "taken aback." He called one of the wives about it, and "she said she understood it was coming in; that it would be all right." The procession of strange men bearing currency continued until the needed total of $190,000 had been brought in.

Q. (*By Halley.*) Who brought it in?
BERNSTEIN: I wouldn't know who the men were.
Q. Did you speak to them?
A. No. They came in and said, "Mr. Bernstein?" I said,

"Yes." They said, "This is for Mr. Campagna's tax." Or some said, "This is for Mr. De Lucia's [Ricca's] tax." . . .

Q. Did you ask their names?

A. I wouldn't think of asking their names, because it made no difference to me. . . .

Q. As this money came in, you kept tally of it; is that right?

A. That is right.

Q. Did you keep reporting to anybody how much you had?

A. I did not; no, sir.

Q. So somebody obviously was adding it up and knew when to stop at the $190,000.

A. That was obvious.

It was all very strange, even disconcerting, Bernstein went on. "Sometimes," he related, "they brought it to my secretary in the office—left it with her on several occasions. I know of one gentleman outside wanted to know what in the world they were leaving that kind of money around there for."

"You have very fine farsight," Counsel Halley challenged Attorney Bernstein. "Isn't it really because of the fact that you knew these questions would be asked that you didn't want to know who brought the money?" The attorney snapped back: "That is your opinion and I resent that, too. . . . I don't propose to have my intelligence insulted."[2]

When all was settled Bernstein went to Leavenworth again to see the boys out of the penitentiary and accompany them home. In this connection, he revealed a further cozy little arrangement. At the Kansas City airport Tony Gizzo, the mobster and alleged Mafia chieftain, would meet them and drive them to the penitentiary. Gizzo also would arrange for airplane tickets and hotel suites, as needed, for the Chicago contingent. "What was the close relationship between Gizzo and your client?" Halley asked. "What was the reason for this very great assistance you would get . . . ?" Bernstein re-

[2] Of Attorney Bernstein's part in the $190,000 deal, the committee's report said: "The connivance in this plot of a lawyer who obviously could provide the essential clues, if not the actual answers, brands the entire matter as even more shocking."

sponded, "I don't know. I think when I went down for the first time with Accardo, I think it was all arranged at that time." It was the committee's contention, of course, that close ties exist between all the local mobs in the nationwide crime syndicate.

Before Attorney Bernstein had concluded his several appearances before us we had collected a number of interesting opinions from him. For instance, Counsel asked him at one point why he took exception to the statement that Tony Accardo was a gangster. The following colloquy ensued:

BERNSTEIN: The word "gangster" has a different connotation to me than it may have to other people. A gangster is an individual who goes out and, by means of force, duress, obtains sums of money. If you and I go out and do certain things legally, and place funds in his possession without duress, at our own direction, and then he does something with that, that would not be gangsters. Gangsterism is very definitely a form of violence.

HALLEY: A gangster is a man who belongs to a gang, isn't he?

BERNSTEIN: Then you and I are gangsters. . . .

HALLEY: What gang do I belong to?

BERNSTEIN: We belong to the human race. We belong to a political party. That may be a gang.

At another point, when Counsel was probing Bernstein as to the loose habits of his gangster clients in submitting facts to back up their claims of income and deduction for tax returns, Bernstein asserted: "I have no reason to believe that my clients would lie to me or make a false return to the government, especially since they have been audited and found to be accurate." Counsel pointed out that one of Bernstein's clients, Guzik, was convicted for an income tax violation and sentenced to the penitentiary. "That," Bernstein replied, "is when they [sic] learned their lesson. The men have paid their penalty and they are trying to do what is right." He also made a spirited defense of Murray (The Camel) Humphreys, saying that he was "forced" out of a legitimate laundry business because of "political activities."

HALLEY: . . . What do you mean "political activities"?

BERNSTEIN: I mean because these men tried to go into legitimate business and they were not permitted to.

Q. Why not?

A. Just because of the newspapers and other people that keep on pushing them around.

Q. Is that why Accardo and Guzik were forced back in their policy racket?

A. I don't know, sir. I don't know what racket they are in.

Concerning taxes, this experienced attorney at law gave us still another bit of advice. We just did not understand the *modus operandi* of the men we referred to as gangsters, he told us. "These people don't tell you anything," he explained. "They say, 'Here are facts that I have,' and I prepare the [income tax] return on what I have. They take full responsibility for their returns. . . ." Halley inquired, "Is there any disposition on your part not to want to know anything?" Said Bernstein: "No, sir. If I feel a client wants to give me information, that is up to him."

This exchange, the committee felt, was a highly revealing exposition of what, in general, is wrong with the income tax returns filed by gangsters. It also fortified my determination to seek passage of an amendment to the internal revenue laws, specifically requiring persons who admittedly profit from illegal operations to file complete financial statements, along with their annual tax returns, itemizing their sources of income. I am strongly in favor of any weapon which will enable internal revenue agents to get at the truth and to start collecting some of the sorely needed millions of tax dollars which these hoodlums now are concealing and withholding from the government.

We ran up against the same stone wall when we sought to learn from Ricca and Campagna—and later from Tony

Accardo—who might have put up the $190,000. "Why, I would be glad to find out who did that for me," the white-haired, fifty-two-year-old Ricca blandly told us. And when I told him bluntly that I thought he was committing perjury he protested: "Oh, I am telling the truth!" When Senator Hunt taxed him with the preposterousness of his story he offered the explanation that all the publicity about the mysterious donations must have scared off the donors and they thought "it was better to lose the money . . . than to get the publicity in the paper and all that." But, he added, "someday they come along, and I reimburse." Campagna, too, said he just never got around to asking Bernstein how the money was paid. "It sounds fantastic, but it is true," Campagna told us.

Ricca and Campagna gave interesting accounts of themselves. Campagna, who sometimes used the name of Carmini and other aliases, once was a $50-a-week guard for Al Capone's beer and alcohol trucks. Originally he was a Brooklyn gangster, which accounts for his sobriquet—Little New York. He told us he made his big money operating horse books and other gambling enterprises in Cicero and Chicago. He owns 950 acres of farmland in the vicinity of Fowler, Indiana, for which he said he paid approximately $122,500. The committee had some trouble with Campagna when it caught him in an outright lie about a certain sum of money which he had hidden in his basement while he was in the penitentiary. First Campagna told us he had the cash concealed in "some fellow's house," then he admitted he was the "fellow." He told us his hoard was approximately $30,000, but later admitted it "might be" as much as $75,000. These inconsistencies in his testimony, which was given under oath, were referred to the Federal District Attorney.

We had heard from the Chicago Crime Commission that Ricca had been known in Italy as Maglio. Ricca himself claimed his correct name was De Lucia, and that he used so many aliases he couldn't remember them all. "Any place I go I mention any name that comes to my mind . . . just a habit," he explained.

This man of many names went on to tell us, under questioning, that he made his big money as a gambler. When he went to the penitentiary late in 1943 he had accumulated some $300,000 in cash as the profits from gambling, mostly on the horses. He kept a great deal of money hidden around his house, and he also had a safe deposit box in which he sometimes kept as much as $100,000 in cash. His principal gambling activity was taking bets at the race track from big gamblers who did not want to put up their money at the legalized pari-mutuel windows because large wagers would cause the odds to go down. As Ricca explained his highly personalized operation:

"I used to go out to the race track. Somebody . . . wants to bet $10,000 on a horse, and if he put it in the totalizer, naturally the price go down, so I used to hold the bet. If I thought it was all right, I hold it."

Associate Counsel Robinson asked:

Q. Who bet with you?
A. A lot of people bet with me. I don't recall. That is a long time ago.
Q. Can you recall any of the larger betters with you?
A. Yes; Al Capone was one. . . . Al was a big better. He would bet $10,000 on a race . . . but he would spread it around. Sometimes I take a piece, sometimes I don't.
Q. How large a sum would you handle in gambling over a space of a year? . . .
A. Gee, I don't know. I suppose sometimes I would make $100,000 a year or something like that, sometimes less.

Ricca today is a man of considerable substance. He told us he owns a home at River Forest, Illinois, an elaborate summer house at Long Beach, Indiana, with swimming pool and tennis courts, and an 1100-acre farm in Kendall County, Illinois, which he said cost him approximately $230,000. These assets—plus certain stock holdings and the $300,000 cash Ricca said he had on hand when he went to the penitentiary—made the committee look askance at the story we dug out about how

Ricca, after his parole, borrowed $80,000 from one Hugo Bennett, formerly Benvenuti, a $22,500-a-year auditor for the Miami Beach Kennel Club and the National Jockey Club at Sportsman's Park at Cicero, a Chicago suburb.

The situation regarding the Chicago and Miami horse and dog tracks is so involved that it required some clarification. The president of both the National Jockey Club and the Miami Beach Kennel Club is William H. Johnston, who in 1948 arranged for a $100,000 contribution to Fuller Warren's gubernatorial campaign, a story which we explored thoroughly in our Florida investigation. Formerly the president of the Cicero track was one Edward J. (Eddie) O'Hare, and the secretary-treasurer was John Patton, for many years famed as the so-called "Boy Mayor" of Burnham, a Chicago suburb which Virgil Peterson described as a hide-out and a "center of vice, gambling, and booze for the Capone Syndicate." Johnston sparred at great length with Counsel Halley as to whether any of his tracks had links with the Capone gang, but Peterson stated in his testimony: "During the heyday of Al Capone the Capone Syndicate was in control of dog tracks in virtually every part of the country including Florida. The Capone Syndicate czar of dog racing during that period was Edward J. O'Hare. . . ." In November 1939, O'Hare was having a conference with Johnston and Patton in his office at Sportsman's Park, cleaning his revolver as he talked. As he left the track with the revolver in his pocket he was ambushed and killed by the familiar shotgun method—another episode in the chain of what Peterson called "gang warfare" killings.

Halley hammered at Johnston:

Q. Do you not know that it was reported in the newspapers at the time you went to work for Sportsman's Park that O'Hare was running not only Sportsman's Park but the Hawthorne Kennel Club for Guzik, Nitti, and Al Capone?

A. No, sir.

Q. Did not the newspapers actually state that Al Capone had so told the police?

A. Not that I know of. I never seen it.

Q. Was not that public knowledge throughout Chicago?

A. It wasn't. That was not public knowledge. . . . None of this stuff was common knowledge, or ever came into the newspapers until 1939 when Mr. O'Hare was killed.

Q. I can show you clippings going back to 1930 in the newspapers.

Anyway, when Ricca, the Capone Syndicate gangster, came out of the penitentiary and wanted $80,000 for the purpose, he said, of making improvements on his farm, he turned to his old friend Bennett, the auditor at the track where Ricca, with other Caponeites, had gambled. Bennett obligingly let him have the $80,000 in two installments of $40,000 each, the first in 1948 and the second in 1950. Bennett told us he had to borrow all but $5000 of the first $40,000 to lend Ricca. He obtained $20,000 from his boss, Mr. Johnston, and $15,000 from a concessionaire, Max Silverberg, who did business at Johnston's various tracks. The security and interest provisions in connection with the loans to Ricca were vague; on the first $40,000, Bennett said, there was an "oral agreement" that Ricca would pay no interest at all during the five-year term of the loan, but at the end of that period he either would have paid off the $40,000 in full or would pay interest for the whole period at the rate of four per cent.

Bennett insisted he made this unusual loan to Ricca out of "pure friendship" and nothing more. To date, he acknowledged, Ricca had not paid back any of the money.

There also was another complicated coincidence. When Ricca applied for the second $40,000 in 1950, Bennett, who was not a man of great means, just happened to have that exact sum on hand. How had he acquired it? Well, a little real estate deal had just taken place, in which the stockholders of the Miami Beach Kennel Club—Bennett was a minority stockholder, too—sold to the Miami Beach Kennel Club the land on which the club was located. The stockholders took a profit for themselves of approximately $750,000 on this deal. Bennett's profit was about $28,000, which, with his original investment, gave him the $40,000 that he turned right around and loaned to Ricca. "Just a coincidence in arithmetic?" Halley asked him. "Just coincidence, yes," Bennett replied.

Bennett also insisted that neither Johnston nor Silverberg knew he was borrowing the money from them to loan to the Capone henchman. We recalled Johnston to question him about this. He said that Bennett merely told him that he wanted to borrow $10,000 because "he was going into business."

"I said, 'Do you know what you are doing?' " the free-handed track boss related. "He said, 'Yes.' So I said, 'All right,' and give it to him." (Without interest, too, Bennett had told us.)

Toward the conclusion of our exploration into the details of this remarkable transaction Counsel Halley finally asked Bennett: *"What did he have on you? . . .* He [Ricca] had great assets, two homes, a farm, cash money. You had to . . . borrow the money, and you didn't even say to the man, 'Look, if I lend you this money, I will have to borrow it'?" To which Bennett replied: "Well, I guess it is my silly pride or something. . . . I just didn't say I didn't have it."

All these complicated transactions—the mysterious bundles of cash for Ricca's and Campagna's back taxes; the money which The Waiter and Little New York said they had stashed away but didn't use, and the loan by Bennett of money that was traced right back to the race tracks which Mr. Johnston assured us had no links with the Capone Syndicate—added up to a picture that we could view only with considerable skepticism.

Other phases of Ricca's activities since his parole have aroused curiosity. For instance, when his daughter was married in January 1948 he gave a wedding party for her at one of Chicago's leading hotels that cost him in excess of $15,000. The bill for the hotel services alone was $12,324.58, which Ricca, according to investigators, paid in $100 bills. It has been charged that he failed to make a truthful report of these expenditures to his parole officer.

Following our investigation of the whole question of the parole of Ricca, Campagna, and Gioe, the government instituted proceedings to revoke the parole of all three. This case was pending before the Supreme Court and had not been decided as this was being written.

CHAPTER 5

GREASY THUMB, THE ENFORCER,
AND SOME CHICAGO POLITICIANS

Two Chicago hoodlums in whom the Senate Crime Investigating Committee had particular interest were the frequently mentioned Jacob Guzik and Anthony Accardo. We felt that these infamous and rather strangely assorted partners might hold a key to the whole question of organized interstate crime in the United States, so widely dispersed were their nefarious interests. We were forced, however, to wait a long time before we could question Messrs. Guzik and Accardo, for both were elusive witnesses.

Accardo is a thoroughly vicious character. He used to operate under the appropriate alias of Joe Batters back in the days when he was a strong-arm man in Chicago's underworld and reputedly a bodyguard for the late Machine-Gun Jack McGurn. In 1929, as Virgil Peterson testified, Accardo was suspected and questioned as one of the alleged plotters of the St. Valentine's Day Massacre in which seven members of the Bugs Moran gang died; nothing, however, ever was proven against him in this connection. In 1931 Accardo was labeled a Public

Enemy by the Chicago Crime Commission. After several months of dodging a committee subpoena, Accardo finally appeared before us in Washington on January 5, 1951.

I never shall forget the anticlimactic manner in which Tony the Enforcer, as he is sometimes called, finally put in his appearance. Instead of sitting down in the hearing room of the Senate Office Building, Accardo skulked in the corridor near a men's washroom. When we were ready for him his attorney, a balding young fellow from Chicago, walked out in the hall, clapped his hands sharply twice, and the redoubtable Enforcer shuffled in. A swarthy, gorillalike individual, Accardo now observes the approved code of the more successful gang leaders of imitating a gentleman in dress and outward habits; hence his clothes were of unostentatious pattern and of expensive cut and fabric, and his cravat bore the trademark of one of the most fashionable dining and wining places in the East. The only jarring note in the appearance of our *ersatz* gentleman was a curious mark on his right hand—a flying dove, tattooed into the crease between thumb and trigger finger. When Accardo squeezed his finger the dove looked as if it were flying. Tattoos, like blood, will not wash off.

Guzik, a pouchy-eyed little man of sixty-four, with a ravaged face that looks as if it were made of wax left too long near a hot fire, was even more difficult to find. The warrant for his arrest as a missing witness was not served on him by the Senate sergeant at arms until the final week of our scheduled public hearings. Guzik is a manipulator rather than a muscle man; he acquired his nickname—Greasy Thumb—from the fact that he used to be the business manager and pay-off man for Al Capone. It is a strange quirk of gangdom that these two men should be partners and joint leaders of the Capone Syndicate, for police records show that Accardo, in 1945, was picked up for questioning in connection with a gang-style kidnaping of none other than Guzik. Guzik at that time, according to talk in gang circles, reputedly had to pay $75,000 to regain his freedom. But nothing ever came of this episode, for Guzik stoutly insisted the whole thing was just a misunderstanding over a "business transaction," and now the two men are firmly united in what they euphemistically call a business partnership.

We didn't learn much directly from Guzik and Accardo. Accardo answered only a few elementary questions, refusing even to give us information about things which definitely were part of police and court records. There were approximately 140 instances of his refusal to answer what we and Counsel considered legitimate questions. The Senate, at the committee's request, cited him for contempt.

The gray-visaged Guzik was even worse: he appeared without an attorney and carried his refusal to answer questions down to the point of outright silliness, such as when we asked him, "How old are you?" and he refused to answer on the grounds that it might "incriminate me or tend to incriminate me or lead by some devious ways to incriminate me." After he had parroted this monotonous phrase some eighty times Senator Wiley asked him if he had consulted with a lawyer, and Guzik answered that he had not. "Where did you get this phrase you have been using all the time?" asked Senator Wiley. "I have heard it on television," Guzik said. At the end of his defiant performance the committee ordered that he be held under $10,000 bond pending further action, and he, too, was cited for contempt. All Guzik had to say in his tired, flat voice was, "When can I make my bond?"

Though we did not learn much from Guzik and Accardo, we learned a good deal about them. One of the topics which we explored with interest was the shadowy association of Guzik and Accardo with the "policy wheel" operations of the Manno brothers of Chicago. Before developing this topic, it might be well to explain here the significance of policy wheels in Chicago. In the big city's teeming Negro district policy wheels—a variety of the "numbers" racket whereby daily drawings for combinations of winning numbers are conducted—have come to be big business. Associate Counsel Robinson estimated that in the past five years $1,500,000,000 has been played on the policy wheels in Chicago. Operations of this magnitude, of course, could not exist without graft being paid to dishonest police officers for protection. None of the policy wheel operators whom we questioned, however, would admit such payments.

There is a melancholy moral in the size of the policy operations when one considers that the staggering sum is amassed from the nickels, dimes, and quarters of the inhabitants of some of the worst slums in America. There are numerous wheels operating—with fanciful names such as the Roman Silver, the Calcutta-Green Dragon, the Jack-Pot Whirlaway-Alabama-Georgia, and so forth—and the racket has resulted in multimillion-dollar profits for the operators.

The Capone mob, of course, could not keep its hands off such a bonanza. Coincidentally numerous instances of violence—kidnapings, bombings, and such—began cropping up.

One witness summoned before us was Edward Jones, who had been living in Mexico City for the past seven years. Jones, a onetime Pullman porter, was a partner with his wife, mother, brother, and two men named Theodore Roe and Clifford Davis in the operation of a policy wheel known as the Maine, Idaho, and Ohio. This was a profitable operation. Net profits, for the four-year period, 1946 through 1949, after sizable deductions for overhead, came to $3,656,968.22, according to the partnership's own records. The banner year for operation of the wheel was 1946, when the reported net profits were $1,120,413.87. That year Edward Jones was kidnaped and held until his family paid $100,000 ransom. Even though five years had elapsed since the kidnaping at the time we questioned him, the ex-porter, who wore a huge star-sapphire ring, was exceedingly timorous about speculating as to who might have kidnaped him. He insisted he did not even know whether his abductors were white persons or Negroes because they were "blindfolded" when they snatched him. He said they kept him a week—he was blindfolded all the time—until the ransom was paid. When we asked him if he could not distinguish from their speech whether they were white or colored he demurred: "Well, that is very difficult . . . there wasn't that much exchanged in words." His partner, Roe, was telephoned once by a party purporting to deliver a message from the kidnapers. "It didn't sound like no colored person," Roe said, "but I wouldn't know what nationality."

Whether the kidnaping of Jones was a crime conducted solely for the ransom money, or whether it was part of a "muscle" operation whereby gangsters took over part of the business, never has been established. Jones himself denies that the Maine, Idaho, and Ohio wheel has been "muscled." It is significant, however, that Ed Jones and his brother George—though each continues to draw a twenty per cent share of the profits—have lived in Mexico City since the kidnaping.

Another profitable policy operation in Chicago—the so-called Roman Silver wheel—was run, according to evidence in the record, by Peter Tremont and a suave character named Patrick Manno, alias Manning. According to evidence developed in a sensational Texas case, Manno was an important man in the policy end of the Chicago Syndicate. Three of his brothers, Tom, alias Mousey, Nick, alias Jeff, and Fred, worked with him in the Roman Silver operation.

A rival setup was the Erie-Buffalo wheel, which for years had been the family enterprise of the late Julius Benvenuti, so-called "policy king" of Chicago. Julius had once done a favor for Al Capone, so the mob granted him amnesty. But when Julius died and his two brothers, Leo and Caesar, took over, the "debt" was discharged.

The Erie-Buffalo wheel was a tempting tidbit; our records showed that the two Benvenutis in 1947 reported a gross income of $2,317,048.69 and split a net profit of $205,920.20. All of a sudden a series of significant events began to take place. First the homes of the Benvenutis were bombed. Soon after, it came to pass that there were two new partners in the Erie-Buffalo wheel—Tom (Mousey) Manno, brother of the influential Patrick, and one Sam Pardy. Exactly what conversations led up to this arrangement the committee did not establish, because neither Tremont nor Pat Manno—both of whom have been cited for contempt—would talk, and Pardy and both Benvenutis were on the list of missing witnesses. In fact when the committee was looking for them the Benvenutis were reported to have cleared out entirely and gone to Italy.

However, the committee had a powerful weapon that enabled us to complete the picture. President Truman had facilitated our investigation tremendously by giving the committee authority to examine income tax returns. As lawbreakers—ever since "the man with the whiskers" sent Al Capone to jail—are mortally afraid of monkeying with tax returns, we found important segments of our answer there. It went like this:

In 1947 both Sam Pardy and Mousey Manno, income-wise, were small fry; that same year the Benvenuti brothers each reported more than $100,000 income. But in 1948, after the muscle-in, Sam and Mousey *each* drew $307,565.53 from the Erie-Buffalo, while the Benvenutis received only $50,000 apiece. In 1949 a partnership return for "Pardy and Manno" showed gross receipts of approximately $6,000,000, and a gross profit of $286,822.89. That year Pardy and Manno split the net profit fifty-fifty, and Leo and Caesar Benvenuti, now demoted to "associates," again drew a mere $50,000 apiece. But under "Salaries, Fees, Commissions or Other Compensations," there was a payment of $278,667.89 to Anthony J. Accardo. For "Special Service," it was called.

The final step was to look up the partnership return of Guzik & Accardo for the same year. It showed that Guzik & Accardo received—and split—$278,667.89 from the Erie-Buffalo policy wheel. As Associate Counsel Robinson summed it up in a report to the committee, the sequence of events added up "to only one conclusion—that the Benvenutis were muscled out of a very lucrative policy wheel by members of the mob."

As for interstate crime links, the committee further established a picture of Pat Manno as an out-of-state negotiator for the Guzik-Accardo wing of the Capone Syndicate. Manno, according to testimony of Lieutenant George Butler of the Dallas (Texas) Detective Department, was tied up with a brash and overly talkative Dallas and Chicago criminal named Paul Jones, who had once served time for murder. Jones, representing himself as acting for Manno, was attempting to buy protec-

tion for the Chicago Syndicate to take over gambling in Dallas
County. He made the mistake of thinking Lieutenant Butler
and Sheriff-Elect Steve Guthrie could be bribed. They set a
trap for him and recorded their conversations, including one
revealing conference attended by Manno himself. Jones, a boastful punk, once told Butler, the lieutenant testified, that his
syndicate "operates from coast to coast" and also "in Canada
and Spain." Butler testified:

"He [Jones] . . . could go into any fairly large city in the
United States and his syndicate would have some connection
there. In case he ran into any local trouble he could call his
office long distance, and they would send him all the money
he needed or all of the men he needed."

Q. Do you remember any of the towns he named?
BUTLER: He named St. Louis, Kansas City, New Orleans,
Little Rock, to name a few. He says [these towns] . . . were
well oiled, and everybody was making money.

Jones was even indiscreet enough to name Guzik as the head
of the syndicate, and Murray Humphreys as another prominent
member. Manno, Butler testified, was said to have been
"Number Five" in the setup.

Under the methods of the high-powered, efficient Chicago
gangsters, everything would be extremely "safe" and businesslike, Jones assured the Dallas officials. If the sheriff wanted to
enter into the deal, which involved both a weekly payment and
a percentage of the gambling profits for him, he would "make
$150,000 a year, maybe more," Jones promised. The Chicago
Syndicate would send down expert operators and "a good,
well-coached accountant to handle the books for Uncle Sam's
sake," and would handle any other mobs that tried to
muscle in.

At the recorded conference into which Manno blundered
Jones blabbed that "we have told Steve [the sheriff-elect] that
he's going to have a clean administration and that we're going
to help him and advise him . . . rather than embarrass him in

any way, shape, or form. . . . The program is that we have horse booking, slot machines, dice, numbers, everything. We're going to keep it clean. We're going to take over quietly. . . ." Manno himself, evidently relishing his role as the Chicago big shot, loftily explained to Lieutenant Butler and the sheriff-elect —with the hidden microphone recording every word of it— that his people didn't believe in low stuff like dope peddling, prostitution, etc., nor did they like to run a lot of joints in a town. "I like one big spot, and that's all," he opined. "Out in the country, out of the city entirely."

The audacious Manno went on to assure the sheriff-elect that if he'd only turn crooked and give the Chicago boys the exclusive gambling franchise he'd "be doing well in ten or fifteen years." Describing the rosy lot of those fortunate enough to tie up with the syndicate, the persuasive Manno continued:

"Everybody's happy. Everybody's got beautiful homes, living comfortably, go away a month or two at a time." He added: "You see, I try to be frank and honest with you. I come here. I want to listen to you. I really want to be honest and frank. That's what you want, isn't it?"

These are the sort of riffraff who are corrupting many of our law enforcement officers. Fortunately, in Dallas, they picked the wrong parties, and the trap was sprung on them. Paul Jones was convicted of bribery in connection with the case, and while he was appealing his sentence the government caught him smuggling narcotics—that evil crime which his boss, Manno, had loftily denounced in the recorded conversation—and he is serving time in a federal penitentiary. Manno, Guzik, Accardo, and the others, unfortunately, remained at liberty.

Our Chicago hearings also provided us with a significant case history of how a onetime hoodlum can establish himself in a legitimate business and become enormously wealthy. The case into which we delved was that of Joseph Charles (Joe) Fusco, forty-eight years old, now the operating vice-president of Gold Seal Liquors, Inc., wholesale distributors; a stockholder in four other liquor distributing companies; and part owner of a brewery. From a sales volume standpoint, Fusco boasted, Gold Seal was Chicago's Number One dealer. His own net worth was possibly $1,000,000, and the book value of the Gold Seal corporation alone, of which he owns twenty-five per cent, was $2,200,000, he told us. He said his annual income was around $110,000 to $120,000, which had enabled him to establish the "Joseph Fusco Foundation" to "handle any charity operations that I want to give money to." He also said he wins large sums of money annually—$37,000 in 1949, for example—on the horses.

In his testimony before the committee Virgil Peterson of the Chicago Crime Commission gave us this thumbnail report on Fusco: "Joe Fusco, designated several years ago as a public enemy, during the prohibition era was a principal lieutenant in the Capone Syndicate, handling the manufacture and distribution of illicit beer. He is presently suspected of being the respectable front in the liquor industry for the syndicate. . . . It has been stated that the syndicate owns or controls at least seventeen per cent of the retail liquor stores in Chicago. . . .

"On June 12, 1931, Fusco was indicted with Al Capone and other members of the Capone mob in federal court, totaling sixty-nine defendants, charged with liquor conspiracy. The indictment was dismissed after Al Capone was convicted of income tax evasion and sentenced to the federal penitentiary. On June 7, 1934, when he [Fusco] was arrested, he was in the company of Matt Capone, Ralph Capone, brothers of Al, and Dennis Cooney, who was a powerful figure in the Capone Syndicate."

Peterson also identified Rocco De Stefano, with whom Fusco admitted doing business. Peterson called De Stefano an "important syndicate man" and said he "has come into prominence recently as an affiliate of such well-known members of the syndicate as Joe Fusco, vice-president of Gold Seal Liquors; Jake Guzik and Charles[1] and Rocco Fischetti. De Stefano con-

[1]Charles Fischetti, the late Al Capone's cousin and one of Capone's successors to leadership of the Chicago Syndicate, died of a heart attack at Miami Beach in April 1951, after he and his brother Rocco had been taken

trols a chain of retail liquor stores in which Fusco is supposed to have an interest or did have an interest."

Fusco was a cocky and arrogant witness. He started off by indicating the witness chair and asking me, "Is this the hot seat?" He denied the picture Mr. Peterson painted of him as an ex-hoodlum and present affiliate of the Capone Syndicate. He did admit, however, that he sold illegal beer in Chicago in the early twenties and that he had known Al Capone. Though he admitted Al had helped him on at least one occasion with some helpful advice on where he could buy beer, Fusco denied he had worked for Capone. He did not deny his acquaintance-ships with numerous underworld figures from Chicago and elsewhere, including the above-mentioned Rocco De Stefano, to whom Fusco admitted he extended unlimited credit. Fusco said he also brought De Stefano into his brewing company as a stockholder.

Fusco admitted he had been arrested on a whisky charge; however, it was ever so innocent, he told us—just as we were told by scores of underworld characters that their various arrests were either accidents, coincidences, or frame-ups. In Fusco's case, he was just a "punk kid" of eighteen when some fellows asked him if he would mind being one of three signers necessary to incorporate a trucking outfit known as the World's Motor Service Company. So he signed the papers, though he really "had no investment or interest" in the company. When he stopped working for the trucking company, "not knowing too much about corporations or anything like that, I even forgot I was ever an officer there," Fusco went on. "In 1924 or whenever that time happened, they found some whisky in this company's garage. On account of my being an officer, I was arrested as being one of them." But the case against him, he added, was dismissed.

The only conviction for any criminal offense on his record, Fusco said, occurred around 1919 or 1920 when he was driving

into custody on a Senate arrest warrant. Fischetti, who liked to pose as "Dr. Charles Fischer, noted art connoisseur," and his brother had evaded a committee subpoena for months by hiding out in Brazil.

a truck for the same company. He was hauling a load which was "supposed to be near beer" and, as he informed us with some vehemence, "I tell you to this day at the time I went for this beer it was supposed to be near beer. I didn't know any different." But agents stopped him on the highway, and what do you suppose they found? It wasn't near beer after all, it was real beer. It wasn't until years later, when Gold Seal, with which Fusco had become affiliated, was applying for a permit to handle alcohol and some question was raised about his record, that he "found out that someway, somehow, the case was disposed of." "I was supposed to have gotten a fifty-dollar fine . . ." he said. "That was the first time I ever knew I had a fifty-dollar fine against me."

Fusco said he began working with Gold Seal as a salaried salesman in 1935. In 1942 he began buying stock and was made an officer of the company. He traced his dealings with various distillers; told of how he had scrapped to keep up his whisky allocations during the World War II shortage period, and how today he was the exclusive distributor for many leading brands. At one point Fusco, losing patience with Halley's persistent questioning, delivered a long and rather revealing pronunciamento, part of which was as follows:

"I am going to tell you about Gold Seal. I defy any liquor company in the United States has run a company [sic] any cleaner than Gold Seal, for the simple reason that Joe Fusco is connected with that company. I want you to know that. . . .

"I tell you the reason why I am here and I am tickled to death to be here, for the simple reason that maybe once and for all everybody concerned with the government—I don't care about John Doe Public because he doesn't mean nothing to me —are satisfied that we are running that business one million and one per cent on the up and up. I would like you to go in there, and I mean turn those books inside out, really go in there and give it a good cleaning, to see if you can find anything. By God, if you can find anything, you can say to me, 'Fusco, we want you to step out of there,' and I will be more than glad to step out of there tomorrow morning!"

Painfully, and with the witness making long speeches at almost every question, Halley extracted from Fusco some of the details of how he gave away twenty to twenty-five cases of whisky as Christmas gifts to public officials and other friends. Practically every cop in the district came around at Christmastime for a bottle or two of whisky, Fusco said. The whisky dealer became belligerent when asked who received his Christmas liquor. "If you were in Chicago," he barked at Halley, "maybe I would send you a case too." Halley retorted: "Maybe I would return it to you." "I don't know," said Fusco in a manner that revealed the arrogance of this type of person. "I have never got any back."

Before Fusco left the witness stand Halley asked him pointblank: "Are you able to say whether or not you or any of your associates have used intimidation as a method of getting business in the liquor industry?" Fusco snapped: "Positively not." Halley pressed him further: "Have you heard charges made by various of your competitors that you have used it?" Fusco answered: "Not directly."

All throughout our investigation we found it extremely difficult to establish definite proof of "muscle" tactics by the mob interests which infiltrated legitimate business. We tangled with "reformed" mobsters all along the line on this point.

In Chicago one witness, Max Bloom, whose family has been in the wholesale tobacco and liquor business for fifty-five years, testified that his firm's annual liquor business had dropped from a volume of nearly $900,000 down to $300,000 after Gold Seal, under Fusco, "got big." More recently, he said, mob interests were muscling into the tobacco field, and he "felt the same thing was going to happen . . . that it was going to be a question of being muscled out of accounts." Bloom told of losing one old customer, who owned a chain of liquor stores, to "one of the element." "In talking to him," he testified, "he just told me in plain English he can't even talk to me." Bloom also told us that the legitimate operators in his field are "just scared to death" of the new element that is taking over.

There was an ugly and significant aftermath to Fusco's appearance before us. As indicated by the portions of his testimony which I quoted, Fusco certainly did not tell us much. His testimony, however, was given in executive session and was not released at the time. Apparently the mob got the idea that Fusco had "talked." Ten days after his appearance before us a black powder bomb went off in the doorway of his Gold Seal warehouse. The newspapers captioned a picture of Fusco inspecting the damaged warehouse as follows: "He Talked to Kefauver." One newspaper quoted Chicago police as expressing the opinion that "the bomb might be a tip to Chicago's underworld, both respectable and unrespectable, to keep their mouths shut when the Senate Committee returns here in December."

Everywhere we went the committee found a certain amount of political immorality, but in Chicago the rawness of this sort of thing was particularly shocking. I previously mentioned the case of Dan Serritella, who was simultaneously a state senator, scratch sheet operator, and business partner with Greasy Thumb Guzik. We accumulated a mass of evidence that conclusively proved the interests and connections of the Capone gang with politicians of both major parties. The mobsters played politics strictly for their own interests. When we asked the witness Philip D'Andrea, the ex-Caponeite, whether Al Capone had been a Republican or Democrat, D'Andrea replied: "He was a Republican when it fitted his clothes, I guess, and a Democrat otherwise." I asked him: "You mean the whole group played both sides of the street?" "That is right," the witness answered.

Frederick Pretzie, Jr., administrative assistant of the Chicago Crime Commission, told us of having been profanely heckled and even threatened with physical violence by certain legislators who were members of the so-called Chicago West Side bloc, friendly with the Capone mob. These incidents occurred during the legislative battle over passage of the so-called Crime Commission bill, backed by Governor Adlai Stevenson, but defeated largely through political trades effected by the influential West Side bloc. Pretzie himself witnessed a near fight in a hotel lobby between one member of the West Side bloc, Representative James J. Adducci, and another member of the legislature who was on the other side of the fence. The other legislator told Pretzie afterward that the West Side bloc "had threatened not only violence" but told him they would "spend $25,000" to defeat him in his district if he did not change his mind and vote against the Crime Commission bill.

The pro-Capone bloc in the legislature was bipartisan and included Democrats and Republicans alike. For instance, Virgil Peterson testified that Senator Roland Libonati, a Democrat, "has been pictured with Al Capone and with Machine-Gun Jack McGurn, and was picked up after an election raid one day by the police, around 1930," in company with Paul Ricca and other members of the mob. Another member of the bloc was the previously mentioned James J. Adducci, a Republican and for eighteen years a member of the Illinois legislature. Mr. Adducci appeared before us and outlined his political philosophy and certain facets of his career. He has been a friend and consort of numerous notorious Capone gangsters, and admitted having been arrested frequently himself on numerous charges—including kidnaping—but never convicted.

For eight years, Adducci testified, he has been getting a commission of "between $5000 and $6000 or $6500" by selling stationery and envelopes to the state. He also boasted of having control of about forty patronage jobs, including ten men on the staff of the sheriff of Cook County, and "a couple of highway police." Adducci cynically told us that "my conscience made me" oppose the Crime Commission bill. When we asked him if he ever had studied the bill Adducci roughly answered: "Hell no, I didn't study it!" He also told us—and I quote from the record:

ADDUCCI: I come from a very funny district. I have every element there is in the world, I guess, in my district. I have the pimp, the jack-roller, the safeblower, the dope fiend, and every-other god-damned thing in there. I mean, I come from the

West Side of Chicago, a very poor district. All those elements
are in there. Skid Row, you may have heard of Skid Row. That
is in the heart of my district, where all those so-called hoboes
come in and congregate in there. There are so many hunt-and-
—— joints, they call them, saloons where they buy their pint
of wine and stuff.

THE CHAIRMAN: You never have any trouble getting elected,
do you?

ADDUCCI: No, I don't, Senator.

THE CHAIRMAN: When is your term up?

ADDUCCI: It is up right now. I was nominated in April, and
I have no opposition in November.[2]

There was no doubt in the minds of any of us, after the sort
of testimony we heard in Chicago, that organized crime and
political corruption go hand in hand, and that in fact there
could be no big-time organized crime without a firm and
profitable alliance between those who run the rackets and those
in political control.

[2]Adducci was re-elected.

CHAPTER 6

CORRUPTION OF A SMALL TOWN:

A CASE STUDY

THE pattern suggested so far is that crime and contempt for the law are big-city operations. This is not necessarily so. The smaller cities and towns have it too. Sometimes, as the committee was to learn, crime in the smaller places was conducted as a suburban, or branch, operation of the nearest big-city gang. This was particularly true in the Chicago and New York areas. On the other hand, there also is the phenomenon of the wide-open small town, free from big-city gang influence where the local operator—usually a single "strong man"—is able to operate without paying any particular tribute to the law.

Had time permitted, I should have liked the Senate Crime Investigating Committee to conduct at least one complete case study of such a small-town operation. The small cities and towns, as has often been said, are the backbone of America. If corruption threatens to take over the small towns it is important that we find out about it and turn the spotlight of exposure upon it, so an aroused public opinion can get to work on cleaning up conditions. In many big cities young people come to maturity with an attitude of contempt for the law, because almost daily they see and hear of instances wherein criminals, through alliances with conniving politicians and crooked law enforcement officers, are bigger than the law. It would be a frightful thing if this same disillusionment should spread to the small-town youngsters of America.

The committee touched briefly on one such case study in its questioning, both privately and in public hearings in Chicago, of a man named Thomas J. Cawley. In a way Cawley, a stocky, unabashed, monosyllabic witness, was a refreshing change from the procession of hoodlum witnesses whose carefully rehearsed refrain, "I refuse to answer on the ground it might tend to incriminate me," became so monotonous to our ears. He at least made no bones of the fact that Thomas J. Cawley was the undisputed gambling king of two small towns in Illinois. One was La Salle, population 12,023. The other was Streator, population 16,442. The two towns, both in La Salle County, are about twenty-seven miles apart.

For what it is worth, I should like to quote simple and unadorned excerpts from the official record of the examination of this small-town gambler.

Cawley's first appearance was in executive session, October 18, 1950, U. S. Court House, Chicago. Associate Counsel George Robinson examining:

Q. State your full name.
A. Thomas J. Cawley, C-a-w-l-e-y.
Q. Where do you live?
A. La Salle, Illinois; born and raised there.
Q. What is your business, Mr. Cawley?
A. A cigar store operator.
Q. What other business do you have?
A. I operate a farm and a book. . . .
Q. Where do you operate your book?
A. 621 First Street, La Salle, Illinois.
Q. Is that the only book you operate?
A. I operate one in Streator, Illinois. . . .

Q. Is it [the Streator operation] solely a book?
A. Well, it is a gaming room, is what it is. We have dice.
Q. You also have gambling equipment?
A. Yes.
Q. What type of games do you run?
A. Dice.
Q. Crap tables?
A. That is correct.
Q. Roulette?
A. Roulette, La Salle, and that is all.

Cawley went on to say that he employs about sixty-five or seventy persons in La Salle; this includes his restaurant, bar, and cigar store employees, in addition to the gambling help.

Q. How long have you operated the book there?
A. I imagine . . . around fifteen years.
CHAIRMAN: Is that in La Salle?
A. In La Salle; at Streator, I would say ten years. . . .
Q. Who is the sheriff of that county?
A. The sheriff now is Ryan.
Q. How long have you known him?
A. I hardly know the man. . . .
Q. Did you know Mike Welter?
A. Yes, sir. . . . He was sheriff three terms. . . .
Q. Did you contribute to the campaign funds of any of the other sheriffs?
A. No, sir; only Mike Welter.
Q. How much did you contribute to his campaign?
A. Five hundred dollars.
Q. Mike Welter knew what business you were in?
A. . . . I wouldn't know whether he would or not.
Q. Why?
A. I never asked him. . . .
CHAIRMAN: What we want to get at is: how can you run wide open down there without the sheriff knowing about it

and doing something about it? It is generally known, is it not, that you operate these places?

A. That is right. I was born and raised there. I had a good friend, the mayor of the town, and he wouldn't let none of them politicians come into our city. . . .

CHAIRMAN: He would not let any politicians come in?

A. He wouldn't let them politicians come from the county into the city from La Salle.

CHAIRMAN: He would not let the sheriff come in?

A. That is right.

CHAIRMAN: So he is the one who let you keep on running; is that it?

A. He never let me keep on running. He didn't do any more for me than he would for anybody else. Anybody can go down in that town right today and open up, and it doesn't cost them a five-cent piece.

CHAIRMAN: The sheriff does not bother you?

A. That is right.

CHAIRMAN: Do the people like it, you think?

A. I think they do—ninety per cent of them.

Associate Counsel Robinson resumed the questioning:

Q. What is the present chief of police's name?

A. Eddie Kasprowicz, something like that. . . .

Q. He knows what business you were in?

A. Yes. Everybody in town knows what business I am in.

Q. Do you pay money for protection?

A. No, sir.

Q. Never have paid any money?

A. No. When I do, I will get out of business.

Q. Do you contribute any money to political parties?

A. I might contribute to both parties a check . . . a hundred dollars here or a hundred dollars there; yes. . . .

Q. That was to the political party, but to no particular individual?

A. That is right. . . .

Q. Have the mayor or chief of police ever done anything to put down your book?

A. No.

Further questioning revealed that Cawley's business was a family enterprise of which he owned fifty-two per cent. His share of the net profits the previous year (1949) was approximately $67,000. He said his partners were a brother and two sisters; that they "absolutely" were not connected "with anyone from Chicago" or elsewhere, and that "when they [the Chicago element] come in, I go out."

We next delved into Cawley's connections with the racing wire service. He was in that business, too, in both towns. His ticker service, which he bought from one of the Continental Press distributors, was cut off at La Salle shortly before he testified but still was operating at Streator.

Q. You had never been raided?

A. Yes; I was raided once. . . . I have had one conviction.

Q. What was that?

A. Well, running a gaming house.

On December 20, 1950, the committee had Mr. Cawley back in Chicago for examination in open hearing. In the meantime we had read in the Chicago newspapers that, the day after he told us in executive session that he ran without interference, his place in La Salle was shut down tight by order of the mayor; in Streator the police chief was quoted as saying he had called at Cawley's Paddock Club but found "nothing but punch-boards and lucky bowls." But the following is what we heard from the still unruffled Cawley when Associate Counsel Robinson started off the questioning:

Q. Do you still have an establishment in both places [La Salle and Streator]?

A. That is correct.

Q. Are they still operating?

A. That is right.

Q. Have they been down to speak of for any period of time in the last two or three months?

A. Very little.

Q. You have no trouble operating now?

A. That is right.

Q. Everything is going the same as usual?

A. Yes.

Q. Your books are operating . . . and your crap games are operating?

A. That is correct.

Cawley went on to enumerate, perfectly frankly, in response to questions, all the forms of gambling in which he was engaged. In addition to the horse books he listed a baseball pool, punchboards, roulette, and a small poker game. Slot machines had been out for some time.

Still curious as to how he got away with it, I picked up the questioning:

Q. How do you account for the fact that you can operate the way you can, Mr. Cawley?

A. Well, it has been going on down there for twenty-five years.

Q. You said ninety per cent of the people like it?

A. That is right. We had an election down there that proved that.

Q. Tell me about that.

A. The sheriff—two sheriffs run, one run on an anti-gambling ticket and the other fellow run on an open ticket, and the fellow on the open ticket win the election. . . .

Q. Don't you sell liquor in your places?

A. . . . They took my liquor license away from me.

Q. And when did they take the liquor license away from you?

A. After I got back from this meeting the last time. (Laughter in the hearing room.)

Q. But you still sell liquor?

A. That is right. . . .

Q. But it hasn't made any difference in your operation?

A. No. No.

CHAIRMAN: Very well. Thank you, Mr. Cawley.

CHAPTER 7

MIAMI: POLLUTED PLAYGROUND

IN THE spring of 1950 as Senator Hunt and I opened hearings in the Miami area, a great feeling of sadness oppressed us over the realization that an area so blessed by God and nature could be so polluted by man. Miami Beach was the focal point for a vicious pattern of criminal and political corruption that extended to other resorts all along the fabulous winter playground coast. The area had become the plunderground as well as the playground for America's most vicious criminals, who, with the acquiescence of well-paid so-called law enforcement officers, had taken over most of the Florida gambling rackets and were reaching out for more. Not satisfied merely with the illegal rackets, the mob interests had created a further potentially dangerous situation by infiltrating legitimate fields such as hotels, real estate, and the construction business. The hotel infiltration facilitated the establishment of headquarters for the various mobs and, in effect, made Miami the winter capital of the national crime syndicate.

A great deal of this bad situation has been changed. The committee's investigation of the Miami area, we were told, provided the impetus to the efforts of Miami's decent citizens and civic organizations to strike back against the underworld. Our hearings not only turned the national spotlight upon the crooks but started a chain reaction that swept complacent sheriffs out of office and reached high into state politics. The Florida legislature appointed its own commission to study crime conditions. These results reflected great credit on Miami's aggressive daily newspapers—and certain newspapers elsewhere in the state—and on the Crime Commission of Greater Miami, led by Colonel Jack Younger, president, and Daniel P. Sullivan, operating director, which long has spearheaded the fight against crime.

Even months after our disclosure in Miami the lid still was clamped tight upon illegal bookmaking, in so far as any large-scale activity was concerned, and many of the gambling casinos run by out-of-state hoodlums were shut down. The state was receiving greater revenues from legalized pari-mutuel betting, and, with tourists losing less money to the gamblers, merchants were reporting better business.

Broadly speaking, the committee, in its Florida hearings, explored four avenues. First was the subornation of law enforcement officials—sheriffs, deputies, constables, and policemen—and other elected public officials. Second was the penetration by the out-of-state hoodlums of the vastly profitable gambling dives, coupled with the infiltration of hotels and other legitimate enterprises; if ever we found concrete evidence of the interstate nature of organized crime it was in the Miami area. Third was the question of a $100,000 contribution from racetrack interests to the political campaign of the governor of Florida. Finally there was the saga of the S & G Syndicate, a powerful local organization that was the evil mentor behind a multimillion-dollar bookmaking ring. If Continental Press was Public Enemy Number One in the United States, S & G was Public Enemy Number One in the Miami area. Now, as the result of a combination of factors, including the Crime Committee's exposures, the once mighty S & G, at the moment at least, is out of business.

Let us begin the Miami area story with the case of the since deceased Walter Clark, sheriff of neighboring Broward county, of which Fort Lauderdale is the seat. Since 1933 the Broward voters had been electing the forty-six-year-old Clark, a onetime butcher and grocer, to office. Some years ago a governor of Florida had removed Clark from office, but the legislature reinstated him and the voters kept re-electing him. In Sheriff Clark's bailiwick there were three notorious gambling joints— Club Boheme, Colonial Inn, and Club Greenacres. Among the out-of-state gamblers and racketeers associated in these operations, Daniel Sullivan, operating director of the Greater Miami Crime Commission, testified, were the infamous Joe Adonis, the notorious Lansky brothers, Meyer and Jake; Vincent Alo, alias Jimmy Blue-Eyes, and bookmaker Frank Erickson (since imprisoned), all of New York City and New Jersey; and, from Detroit, Joe Massei and William G. Bischoff, alias Lefty Clark. Smaller fry from Chicago and Florida also had pieces of the Colonial Inn operation. But when I called Sheriff Clark's attention to the open and notorious operations by gangsters in his county the sheriff's answer was: "I haven't had any knowledge of any gambling."

We fenced a bit on the question of how recently these casinos had operated—apparently they were closed for the time being; then I asked Clark why he violated his oath of office by ever letting them operate. He gave the brazen reply:

"I was elected on the liberal ticket, and the people want it and they enjoy it. . . . I let them have what they want for the tourists down here."

At a later session I asked this astonishing sheriff to define what he meant by "liberality." "Well," he said, "I am not going around snooping in private businesses and homes."

Clark went on to admit that he had been well acquainted with gambler Jake Lansky for twelve or fifteen years. I asked:

Q. Sheriff, do these people pay you off?
A. No, sir.
Q. Do they contribute to your campaign?
A. They contribute to the campaign.

Q. Did Lansky?

A. The boys in the South end handle the campaign.

Q. What do you mean "the boys in the South end"?

A. I have friends down there and they go to these fellows and they contribute to the campaign.

Q. How much do they contribute?

A. I don't know. I never asked and never looked to see.

Later, however, Clark admitted to Counsel Halley that he had been told directly by Lansky that a campaign contribution was forthcoming.

We went into great detail with Sheriff Clark about his various interests, properties, and investments. He told us his salary was $7500 a year, plus certain fees, and that his total annual income ran anywhere from $15,000 to $35,000. He mentioned a good number of enterprises in which he was interested, but one which he did not mention was a one-quarter interest in the Broward Novelty Company. His brother Robert, who was chief deputy sheriff, also owned a similar share. The Broward Novelty Company, as the committee noted in a report to the Senate, "operates an illegal *bolita* [a Cuban "number" lottery] and slot-machine business."

"During 1945 to 1947," our report continued, "the gross sales from this illegal bolita and coin (including slot) machine business amounted to approximately $1,135,420.43, of which sum Sheriff Clark's and his brother Robert's share in 1945 was declared by them as $12,910.89 each, representing one quarter each in this business. In 1946, their declared income amounted to $16,710.09 each from this business, while in 1947, they declared an income of only $4,221.15 each. . . ."

I taxed Sheriff Clark with his failure to tell us about the Novelty Company business when we examined him the first time. His reply was, "I never thought about it at the time."

At the end of our examination of Sheriff Clark the committee concluded: "There is no doubt that he completely failed in his duty to enforce the laws of the state of Florida and that he not only aided and abetted violations, but that he personally participated in a major violation." A few months later Clark was removed from office by Governor Fuller Warren.

In Miami (Dade County) we looked into the activities of James A. (Smiling Jimmy) Sullivan—no relation to Crime Commission Director Daniel Sullivan—a former traffic policeman who had been sheriff since January 1945. The voluble Jimmy, who wasn't smiling much toward the end of his examination, admitted that his assets had jumped from $2500 to approximately $70,000 during his five years in office; his salary in that time had started at $7500 and never exceeded $12,000 a year. We also heard testimony that Mrs. Jimmy Sullivan had taken large amounts of cash—more than $25,000 in all—to relatives in Maryland.

We learned that Sullivan had pocketed approximately $10,600 which had been given him as political contributions in his two campaigns and which he happened to have "left over." The story of the pocketed political contributions came to light because of an investigation of Sullivan's income tax returns, still pending as this was being written.

In tracing his various financial activities and real estate deals for us, Smiling Jimmy admitted that he frequently had large sums of cash on hand. He was one of the first of a small army of sheriffs and deputies we were to encounter who were "mistrustful" of banks and kept their money secreted at home. When asked where he kept it the sheriff rather shamefacedly replied: "Well, I keep it rolled up in an old blanket and hid up on a shelf." This, at least, was an innovation from the traditional tin box! Sometimes his hoard was as high as $12,000.

In an earlier exchange with the Miami Crime Commission, which charged that gambling and bookmaking were wide open in Dade County, Sheriff Sullivan had insisted indignantly that such charges were "pure fabrications" and that it all was part of a political plot to "get" Jimmy Sullivan. The Senate Committee, however, heard testimony from a procession of former Sullivan deputies, adding up to the inescapable conclusion that graft—in exchange for "protection"—was rampant in the sheriff's office.

Of Smiling Jimmy's performance on the witness stand, the committee, in its report, had to conclude: "Much of Sullivan's testimony was vague and evasive and the committee does not consider it credible."

The fantastic aftermath of the Sullivan affair, however, was this: after a Dade County grand jury returned an indictment against Sheriff Sullivan, charging him with neglect of duty, failing to enforce gambling laws, and permitting deputies under him to accept bribes, Governor Fuller Warren, in October 1950, suspended Sullivan from office. Early in April 1951, however, the indictment having been dismissed on a technicality, the governor reinstated him, stating that his study of the evidence "does not show the violation of any law of the state of Florida by Jimmy Sullivan. . . ." The governor's action took place just before the state Senate was scheduled to take action which Florida political observers believed would have made Sullivan's removal permanent.

Immediately the most violent political controversy to rock Florida in years broke upon Governor Warren's head. In front-page editorials, which were echoed in the Florida legislature, both Miami daily newspapers demanded his impeachment, a cry which was taken up by aroused citizens. In words strong even for politics, the Miami *Daily News,* which ran a black border around its editorial, demanded: "How lousy, stinking—and obvious—can a governor of Florida be before the people rise up and strike him down?"

Apropos of this situation we reported to the Senate: "The committee cannot understand and strongly condemns the reinstatement by Governor Fuller Warren, of Florida, of Sheriff James Sullivan without a full and public investigation of all the facts brought out by this committee and by the Dade County grand jury."

A tragic story on alleged corruption of the law in the Miami area was told us by George Patton, a former deputy under Sullivan. Patton, whose name originally was Petemezas, was a young American of Greek descent who, after serving this country honorably in World War II, became a Miami Beach policeman and later a deputy. He told us he had intended to be a decent, honest officer but soon after joining the force he "learned for the first time that law enforcement didn't always operate the way I thought it did."

Patton told us he became a grafter on the police force and that when he later became a deputy in Sheriff Sullivan's criminal division he collected "close to $50,000" in bribes over a period of nine months for protecting gambling on Miami Beach. He was the "bag man," or collector, he said; he stated he kept $15,000 of this money for himself. He also agreed with Counsel Halley that what he collected for himself and his partners was only a small part of the over-all graft picture.

One of the incidents he described was the alleged fleecing of a wealthy oilman at a beach casino. A gambler, admittedly a member of the so-called "Little Syndicate" on the beach, who was paying Patton for protection, told him, the ex-deputy said, that the sucker lost $800,000 in two nights and settled the debt for a cool half million.

Patton finally resigned from the sheriff's office to run for constable, but he was defeated. He told us he had hated being dishonest but he found himself deeper and deeper in the mess. The committee's position was that the young man's original moral weakness could not be condoned, but that he had made a commendable effort to square his debt to society by telling what he knew. His future is in doubt, as, after Sheriff Sullivan's return to office, he was picked up on a charge of alleged perjury, based on an information signed by the acting county solicitor, in connection with his testimony in two appearances before Dade County courts.

We also explored alleged links between the Miami Beach Police Department and the gambling interests. City Councilman Melvin J. Richard, a vigorous anti-crime crusader, played for us a recorded transcription of a telephone conversation between himself and Police Lieutenant Phil Short, a former Miami Beach police chief, in which Short acknowledged having been instructed some years ago not to interfere with a certain card game at one of the gambling clubs. Richard asked: "Who would give you orders like that?" and Short laconically replied: "Chief of police."

The councilman further testified that the police officer told him in a later conversation of having shut down gambling almost instantaneously on one occasion when he was chief of police, merely by telling Detective Pat Perdue, the department's one-man gambling "squad," to go out and put the lid on. "I asked him," said Richard, "how it was possible for Pat Perdue to accomplish that, and he said all he [Perdue] had to do was to go out and tell the boys that the 'heat was on' and they closed up."

Lieutenant Short himself testified: "When I was inaugurated as chief of police I made up my mind I didn't want to get involved with anything pertaining to horse bookmaking. I had nothing to do with it. I called Pat Perdue in and said that 'you understand what these fellows are doing, just carry on, I don't want to know anything about the bookmaking or how they run it.' "

THE CHAIRMAN: Mr. Short, why didn't you want to know about bookmaking, if you were chief of police? Wasn't that your job?

SHORT: I have been an officer for better than twenty years and I knew what "hot potatoes" were.

Concerning infiltration by out-of-state gamblers and the unwholesome penetration of the hotel business in the Miami area by underworld characters, the committee summed up:

"The testimony at the executive hearings established substantially that large numbers of known gangsters and racketeers from New York City, Philadelphia, Detroit, Cleveland, Chicago, and other cities gathered together in Miami Beach and consorted at certain meeting places, including the Wofford Hotel, the Boulevard Hotel, the Sands Hotel, the Grand Hotel, and others.

"These gangsters and racketeers operated at the Colonial Inn, the Greenacres gambling casino, the Club Boheme in Broward

County, and the Island Club and Club Collins in Dade County.

"The group operating at the Colonial Inn, which has since transferred its activities to the Club Greenacres and the Club Boheme, included Frank Erickson of New York; Joe Adonis of New York; Meyer and Jake Lansky of New York; and Mert Wertheimer of Detroit.

"These operations show tremendous profits, the net reported income totaling $348,821.48 in 1948 and $599,073.44 in 1949. In addition, they operated what was known as the 'big New York craps game' conducted by William Bischoff (alias Lefty Clark) and Joseph Massei. This cash operation of a single craps table yielded $222,056.47 in reported income for the 1949 season."

In search of concrete evidence as to the interstate nature of criminal operations in Miami, we developed significant evidence on the activities of bookmaker Frank Erickson, the since jailed associate and lieutenant of Frank Costello in the New York-New Jersey area. We found that Erickson, acting through Abe Allenberg, a New York attorney, invested more than $250,-000 in Tropical Park race track in 1935, and that Erickson's associate in this venture was John (Boy Mayor) Patton, the old friend of Capone gangsters and latter-day associate of Governor Warren's friend, race-track operator William Johnston. Erickson, as has been noted, also had pieces of various gambling casinos. Both Erickson and Patton sold out their track interests in 1941, at which time Erickson financed Allenberg in the operation of the Wofford Hotel. Other partners in the Wofford operation, we later learned, were two men well known to the police of their respective cities, John Angersola, alias King, of Cleveland, Ohio, and Anthony Carfano, alias Little Augie Pisano, of New York. "The Wofford," as we said in our report, "then became the meeting place for notorious racketeers and gangsters from all over the country, and headquarters for Erickson's very extensive bookmaking operations in Florida, which included concessions at the Roney Plaza, Boca Raton, and Hollywood Beach hotels, and very large-scale illegal bookmaking activity within the confines of the various Florida race tracks."

An interesting titbit we picked up from Allenberg was that Sheriff Jimmy Sullivan had given him (Allenberg) a card as an "honorary deputy sheriff."

Two other Miami Beach hotels had special prominence in the operations of mobsters, the committee learned from Crime Commission Director Sullivan and other witnesses. One was the Sands Hotel operated jointly by Alfred (Big Al) Polizzi, one-time Cleveland mobster; and Dave Glass and Benny Street, both of whom had convictions in Philadelphia as horse-book operators. The Sands, Director Sullivan said, "became a gathering place, particularly, for a group of gamblers, racketeers, gangsters from Philadelphia, Pennsylvania, headed up by Nig Rosen." We also learned from questioning Polizzi that his good friend John Angersola silently held half of Polizzi's twenty-five per cent interest in the Sands. Angersola, in addition to his interests in the Wofford and the Sands, had a piece of still another mob-favored hotel, the Grand. As Director Sullivan testified, the area of Miami Beach around the Grand and Wofford, which are only two blocks apart, "became nationally known as a meeting place probably for more nationally known racketeers and gangsters than any one local area in the United States."

A postscript to our investigation of Miami Beach hotel operations was turned in some months later by the Fulbright Committee, which was investigating activities of the Reconstruction Finance Corporation. Senator Fulbright's group, a subcommittee of the Senate Banking Committee, was particularly interested in a $1,500,000 RFC loan to the Saxony Hotel, built and operated by one George D. Sax, of Chicago, who was well known to the Crime Committee as the "king" of the multi-million-dollar punchboard manufacturing industry. Self-styled underworld "elite" such as Frank Costello had taken to stopping at the Saxony, which was one of the most luxurious hotels on the beach. As brought out by the Fulbright group, a number of official guests from Washington had also stayed at the Saxony on several occasions as guests of the management. I read of these disclosures with mingled amusement and relief, recalling that on one of my trips to address a Miami religious

group, while the crime hearings were still in progress, someone had unwittingly made arrangements for me to stop at the
Saxony and to be a guest at a reception given by the punchboard king. Fortunately I learned of it in time and canceled the
arrangements.

The high-level political situation in the state of Florida which
the committee investigated with considerable concern was the
question of the financing of Governor Fuller Warren's campaign for the gubernatorial office in 1948. Purely local and state
political matters, of course, were outside of our jurisdiction, but
we had a legitimate interest in the Warren campaign financing
because of a major contribution that came from the previously
mentioned William Johnston, the Chicago and Miami horse-
and dog-track operator, who, as the committee noted in a report, "has had a long career of close association with Chicago
racketeers of the Capone gang."

The expenses of Governor Warren's campaign, the committee learned, were met almost entirely by three men, who jointly
put up a sum in excess of $404,000. These men were: C. V.
Griffin, of Howey-in-the-Hills, Florida, a large citrus grower
who advanced $154,000; Louis Wolfson, of Jacksonville, Wash-
ington, and New York, who, at the age of thirty-eight, has had
a spectacularly successful moneymaking career and who contributed "in excess of $150,000"; and finally Mr. Johnston, the
race-track boss. Johnston turned over $100,000 to the campaign
fund, of which $40,000 came from his personal funds and
$35,000 from his brother, J. R. Johnston, who is associated with
him in track operations. Another $10,000 of the money raised
by Johnston came from Max Silverberg, the same race-track
concessionaire who (as related in Chapter 4) had let Hugo
Bennett, race-track auditor, have $15,000 which Bennett loaned
to Chicago gangster Paul (The Waiter) Ricca.

As Griffin told it, Governor Warren "asked me to take charge
of his campaign," which "was practically at a standstill for
money to operate." Griffin, in turn, asked Johnston and Wolfson to meet with him, and they each agreed to put up $25,000 as

initial contributions. Griffin said he went to Wolfson because "I just thought he had lots of money." It was the governor's suggestion, however, that Johnston, who had been a contributor to an earlier Warren campaign, be "invited" to help, Griffin said. As campaign collections lagged, the three big contributors found it necessary to put up more and more funds, until they had subscribed something over $404,000.

Mr. Wolfson is a young man who, with his four brothers, less than twenty years ago started a small pipe and supply business in Florida and, by phenomenal growth during and since the war, expanded the family holdings into a fabulous financial and industrial empire. He told the committee that taxes "on an income in excess of $7,000,000" were paid on the family businesses. His holdings presently or in the past have included public utilities (the Wolfsons control Capital Transit Company in Washington, D.C.); a motion picture studio and a theater chain; a construction company, shipbuilding yard, insurance firm, and other interests. Wolfson said one of his companies had sold supplies to the state of Florida for the last twenty years, but that "the only consideration" he expected for his contribution of $150,000 was "for this governor to be an outstanding governor and sell the state of Florida."

Mr. Johnston, when he testified before us in Washington (he was out of the country at the time of our Florida hearings), had a prepared statement on the question of why he gave so much money to Governor Warren's campaign. "I have known Governor Warren as a close and intimate friend for more than fifteen years," the track operator sonorously told us. "My acquaintanceship over this period of time has convinced me that he is an able, competent and honest man—a man who I felt would make and indeed who has made an outstanding governor for the state of Florida. It was this and my strong friendship which prompted me to help Fuller Warren. . . .

"Why the help which I gave Governor Warren should cause such a stir I am unable to understand. I am not a politician but I want to say to this distinguished committee that if a man who has been fortunate enough to acquire a little means cannot help a close personal friend to achieve his lifelong ambition, then we are departing from what I have always thought to be a traditional American practice."

Citrus grower Griffin, at least, made no such claims to sweeping altruism as did the industrialist and the race-track operator. He told us frankly that he and his partner, who split the $154,-000 contribution between them, were interested in securing the passage of certain legislation which they thought would help their business, the citrus industry. "I was going to promote legislation in an attempt to accomplish that end—which we did —and put through the legislature the citrus code," Griffin said.

Q. (*By Halley.*) After Governor Warren was elected, is that right?

GRIFFIN: That's right. He agreed not to veto it, and to support it. . . .

Q. You also wanted to get your partner on the Citrus Commission, didn't you?

A. Naturally I would like to get him in. Naturally I would want my associate as chairman, which he was.

Griffin himself was appointed "chief crime investigator" for the governor. But since the election the citrus grower has fallen out with Warren and has lost his investigator's job. Griffin told us he "might have been" fired because of a feud that developed between him and his ex-campaign crony, Bill Johnston, who was friendly with another crime investigator for the governor, one W. O. (Bing) Crosby, about whom more will be heard later.

The gigantic operation of the S & G bookmaking syndicate was another major avenue of inquiry. The syndicate itself admitted that it grossed $26,000,000 in 1948, while Crime Commission Director Sullivan estimated that the annual gross probably would range between $30,000,000 and $40,000,000, with a net profit of $4,000,000 to $8,000,000 to the syndicate's operators.

The syndicate was started in Miami Beach in 1944 by five "local" boys—Harold Salvey, Jules Levitt, Charles Friedman,

Sam Cohen, and Edward (Eddie Lucky) Rosenbaum—who, operating as independents, practically controlled bookmaking in the Miami Beach area. They decided to get together and pool their activities for greater efficiency and profits. Sam's brother Ben became attorney for the syndicate and, as was indicated by the testimony of George Patton and others, was extremely active in many ways.

These S & G "boys" were slippery and arrogant characters, with many facets. Salvey, for instance, was an old time bookie who told us he had done nothing except engage in bookmaking or finance other bookmakers for twenty years. Salvey didn't do much actual work for S & G—he was "a sort of neurotic and what not," partner Eddie Lucky glibly testified—but he was kept on as a full partner; the fact was that Salvey's close friendship with an influential city councilman, William Burbridge, with whom, as we learned, he participated in profitable real estate deals, made Salvey useful to the syndicate. On one occasion Salvey borrowed $40,000 from Burbridge for a short period, paying interest at a rate which amounted to about twenty per cent. Another time Burbridge himself testified that Salvey had sent him a check for $1000, and neither of them ever had "been able to remember" what it was for. Councilman Burbridge became furious when one of the spectators snickered at this bit of testimony, and, turning to the heckler, said: "You think it is funny? . . . What's funny about it?"

All the partners were missing when we sought to subpoena them in Miami. Later Rosenbaum, Salvey, and Levitt condescended to appear before us in Washington, at which time Eddie Lucky blandly explained he had decided to go "fishing" at the time of our Miami hearing. "You knew sooner or later you would have to come—you couldn't run forever?" Counsel Halley hammered at him. "That's it exactly," Rosenbaum coolly replied. Later we caught up with Friedman and summoned him to testify before us in Chicago. He told us that he had ducked out to the Keys when we were looking for him in Miami "because I thought this was strictly a show." "I think my reputation is as good as any gentleman in the house here, and I didn't want to get embarrassed," Friedman said.

S & G actually was a master organization encompassing a pool of some two hundred local bookies. The name S & G had no particular significance, unless, as facetiously suggested by lawyer Cohen, it meant "Stop and Go." The syndicate bought the wire service from Continental Press's Miami Beach distributor and in turn relayed the information to the bookies. It also arranged for telephone service, handled the matter of "protection" with the law, and acted as a banker when the bookies needed money to buy a gambling concession from a hotel. In turn S & G took a healthy cut of the bookies' "take." Another by-product of the arrangement was that S & G would take "lay-off" bets from its bookie members whenever the smaller members of the syndicate had wagers too big for them to handle. This disclosure of "lay-off" activity was considered important by the committee, for it put S & G itself indisputably in the bookmaking business.

For a long time S & G's monopoly over bookmaking activities on Miami Beach was almost one hundred per cent complete. Even the then powerful New York gambler Frank Erickson, who had paid $45,000 for a three-month bookmaking concession at Meyer Schine's luxurious Roney Plaza Hotel, came to grief when he attempted to buck the local syndicate. Hotel man Schine testified that, after he had broken off an arrangement with S & G partners Salvey and Levitt and had made the contract with Erickson, he (Schine) was visited by Detective Pat Perdue. Schine said that Perdue told him he should not let the contract go to Erickson; that "we don't want any outsiders in here . . . and we would rather that you gave it to our local syndicate."

The hotel man made the mistake, he said, of defying Perdue and permitting Erickson to open up the Roney Plaza book. In about two weeks Perdue descended on the hotel in a highly publicized raid and put the Erickson-Roney Plaza book out of business. Next year, Schine said, "we didn't rent to Erickson any more." Instead, he stated, the concession was leased

"to somebody who was supposed to be associated with the
S & G. . . ."

There was only one flaw in the S & G's highly efficient operation. It became such a profitable and tempting racket that it
aroused the cupidity of the prosperous crimesters from Chicago
who, in the approved manner of upper-bracket hoodlumdom,
spent their winters on beautiful Miami Beach, soaking up the
sun on their daily strolls from hotel to horse parlor. The big-
town boys began thinking it was much too good a thing to be
wasted on five local characters. At this point, as the committee
reconstructed the story, the ubiquitous and sinister partnership
of Guzik & Accardo entered the picture. It is the committee's
contention—a contention which the principals involved either
denied or refused to talk about—that Guzik & Accardo, acting
for the Chicago-Capone Syndicate, dispatched Harry Russell,
alias Weinstein, a Chicago gambler, on a mission to S & G early
in 1949. Russell, the committee believes, delivered to the S & G
partners a proposition reminiscent of the "offer" conveyed to
the late James Ragen of Continental Press by the same Chicago
mob elements in 1946. They wanted to "muscle in."

Understandably devoted to their $26,000,000 business, the
S & G partners didn't want to be "muscled," and they declined
to join forces with Russell. The Chicago interests were disappointed but gentlemanly about it. Nothing crude or violent
transpired. However—just as had been the case when Mr.
Ragen of Continental Press displayed stubbornness—a number
of things commenced to happen. Mr. Russell began building up
a syndicate of his own, and bookies at a number of plush hotels
dominated by the Chicago mob element began flocking over to
Russell. Next, Governor Warren's crime investigator, the previously mentioned W. O. Crosby, known as Bing, appeared in
Miami Beach. Here things get a little complicated: Bing acknowledged to us that he was a friend of both Harry Russell
and the race operator, William Johnston, who had raised $100,-
000 for the governor's campaign fund and who also knew a
number of the syndicate associates in Chicago. Russell, Crosby
admitted, started feeding him a lot of information on various

bookie joints that he might raid, and Crosby started raiding them. The committee was not surprised to learn that these were all places operated by S & G bookies, who of course began screaming loudly over the infringement upon the immunity they long had paid for and enjoyed.

S & G fumbled along for a while, observing with acute unhappiness the defection of customers to the man from Chicago. Finally came the crusher: S & G was buying its wire service from the local distributor of the same Continental Press that already had undergone the experience of being squeezed by Guzik & Accardo. This service was abruptly shut off one day, leaving S & G paralyzed. For a few days it managed to bootleg a little news from a rash Continental Press customer in New Orleans, but it speedily became apparent to all parties concerned that this was an unhealthy thing to be doing.

In just about ten days after the shutting off of the racing news the S & G partners took another look at Mr. Harry Russell and decided they had been wrong. He might be a pretty nice partner after all. They decided to recapitalize their business—though they admitted to us that they really did not need any capital—and to let Russell have a one-sixth interest. The price they asked for this one-sixth interest in a business that had grossed $26,000,000 by its own figures the previous year was $20,000. When questioned by the committee, the S & G partners and their attorney unanimously maintained that it was they who had approached Mr. Russell and not the other way around, as the committee contended.

At the same time Mr. Russell bought into S & G for $20,000 —and this illustrates the finesse of our up-to-date crimesters— the S & G "boys" happened to buy a boat named the *Clari-Jo*. The price of the *Clari-Jo* happened to be $20,000, and the owner of the boat—lots of coincidences here—just happened to be Tony Accardo. Even though we introduced the canceled checks from S & G to Accardo in payment for the boat, Accardo, when we had him in the witness chair in Washington, refused repeatedly to answer questions about it. Finally, however, Senator Wiley innocently inquired, "Who baptized that name, *Clari-Jo?*" and Accardo, momentarily off guard, replied, "That is my wife's first name and my middle name." As spectators roared with merriment the crestfallen hoodlum, rubbing his jaw with the hand that had the dove tattooed between the thumb and trigger finger, blurted: "I fell into that one!"

The only thing wrong with the S & G squeeze was that it hit lemons instead of the jackpot. The combination of the Senate Committee's disclosures and the opposition of the law-abiding elements in Miami Beach finally generated a heat that even the S & G Syndicate with all its powerful friends could not cool off. Abruptly "the boys," without consulting their Chicago associate, Mr. Russell, decided to go out of business. As lawyer Ben Cohen privately told us, "the boys" grew weary of being painted "the worst monsters in the world." "It is true," Attorney Cohen acknowledged, "that they had been law violators." But they never had done anything worse than gambling, and "to fight the world, it isn't worth it."

As for Guzik and Accardo, they never have admitted having anything at all to do with the Russell-S & G deal. Neither would Russell tell us anything. But Guzik and Accardo were vulnerable on one point. As committee Counsel brought out during examination of Accardo in Washington, and of Accardo's tax lawyer, Eugene Bernstein, in Chicago, the 1949 tax return of Guzik & Accardo showed that the partnership claimed a $7252.81 loss due to "S & G Service," and this, the committee noted in its report, was further evidence that the Capone mob merely muscled into the lucrative S & G Syndicate, using Russell as a pawn. The inference is obvious.

As this was being written Harry Russell and the S & G partners were awaiting trial on an indictment returned by a Dade County grand jury. Attorney Cohen, who had been prosecuted by the state of Florida in connection with the S & G operation, had been acquitted, however, by a directed verdict of the Court.

CHAPTER 8

TAMPA: THE STRANGE DOMAIN OF
A SHERIFF CALLED "MELON HEAD"

Some months after our Miami investigation was completed the Senate Crime Committee returned to Florida to investigate crime in the city of Tampa. The hearings in this industrial port were conducted by Senator Hunt, and the situation uncovered there was a repellent combination of sordidness and violence. In so far as interstate crime was concerned, it was well known that Tampa was an important subcapital of the nationwide Mafia-backed narcotics ring. On the national scale, we found shadowy but sinister links between Tampa, Miami, New Orleans, Kansas City, Chicago, Cleveland, New York, and even Havana, Cuba, in the narcotics, gambling, and murder-for-hire traffic. And on the local level, law enforcement was so thoroughly corrupted that even the Cuban gamblers who ran the profitable bolita racket referred contemptuously to the sheriff of Hillsborough County as *Cabeza de Melón*—"Melon Head." Human life in Tampa was almost as cheap as the sands of the beach: in nineteen years there have been fourteen murders and six attempted assassinations in the Tampa underworld—and only one conviction.

The explosive element that keeps Tampa in a ferment of violence is the long-standing rivalry between two equally hot-blooded gang factions. One is the Mafia-backed clique composed of criminals of Sicilian or Italian extraction.[1] The other is the numerically larger Cuban faction. Mixed in with these, of course, is a leavening of racketeers native to the section. The situation is not helped by the seeming willingness of some law enforcement officials—and the apathy of others—to go along with the underworld.

The two principal characters in the Tampa story were Salvatore (Red) Italiano, Italian-born ex-convict and one of the reputed strong men of Tampa's underworld, and Sheriff Hugh Culbreath, the official known as "Melon Head." Italiano was among the missing when the committee came to Tampa seeking to question him. From Culbreath committee Counsel extracted a fantastic story of how he had managed to make deposits of at least $128,000 in half a dozen banks scattered throughout Florida and Georgia during his nine years as sheriff. In the background of the Tampa story in roles of varying prominence were other public officials accused of taking graft to permit operations of the rackets, and a procession of small-fry Cuban gamblers who made the accusations.

One of the purely local racketeers whom the committee interrogated was Charles M. Wall, a nonchalant, almost whimsical, seventy-one-year-old gambler. Wall, who stated he has "retired," said he began his gambling career as a "crap dealer" in Tampa. J. Rex Farrior, the State's Attorney of Hillsborough County, testified that Wall at one time was the "recognized and admitted, and by the public records, the self-confessed and

[1]The committee report noted: "The committee could not make an adequate investigation of the Mafia background . . . because all suspected Mafia adherents vanished from their homes and usual haunts when it became known that the committee intended to investigate their activities. Months have passed since the committee's visit to Tampa, but these men have continued to evade process. It is freely stated in the particular circles in which they operate that they intend to remain in secret refuges until the life of this committee expires.

". . . One of the fugitives from the committee's process was Santo Trafficante, Sr., reputed Mafia leader in Tampa for more than twenty years. . . ."

public-recorded head and brains of the underworld." The committee questioned Wall about at least three attempts by presumably "unknown" parties to assassinate him. Almost humorously the old man told us how he was wounded by the buckshot from shotguns on two of the occasions. "It kind of— as they say—it glimpsed me," Wall gaily said. He assured us he had reported all he knew about the attacks to police, but nothing ever had come of the investigations—if there were any. "I wasn't much interested in who it was that was doing it," Wall told Associate Counsel Downey Rice. "I was interested in keeping from getting killed." Said Senator Hunt dryly: "You seem to display a remarkable lack of interest in the target that these people were making of you."

As Red Italiano could not be found, we summoned Vincent Spoto to answer a few questions about the missing man. Spoto identified himself as president of Anthony Distributors, a wholesale beer and wine corporation owned by the Italiano family. President Spoto earned $100 a week, not, he explained, for his duties as president, but for work he did in the shipping department. Italiano drew $300 a week as general manager. Spoto said he had not seen Italiano for some time, but that just a few weeks before the Crime Committee hearings in Tampa, Italiano "wrote us a letter that he was resigning from the corporation." Since then Red's son Anthony has been general manager of the corporation at $250 a week. A daughter Elinor is treasurer. Red Italiano was only one of many criminals the committee found throughout the country who, despite convictions for liquor and other violations, had managed, contrary to state and federal regulations, to infiltrate the liquor business. After reading Italiano's lengthy criminal record, which included time served in the Atlanta Federal Penitentiary for violation of the National Prohibition Act, Associate Counsel Rice asked: "How does it happen, then, that Italiano, being a criminal, can be general manager of a licensee?" Spoto answered: "Well, I don't know about that."

From other witnesses the committee heard allegations that Italiano was a big shot in bolita, the Cuban lottery played with

100 numbered balls. Oscar J. Perez, formerly chauffeur to a murdered bolita racketeer, Jimmy Velasco, told us Italiano and Velasco had quarreled violently. Perez also testified that Italiano's chauffeur and bodyguard, a man named Joe Provenzano who was tried—and acquitted—for Velasco's murder, used to carry shotguns in the front seat of his car when he drove on Tampa's main streets. "He was going hunting on Franklin Street," Perez joked grimly.

Noah W. Caton, a marine engine mechanic, told of a strange alleged tie-up between Sheriff Culbreath and Red Italiano. Caton and Sheriff Culbreath had made plans, Caton said, to go into the fish business as partners; the sheriff was to finance the operation and Caton was to do the work. Accordingly Caton found a suitable property, which he said the sheriff finally agreed to purchase for $19,000. On the day the settlement was to be made Sheriff Culbreath failed to show up. Instead Red Italiano appeared and announced he was there "to represent Mr. Culbreath in the deal"; he said he was going to take title to the property in the name of Anthony Distributors. "Italiano assured me right across the desk that he was only negotiating in this deal for Mr. Culbreath," Caton testified. After the deal was closed, Caton (who ran the fishhouse for a while) said, he drew some money for operations from Italiano and directed bills for gasoline and supplies to the sheriff. Finally, Caton said, Sheriff Culbreath claimed that he (Culbreath) was all through with the deal and Caton found himself frozen out. He suspected, however, that the sheriff was not telling the full story, so he checked up and discovered, he said, that Culbreath was still paying taxes on the property.

From Mrs. Anthony Di Lorenzo, estranged wife of a special deputy for Sheriff Culbreath, the committee heard that in 1947 Red Italiano obtained a deputy's commission for her husband, "to do special duties." Thereafter, she testified, both Red Italiano and Sheriff Culbreath regularly telephoned Di Lorenzo to give him instructions as to his "special duties." Di Lorenzo also collected his $200-a-month "salary" from Italiano, Mrs.

Di Lorenzo testified, adding that she frequently went with her husband when he collected it.

Q. (*By Rice.*) What was your impression of what he was doing as a result of these telephone calls? What were his duties?

Mrs. Di Lorenzo: Well, he was checking different places with them, different bolita places. . . .

Q. Was he collecting from them or was he arresting them?

A. He was just more of a go-between between the underworld and the law, as a messenger between those.

The sinister part of Mrs. Di Lorenzo's testimony was the picture she painted of her husband as a man who carried two revolvers and owned both a regular and a sawed-off shotgun. Just before one of the unsolved killings in Tampa, the murder of a bolita operator named Jimmy Lumia, Di Lorenzo was in a disturbed mood, Mrs. Di Lorenzo testified. Associate Counsel Rice asked:

Q. How was he acting just before Lumia was killed? What did he say? How did he talk?

Mrs. Di Lorenzo: Well, he told me that someone was going to be killed. He said something about they had him on a spot, that there wasn't any other way out, that he had to do it or he had to do the job—something in those words. He didn't say he had to do the killing but he said he had a job to do. . . .

Q. Did he say anything a couple of weeks before?

A. Yes; he said someone was going to get it—"I am on the spot." He said he had to do what they said to do because he was in it so deep that he couldn't get out. He said he was in it too far, and he said, "Once you are in there is no out."

Di Lorenzo himself, called as a witness, insisted he was an honest man who never received any money from Red Italiano and whose "special work" for the sheriff consisted of "trying to find out something about this gambling going on here." He said he first heard of Jimmy Lumia's murder the morning it happened when he heard newsboys yelling about it.

The first witness to accuse Culbreath of having received money from the gambling interests was Paul Giglia, a former bolita peddler for the late Jimmy Velasco. During Culbreath's re-election campaign in 1948, Giglia testified, Jimmy Velasco told him "to take some money down to the sheriff." Giglia said he personally delivered $500 in cash to Culbreath. "What did he say?" asked Associate Counsel Rice. Giglia answered: "He said, 'It comes in handy'; that's all." A week later, Giglia testified, he took $1000 to the sheriff.

Giglia also swore that Jimmy Velasco regularly sent money to the "old man"—meaning Sheriff Culbreath. The euphemism for these payments—sometimes $1000 at a time—was "rent," and Giglia testified that "the money was going out faster than it was coming in."

It was Antonio Deschamps, now of Key West, Jimmy Velasco's cousin, who used to check receipts for the murdered gambler, who first told us how the Cuban bolita peddlers called Culbreath *Cabeza de Melón*. He swore Velasco showed him his "pay-off" list, on which there were notations of alleged weekly payments of $500 to *Cabeza de Melón;* the same amount to "R," and $250 to "E.D." Deschamps further testified that Melon Head was Sheriff Culbreath; R was State's Attorney Rex Farrior; and E.D. was former Chief of Police J. L. Eddings.

Similar testimony regarding alleged money-bearing visits by Velasco to the three above-named officials was given by Mario Lounders, now of Hialeah, Florida, and Oscar Perez. Perez said he used to drive Velasco to the county jail, where Velasco and the sheriff would confer in a special inner sanctum called "the rathole." Perez, who said he used to help Jimmy count out the weekly pay-off, declared the amount would vary from week to week. Rice asked:

Q. Why would it vary?
PEREZ: Well, as in every kind of business, I guess you had to balance your budget. (*Applause from the audience.*)

State's Attorney Farrior came to Washington to testify voluntarily before the committee and made a vigorous denial of the accusations against him. Former Police Chief Eddings was quoted in Tampa newspapers as saying the charges against him were untrue, but he failed to accept the committee's invitation to appear before us in Washington and tell his side of the story. Sheriff Culbreath, who appeared before the committee both in Tampa and in Washington, likewise denied having taken graft from the gamblers. He did recall the envelope with the "campaign contribution" from Jimmy Velasco's messenger, Paul Giglia, but he said he didn't "know whether it was a dollar or $500."

The fifty-three-year-old sheriff told the committee some interesting facts about his career and his activities. After Army service in World War I he worked as a helper in a Tampa meat plant until about 1929, when he became a deputy under a sheriff who later was removed from office. Then Culbreath went back to the meat business until 1932 when he was elected constable. He operated a private fishing business during the period he was constable, but filed no income tax returns on his earnings. In 1938 a Tampa grand jury returned indictments against "seven of the most prominent gamblers of the city and nine public officials without whose acquiescence or co-operation these flagrant violations of the law could not have continued." One of these officials was Constable Culbreath, and the grand jury publicly requested the then governor of Florida to remove Culbreath, along with others, from office. Nothing, however, happened. In 1941, Culbreath became sheriff.

The sheriff insistently denied he ever had any dealings with Red Italiano, except to call on him occasionally in search of information that might help him to solve crimes. Also, Culbreath said, "I may have at election time asked him to support me or something like that. . . ." Associate Counsel Rice taxed the sheriff about asking support from an ex-convict of Italiano's reputation, but the sheriff replied: "I find a vote is a vote."

At one point Sheriff Culbreath, who said he couldn't remember exactly how much cash he had in a safe at home, tried to convince the committee that he really wasn't very bright. "I am not a smart boy . . . and never was," he said, assuring us he couldn't even remember the street address of a friend he visits three times a week. He also said he could qualify as a prime example, or "Exhibit A," of how a fellow in public life could be abused falsely by "harping critics, jealous and disgruntled politicians, discontents, malcontents, has-beens, would-be's," and what not.

For a "not smart" boy, "Exhibit A" had done rather well for himself. Associate Counsel Rice—and the process was as painful as dragging an obdurate steer to the branding fire—guided Sheriff Culbreath through a recital of his income over the past nine years, and his present assets. The committee explored the deposits in the six banks; the profits from real estate and numerous other business deals, and finally, when the sheriff's memory failed him again, sent the sheriff home with an investigator to check on just how much money was in that mysterious safe. At last the committee figured from the sheriff's income tax declarations that his net income for the years 1941 through 1949, after deductions and taxes, had been $36,014.98. He claimed he had had $27,000 in cash at the time he became sheriff in 1941, which brought the total to $63,014.98. On the asset side, the sheriff admitted to having cash, bonds, and property holdings valued at $95,893.52. Counsel was able to establish that at least $128,000 had passed through five of Culbreath's bank accounts in the past nine years, and that, currently, the sheriff had $45,700 divided between his various bank accounts, his safe deposit box, and the home safe; also $6500 in government bonds. Keeping in mind the fact that the sheriff and his wife raised two boys and must have had some living expenses themselves during these nine years, Culbreath had done remarkably well on his $7500 annual salary.

Another bit of fairly low—yet tragic—comedy in the Culbreath testimony was the disclosure by two witnesses formerly connected with the sheriff's office that Ernest (Rookie) Culbreath, the sheriff's brother and his chief criminal deputy, ran a gambling book right at the county jail. Rookie was in partnership with another deputy named Leslie Cathcart, who was on the sheriff's pay roll as a "radio dispatcher," and Rookie and Leslie called their partnership, quaintly, "Briggs & Company." Sheriff Culbreath, however, assured the committee that the story was highly exaggerated. It came about, he explained, because his brother, the chief criminal deputy, is almost entirely blind. "The world is pretty dark for him," the sheriff said, "and the only way that he gets any pleasure" is by joking around with Leslie. "They will joke with you any way you want," the sheriff told the committee, but "there is no such thing as gambling like someone testified. . . ."

Associate Counsel Rice, however, was not quite satisfied with this explanation. He produced a match-book cover which read: "Briggs & Company—Rookie Culbreath and Leslie Cathcart. We do small things big. Everything in sports." What did the sheriff have to say about that "Everything in sports"? "Well, sir," Sheriff Culbreath said, "I think someone that put out matches did this to play a trick on them or did it for them."

Not so funny is the story of what has happened to Sheriff Culbreath since the committee's hearings in Tampa. First, the federal income tax people began an investigation. They were impressed not at all by his disingenuous explanation of why he had filed no tax returns during the nine years he was a constable: he thought, he said, that public officials were exempt from paying any taxes, even on private earnings. (There was a law—since repealed—that exempted public officials from paying taxes on their official salaries, but it had nothing to do with income from private sources.) Culbreath has been required to go back over the nine years and file amended returns, and now is engaged in paying up his back taxes, penalties, and interest. In March 1951 a county grand jury returned an indictment against Sheriff Culbreath, charging him with taking protection money from a gambler; also for neglect of duty on a number of counts, including failure to stop "Briggs & Company" from operating a lottery in the sheriff's office. Culbreath was suspended from office, but in May 1951, after a series of legal maneuvers which resulted in dismissal of most of the counts against him, a local jury acquitted him on the remaining count. Governor Fuller Warren thereupon reinstated him, and Culbreath again was "the law" in Hillsborough County.

The moral of the Tampa story is this: if good citizens of a community shut their eyes to wholesale violation of a law— even if it is a law prohibiting something that a lot of people happen to like—law enforcement and honesty in public office will go to hell in a handcart. It happened in Tampa. It can happen anywhere. Fortunately, in Tampa, there may be a silver lining to the black cloud of criminal and political corruption. Tampa's decent citizens, aroused by our committee's exposures in Tampa, the law-abiding element, have been given new incentive—and ammunition—to do something about making their city a better place in which to live. A Hillsborough County Crime Commission has been organized—just as similar commissions have been set up in other communities where the Senate Committee turned the spotlight on local conditions. The Tampa group was fortunate in obtaining the services of Ralph W. Mills, one of the Senate Committee's expert investigators, as its operating director. Mills and George Martin, also of the committee staff, had conducted much of the investigation which led to our disclosures in Tampa. Under his direction, I am sure, a vigorous cleanup will be prosecuted in the bailiwick of Culbreath, Italiano, et al.

CHAPTER 9

HOW TO TURN BRASS INTO GOLD:
THE BLACK MARKET AND
BUSINESS INFILTRATION STORY

MIDWAY in its investigations of what the late Lincoln Steffens aptly characterized for all time as "The Shame of the Cities," the Senate Crime Committee directed its attention momentarily to a special phenomenon of national scope. We wanted to take a look at black market operations—the ugly racket that had plagued American economy in the price control and rationing days of World War II and that was again threatening to become a menace. We realized we could not explore the entire field of black market operations, but because of the timeliness of the subject—the Korean war then was a few months old, and Congress was being asked to vote price control over certain items—we felt it would be both useful and healthy to dissect at least one example. There was reason to suspect that racketeering money once again was in the black market field, creating a condition that was wrecking an important part of the mobilization program planned by Congress and the Administration; and we wanted to know about it.

The black market investigation, of course, tied in squarely with our investigation of another major threat to American life —the infiltration of legitimate business by members of the organized crime syndicate. If the disciples of Frank Costello, the late Al Capone, and their local counterparts in every major city of the country get a strangle hold on even a minor portion of American business, all I can say is God save America. One of the principal aims of the Senate Crime Committee was to expose the extent of this already dangerous penetration and to suggest protective legislative countermeasures.

For our black market investigation we singled out a particularly flagrant and ugly case involving illegal sugar operations. It was a case that came within the committee's scope for two principal reasons: (1) these particular black marketeers had cut freely across state lines; and (2) there were hints of possible connections with the organized underworld—i.e., the national crime syndicate.

It was a shoddy, dirty story in which none of the principals was particularly clean—though one was very sorry. The case was that of Eatsum Food Products, a candy company owned by a manufacturer named David George Lubben, of Woodcliff Lake, New Jersey. Originally Lubben had been a legitimate businessman, but he admitted he had made the mistake of deciding to cheat on the wartime laws of the land for the sake of personal profit. Before he was through he had been taken for a financial cleaning—and in the course of it had been given the scare of his life—by a clever New York operator who had an ex-convict for a partner.

Lubben had been a merchandiser for a Cincinnati bakery. He came to New York during the war years to go into business for himself as a candy wholesaler and manufacturer. The Eatsum company which he acquired, however, had not been in business long enough, under existing OPA regulations, to have any appreciable sugar quota, so Lubben tried everything he could think of to remedy the situation, including coming to Washington to confer with expensive attorneys and "public relations" counselors who, in Lubben's words, claimed "they knew a man who knew a man who knew a man who knew a man who knew a man who knew Harry Truman . . . or something of that sort." Eventually he fell in with some sharp characters in New York City and soon found himself over his head in the black market.

Then Lubben met up with some new characters, namely, William Giglio, the smart operator, and Frank Livorsi, the ex-convict, who had acquired a jelly factory which had a sugar quota of 14,000,000 pounds a year. As Lubben himself told us, all he could think was that "14,000,000 pounds would make me as big as Hershey." Soon the operator and the ex-convict were his partners in Eatsum, and then came the inexorable finale: Lubben was out and they were in.

The public hearing on the black market sugar case, which had been preceded by preparatory executive sessions in New York City, was conducted in Washington. We began with an examination of Livorsi, the forty-seven-year-old ex-convict, who has had an abominable record as a member of society. An admitted friend of such underworld characters as Frank Costello, Willie Moretti, Trigger Mike Coppola, Little Augie Pisano, and others, Livorsi has been arrested, according to his own recollection, at least ten times, including twice on charges of homicide with a gun. The only conviction, however, was a two-year sentence for importation and transportation of narcotics in 1942. The low ratio of convictions to arrests in the cases of known hoodlums, incidentally, was a phenomenon found all over America that gave the committee much concern.

Could Livorsi think of any legitimate business he ever was in, Counsel Halley asked, before he went to jail? "I can't think of any legitimate business," Livorsi sullenly replied. On being released from prison, Livorsi went to work for two dress factories, one of which was owned by a man who also had been a narcotics convict. In 1945 Frank Livorsi teamed up with smart, smooth-talking William Giglio, then thirty years old. They acquired ownership of the Tavern Fruit Juice Company, a jelly manufacturing business. Livorsi, who never had been in the

Race-track executive William H. Johnston (*right*) testifies. Left to right at committee table: Downey Rice, assistant counsel; Rudolph Halley, chief counsel; Senator Kefauver; Senator Wiley; and Julius Cahn, Senator Wiley's executive assistant

Florida witnesses waiting to testify about S & G gambling syndicate: (*left to right*) Jules Levitt, syndicate partner; Ben Cohen, attorney; Edward Rosenbaum, Harold Salvey, also partners; and Leo Levitt, cashier

Wide World

COSTELLO FACES THE CRIME COMMITTEE. A semigeneral view as Frank Costello (*background, second from the right*), seated beside his attorney, George Wolf, occupies the witness stand in the Federal Court room in New York. At long table in rear (*left to right*): Rudolph Halley, committee's chief counsel; and Senators Tobey, O'Conor, and Kefauver

Acme

Chief Counsel Halley interrogates Frank Costello during the hearings in New York

IN AND OUT

(ABOVE) Frank Costello (*left*) takes his seat in the Federal Court hearing room in New York. With him is his attorney, George Wolf. (BELOW) Frank Costello and his attorney, George Wolf, rise from their chairs to leave the hearing room, as Wolf claims that his client has reached the limit of his "physical and mental endurance"

MEMORY MIX-UP. Louis Weber (*left*), reputed policy racketeer, who claimed that he did not know James J. Moran (*center*), New York Water Supply commissioner, glares at Gerard Martin (*right*) as the latter testifies that Weber was a regular visitor at Moran's office

Harold H. Corbin (*right*), attorney for Frank Erickson, tells the committee that his client would refuse to answer any questions which might incriminate him

Virginia Hill tells her story, as committee—and attentive audience—listen. In foreground (*backs to camera, left to right*) Rudolph Halley, Senator Kefauver, and Senator Tobey

"They were not gangsters or racketeers . . . ."

"I knew what I was betting on . . . ."

"We would go to Europe and all that stuff . . . ."

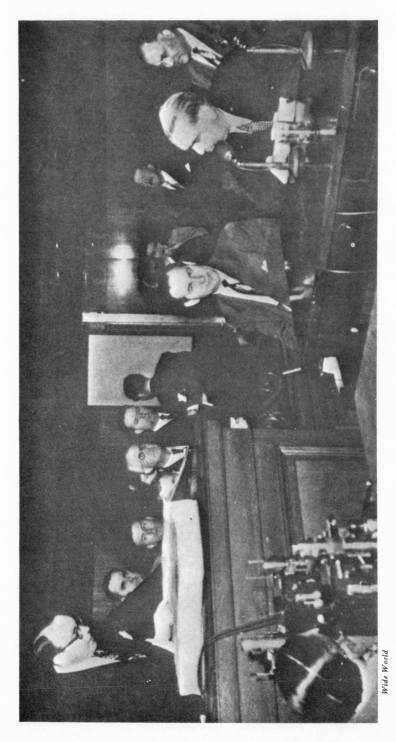

Halley refers to a file of the New York *Times* in questioning Ambassador William O'Dwyer during hearing at Federal Court House, New York City

jelly business before, glibly told us that he "borrowed eight or ten or twenty thousand [dollars] . . . I am not sure about that" to enter the deal. With the company came the precious sugar quota of 14,000,000 pounds.

In executive session Counsel Halley asked Giglio why "a bright young man like you" would choose a convicted narcotics peddler and thoroughgoing hoodlum as a partner. Giglio, alternately an articulate, sarcastic, or injured witness, protested that Livorsi had "paid his debt to society. . . . If he were my brother I could love him no less. . . . He is a very dear friend of mine and if I had the opportunity tomorrow to take him into business with me again and if I could make the man a wealthy man, I would do so." At the public hearing Giglio added: "The reason I took him in is because Mr. Livorsi has a very lovely family. He has three lovely daughters and a lovely wife, and he is a lovely fellow and entitled to a break."

Anyhow, Livorsi testified, the Tavern Company prospered, and there came a time when "Bill Giglio told me . . . that we were going to buy into the candy business." "Whatever he told me," Livorsi added, "was all right with me because I knew he was a capable fellow." So the ex-convict became a partner with Giglio in Lubben's Eatsum candy company. Livorsi insisted that Eatsum was in the "candy business" and entered stubborn denials when Halley, in a series of questions, asked if Livorsi had not been aware that Eatsum actually was buying and selling large quantities of corn syrup in transactions in which the parties concerned passed "large sums of money in cash payment at black market places."

In his new role as jelly manufacturer, Livorsi said, he gave jobs to a number of paroled convicts, including another ex-narcotics dealer, a man known as Big John Ormonte who had been in jail with Livorsi. Big John was paid $100 a week, supposedly to work at the candy factory, but, as we later heard from Lubben, he was such a disturbing influence that Lubben had to appeal to Giglio to take him out of the plant. Big John's salary continued, however, and Livorsi insisted that his old buddy "did his part." As Livorsi explained Big John's duties, "If I wanted to take off and go away from the plant, he would be around the plant seeing that the men did their work. . . ."

There was considerable confusion and debate about just how much Livorsi did draw out of the various jelly, candy, syrup, and sugar operations. He admitted his salary was $1000 a week, but when Halley produced an income tax return "showing you got $290,000 in 1946," Livorsi demurred, saying, "I wish I had seen it." Finally he conceded that the figure "must be right if you have it in front of you." He did recall that on two occasions partner Giglio handed him packets of $100 bills—about $35,-000 in all. "He told me," Livorsi explained, "this is from Eatsum dividends or something." He also said he was able to buy a country home for $50,000 which he later sold for $85,000.

The end of the sugar ride, so far as Livorsi was concerned, was when the little empire founded by Giglio "went broke." There were a lot of unpaid creditors clamoring at the door. "You didn't even pay your income tax, is that right?" Halley asked him. Livorsi replied: "I went broke with it."

HALLEY: What have you been doing for a living since 1947?

LIVORSI: I have been following the horses. . . . I go from track to track. I go from New York to Florida.

Senator Tobey, in his inimitable manner, inquired of Livorsi if he wasn't ashamed of his lifelong illegitimate activities. Livorsi shot back: "Betting horses, shooting craps, or playing cards is illegitimate?" Livorsi further declared, "I am a good American in every way."

When Mr. Lubben took the witness chair the story of the web into which he had fallen—admittedly through his own desire for profit—became clearer and more orderly. It was a tragic story, one that is well worth retelling here in the hope that it may point up a moral to any other potential Lubbens who, in these unsettled and inflationary times, may be teetering on the border between honesty and avarice. There can be no excuse for Lubben's actions, but he has paid dearly, and at least he was man enough to tell the story of his misdeeds to the committee without any attempt at self-justification. Admitting freely that he bought sugar on the black market, he said: "But nobody asked me to go into business. I can't look for anybody to feel sorry for me. I just did it."

Eventually Lubben met up with a man named Ronald Stone, a former attorney who, as Halley pointed out, had been disbarred in connection with subornation of perjury. "The fact that he [Stone] had had this trouble—" Lubben fumbled, "I mean, Jesus, who am I to judge? He was always very nice with me. . . . Everybody was in the act and everybody had an angle. Ronnie Stone was very valuable in getting supplies to us. . . ."

Q. (*By Halley.*) He also helped you get the black market sugar, did he not?

A. Yes, he did.

Lubben told us of having given Stone $10,000 in cash on one occasion to give to a man, supposedly an East Orange, New Jersey, attorney who would be able to get him a legitimate sugar quota. "It was worth almost anything to get a quota . . . not to have to worry about using black market sugar," he said. So he passed over the $10,000, but nothing happened. "We never did hear any more about it." (Stone, in his testimony, claimed the amount was only $1000.)

Explaining why he didn't go to court and try to get his money back, Lubben exclaimed: "How could I go and say I gave somebody $10,000 to use their influence with the government? You have your $10,000 licking and you have to take it and leave it alone." He went on to say that he had "paid two other people since then"—two men in Washington whose names he couldn't recall but which he would "dig up" for the committee.

At this point there was a bit of drama in the hearing room. Senator Tobey, always eager to ferret out information on alleged "influence peddlers," shouted: "I wish you would dig it up! I would like to get hold of these vermin if I could!" Lubben replied, "One of them is in this courtroom now." As Lubben started to point, a well-dressed man, who was heard by news-paper reporters to exclaim that the witness was "lying," stood up and said: "He is referring to me." He identified himself as a Washington attorney named Frank S. Ketcham, whereupon the irrepressible Senator Tobey, who mixed puns with his de-nunciations, demanded: "Did you catch him or did you not?"

Ketcham went on to say that he had been consulted by Lubben on how he could get a quota, and that he gave him ad-vice and worked on the case approximately six to eight months. "It was a very difficult job to attempt to do and I could not pro-duce any results," Ketcham said. For this, the attorney said, Lubben was charged "fairly and reasonably" a fee of $2500.

Then, Lubben testified, he consulted another man in Wash-ington who "was supposed to have been Harry Truman's cam-paign manager in Missouri." "How much did you pay him?" Senator Tobey inquired. Lubben answered: "I think the first time we gave him one thousand bucks, sir, but we weren't the big time for the man. He had more pictures in his office of more of you senators shaking hands with different people than any place I have been in this town.

"If you were just ordinary John Q. Public," Lubben went on, "and you wanted to get something done and you went into this man's elaborate suite of offices and saw a lot of beautiful pic-tures in the office—a gorgeous place—you would think this man was very successful because he certainly didn't get all those pic-tures staying home at night. I thought really truly that this was a man who was going to get a job done for me. I would have paid anything to get a sugar quota, sir, gladly."

Finally Lubben, whose memory was "bad" on the subject, re-membered after much urging and a recess of the hearing that the man with the pictures on the wall was named Victor R. Messall, a public relations counselor with offices in one of Washington's newest and fanciest buildings. We called Messall to the hearing and told him what Lubben had said. "Is David Lubben here? . . . I don't even know that I know the gentle-man or not," Messall parried. Lubben stood up and told Messall that they certainly had met; that a Lieutenant Frank G. Harris had taken him to Messall's office to discuss the sugar quota and that Lubben had paid Messall a retainer. Messall denied knowledge of the whole thing; then Counsel Halley produced a letter to Lieutenant Harris on Messall's business stationery, purportedly signed by Messall, discussing the Eatsum matter and saying that the writer had "been given to understand that this allocation will be very substantially increased shortly. . . ." Messall then said that the letter probably had been dictated and written by an employee of his, and that he had so many accounts that he "couldn't, of course, keep up with all of them."

As a further exploration into the sometime ways of Washington, Halley asked Messall: "Do you say you did or did not ever hold yourself as having been a campaign manager for President Truman?" Messall replied: "I suppose if somebody asked me if I had been—a lot of people come to my office and say, 'I understand that you used to be with Mr. Truman.' I don't advertise the fact, but I am certainly proud of it. I was his secretary for six years, from the day he came to Washington in 1935 until his re-election in 1940. I left him in March 1941 to go in private business. I did manage his campaign in Missouri in 1940 when he was elected to the Senate."

In justice to Mr. Messall, there was no evidence that he personally tried to sell himself to Lubben as a wonder-worker or that he attempted to trade on his rather ancient connection with Mr. Truman. The incident, however, does illustrate the extreme care which people in his position should exercise to avoid embarrassing their former associates by giving the impression that they have "inside connections."

Some time after the $10,000 episode, Lubben continued, Stone introduced him to Louis J. Roth, an accountant, of 166 West Thirty-second Street, New York City. Roth was presented, Lubben said, as "somebody that really has connections." Roth in turn, the manufacturer continued, represented himself as being connected with William Giglio's Tavern Fruit Juice Company; Roth said, Lubben testified, that Giglio had a connection with one of the largest baking corporations in the United States, and that Tavern itself had just secured the 14,000,000-pound sugar quota. This figure overawed Lubben, as he had been scrabbling for black market sugar in quantities as low as twenty-five 100-pound sacks at a time.

So Lubben paid a visit to the office building wherein were located the offices of the huge corporation which he claimed Roth had mentioned; he said he had the impression that there was a definite tie-up between the corporation and the parties he was going to see. He walked through the corporation offices and "met a great many people" who were told that "Dave is coming in with us," Lubben said. They finally wound up in an office on the same floor, occupied not by an official of the corporation but by an attorney who represented the corporation, and there was Giglio. Lubben made a deal to transfer a fifty per cent interest in his company to Giglio and Livorsi; it was his understanding that a relative of Giglio's, one Frank Loperfido, also was in the deal. The sale price was around $40,000, but Lubben claimed his new partners actually paid nothing until they had drawn enough profits out of Eatsum to effect a "paper" liquidation of the purchase price. In exchange for half of his business, Lubben said, his new partners "were to see that I got some sugar." But, he mournfully related, he "never got so much sugar that you could sweeten your coffee with" out of his new partners.

Soon after he acquired the new partners, Lubben went on, a number of things began to happen, all of which added up to grief for him. Giglio, he said, insisted that Eatsum move out of its modest uptown offices, for which Lubben paid $135 a month, and into a new place which was "a regular Hollywood suite," the unhappy manufacturer went on. Everybody had "gorgeous" big private offices and Giglio had a fancy bar in his. In all, the move cost Eatsum about $14,000. Then began a series of unpleasant and threatening visits from various OPA investigators, some of whom, Lubben said, later went to jail. There also was an infiltration into the firm of characters such as Big John Ormonte and another chap identified as Big Louie, who wore a "race-track suit" and scared off the women buyers. Lubben said he also began hearing from various sources, including

Louis Roth, that Frank Costello, the New York underworld king, was the "real boss" of the Giglio organization. Whether it was true or not Lubben never found out, but on one occasion, he testified, he did in fact see Costello at the Copacabana night club with Giglio and Livorsi.

Lubben himself was no angel, as was made abundantly clear by his testimony. He confessed that it was he who, in the relatively short period he stayed in business with Giglio, set up the intricate arrangements for buying a vast quantity of corn syrup in the Midwest by making under-the-table black market payments to farmers and selling it pretty much on the same basis. Everything was done for cash and in five months of 1945 more than $400,000 in cash was received from these transactions, Lubben testified. The money, he went on, was kept in "a little green cashbox" hidden in "a panel in back of the bar in the wall" of Giglio's office. Lubben had the key to the cashbox for the first ten days of the operation, then, he said, it was turned over to Giglio's cousin, Frank Loperfido. "The last time I knew about it there was $140,000 in there," said Lubben.

The denouement was that Lubben, after staying in business with the Giglio group for about nine months, lost both his nerve and his taste for the fantastic deal and decided he would get out at any cost. But he had a harder time getting away from Giglio & Co. than Br'er Rabbit had with the Tar Baby. The business at that time, according to Lubben's figures (disputed by Giglio), was worth $940,000—including the $140,000 allegedly in the green box. Lubben claimed he took back the lease on the plant and machinery he originally had in the Bronx and turned everything else over to the Giglio group, with the understanding "that they would pay my income tax for the nine months in which I was a partner." "In fact," said Lubben, "they later on charged me back about $23 because they claimed that some raisins I had in the warehouse shrunk a little bit. They were that methodical."

Senator Tobey asked Lubben if he had not had "a sense of apprehension and fear that if you did not play ball and do what they said, they might do physical harm to you?"

"I did, yes, I did," Lubben fervently replied. "That was the reason I wanted to get away from them." He went on to say that he had counted on receiving half of the money in the cash-box the day he broke up the partnership. But when he asked Giglio about it, Lubben testified, Giglio coldly told him, "You know we had OPA trouble."

"I said," Lubben continued, " 'I don't know anything about it, but certainly you had not $140,000 worth.'

"In that office that day were Frank Livorsi, John Ormonte, and a couple of other people. I looked around there and Giglio said, 'You are not going to get my money. You are lucky we don't charge you for some other things around here. We ought to get more back. You are getting too good a deal.' "

So Lubben, letting discretion be the better part of valor, "walked out and . . . never went back into that office" until some months later when he said Giglio called him down to close out some details. The final snapper to the whole tangled mess was that Lubben never got his income tax paid by his ex-partners, either.

When he went back into business on his own, Lubben concluded, he still fooled around with black market sugar until he finally was able to buy out a company that had a legitimate quota. "From then on I was free. . . . I felt . . . like I had just made a good clean confession," he said. "For the first time in a long time I was able to sleep." At this point Senator Tobey epitomized the feelings of all of us by remarking:

"You make me kind of sorry that I voted for price controls last night, opening up this vista again. History might repeat itself."

What we heard from William Giglio was a different story. He was an evasive and disputatious witness, as the record plainly shows. But step by step Counsel Halley led him through an absorbing recital of the career that Giglio, who gave his address as Ocean Port, New Jersey, had managed to achieve in his thirty-five years.

He began as the owner of a liquor store; worked during World War II as an "expediter for a company manufacturing collapsible masts"; became interested in the syrup business through helping a friend in the Bronx; then, with his ex-convict friend Livorsi, bought into the Tavern Fruit Juice Company. Tavern engaged in a pretty sharp operation, about which Halley and Giglio tangled tartly. The year before Giglio and Livorsi had bought in, the company had had its sugar quota raised to 14,000,000 pounds because, as Giglio himself explained it, all jelly manufacturers were being encouraged by OPA to make as much jelly as they could, for the reason that "in 1944 fats and oils and butter were in short supply and OPA requested of all jelly manufacturers to manufacture more spreads, more bread spreads." Tavern manufactured great quantities of imitation-flavored jellies from the sugar it received under OPA allotment, but—again in Giglio's own words—"all of our imitation-flavored jellies were sold to a very limited number of customers, only the top customers in the country." These customers, it developed, were large cooky manufacturers, short on sugar themselves, who were buying Tavern's products as "baker's jelly" and paying, as Halley charged, a "premium price."

I asked this remarkable young promoter what he thought of the ethics of taking sugar, which the government wanted him to manufacture into jelly in order to save butter and margarine, and selling the jelly to bakeries which turned right around and used it as a substitute for the sugar which they could not get at the time. "Senator," he answered, "this was perfectly one hundred per cent legal."

There was considerable dispute as to how much money Giglio and Livorsi actually had made from their participation in the Tavern and Eatsum ventures. Halley suggested that the figure was more than $500,000 in the year 1946 alone, but Giglio insisted it would be nearer $400,000 for all operations. Giglio also maintained that Lubben was wrong about many details to which he had testified, and, in defending his relationship with his ex-partner, Giglio claimed that he had enabled Lubben's Eatsum company to earn better than $250,000 by wholesaling jellies made by Giglio's Tavern outfit. The brash young man even seemed rather proud of the cozy arrangement, which he described to us as follows:

"Tavern would sell to Eatsum; Eatsum would mark the material up fifteen per cent, which was the legal wholesale markup, and they would, in turn, sell to National Biscuit and Sunshine Biscuit, and so forth. So Eatsum earned some $200,000 or $250,000, not on Eatsum's efforts, but on the sale of materials that I was already selling."

As a sidelight, Giglio related how, toward the peak of his operations, he was able to purchase the estate of the late Senator Barbour in New Jersey. He said he paid $100,000 for it—$50,000 of which was "borrowed" from a new corporation he had organized. Halley asked him if he had any gambling equipment at his country estate, and Giglio admitted there were two roulette wheels.

But he wanted to explain this, the glib young man said, because "roulette wheels are normally considered as gambling equipment and I would not like to be supposed here to be a gambler, because that is something I have never been." What really happened was that a "Panamanian gentleman whom I had met in Florida" had made him a proposition whereby Giglio would get a "legal license to run a gambling casino in the country of Panama." Gambling in Panama, of course, is legal. Giglio "rushed out," as Halley put it, and bought the two roulette wheels before he ever had any kind of contract. But the deal "never panned out," Giglio told us, and "that equipment lay on my property for three years until it was warped and useless" and "I finally burned it to get rid of it."

The grand finale to the Giglio saga was the pyramiding of the assets he had after Lubben was frozen out into an even bigger corporation called American Brands. There was a period of fantastic expansion and great affluence; then a whopping bankruptcy. The whole mess still is in process of litigation, including, as this was written, a federal income tax investigation. Irving Saypol, U. S. Attorney in New York, credited the committee's work with helping the tax probe enormously.

American Brands was a big thing while it lasted, the young

promoter explained to us. It had a lot of interests, including a huge research project directed by Giglio himself (who was neither a scientist nor an engineer), aimed at developing methods of manufacturing sugar from blackstrap molasses, citrus waste juices, grapes, and other products. "I was the only stockholder of American Brands," Giglio said; it did a business of approximately $3,300,000 in 1946. Giglio's salary was $1000 a week, and on top of it he traveled around the country, spending huge sums on "research." Halley, who had studied the books of American Brands, suggested that the cash spent by Giglio on these trips "ran to several hundred thousand dollars," but Giglio, with perfect aplomb, said "I don't believe that." How, I asked him, had he managed to spend even $100,000 traveling around the country in a short time? Giglio earnestly answered:

"This was not for me alone, Senator. I traveled . . . and carried with me eight or ten men, engineers and chemists. We went to New Orleans, eight and ten of us at the time. We went into the Florida citrus region . . . out to Sacramento. . . . It was a failure. It didn't work out."

At another point Giglio said: "I made one big mistake. I attempted to go too far too fast. That was my error." Counsel Halley, agreeing with the witness for once, said, "I will admit you went far and fast...."

At the time he testified before us Giglio—his American Brands Corporation in bankruptcy and under investigation by the Internal Revenue Bureau—had found a new position as general manager, he said, of a pharmaceutical firm known as the Heparin Corporation. Heparin, a heart drug, is "one of the great boons to medical science today," Giglio explained. Personally, I viewed with some alarm Giglio's next assurance that "the Army and Navy procurement division could explain that one to you [the Senate Committee]. They buy great quantities of it."

Throughout our investigations the committee discovered evidence of infiltration of legitimate business fields by crimesters and their associates. We saw it in Chicago, where Joe Fusco, once labeled a "public enemy" by the Chicago Crime Commission, became the city's largest wholesale liquor dealer; we saw it in Miami, where hoodlums took over hotels; and we were to see more of it in every city where we conducted hearings. The committee found more than seventy separate types of businesses into which countless hoodlums had infiltrated, as follows:

Advertising, amusement industry, awnings, automobiles, bakeries, ballrooms, banking, baseball, bonding, bowling, boxing, candy, catering, cheese importing, cigarettes and tobacco, cleaning and dyeing, coal, construction, copper, dairies, dress manufacturing, dress sales, drug manufacturers, drugstores, electrical equipment, fishing, florists, foods of all types (meat, groceries, and fruit, etc., both wholesale and retail), furniture, gambling casinos (legal in Nevada), gambling equipment manufacturers, garages, gas stations, haberdashery, hardware, hotels, ice, importing, insurance, jams and jellies, juke boxes, junk, laundries, linen supplies, liquor (wholesale and retail), lithography, loans, manufacturing (miscellaneous), oil prospecting, olive oil importing and wholesaling, paper, printing, publications (both racing publications and scandal sheets which posed as legitimate but whose operations verged on blackmail), racing operations and race tracks, race news wire service, radio, ranching, real estate, restaurants (including taverns, bars, and night clubs), rubber, shipping, slot machines, steel, surplus property, tailoring, television manufacturing and sales, textiles, theaters (stage and movies), trucking, transportation, unions, and washing machines.

The pattern of legitimate infiltration by the hoodlum element is a familiar and often a vicious one. It begins with the hoodlum finding himself with more money than he knows what to do with, accrued, of course, from his illegal ventures in gambling, narcotics, bootlegging, prostitution, or what not. A good example of this was established in our interrogation of the Newark, New Jersey, gangster, Abner (Longie) Zwillman, a confessed rumrunner and strong-arm man of the prohibition era, named by former District Attorney William O'Dwyer of Brooklyn in his testimony as one of the old leaders of "The

Combination" which ran Murder, Inc. Zwillman's close associates, O'Dwyer testified, were the late Louis (Lepke) Buchalter (electrocuted), the late Bugsy Siegel (murdered), Lucky Luciano (deported), Albert Anastasia (now in the dress manufacturing business), and Joe Adonis (as this was written, in jail). Zwillman wound up the prohibition era with a fortune. Now he is a participant in a tobacco vending machine company (Michael Lascari, who took money to Lucky Luciano in Italy, is one of his associates); a truck sales and parts agency; a trading company that buys and sells auto equipment and used machinery; another company that deals in scrap iron, and a company that places and operates some 700 washing machines in apartment buildings. He also has investments in properties and business held for him in the names of other persons acting as his trustees; he declined to give us information about these trusteeships, stating that he had set it up in that manner because "sometimes my name kills a deal."

I cannot overemphasize the danger that can lie in the muscling into legitimate fields by hoodlums. None of us on the committee would deny the right of an honestly repentant wrongdoer, who has paid his debt to society, to go straight in a legitimate field; indeed, this should be encouraged. But there was too much evidence before us of the *unreformed* hoodlums gaining control of a legitimate business; then utilizing all his old mob tricks—strong-arm methods, bombs, even murder—to secure advantages over legitimate competitors. All too often such competition either ruins legitimate businessmen or drives them into emulating or merging with the gangsters.

The hoodlums also are clever at concealing ownership of their investments in legitimate fields—sometimes, as Longie Zwillman said, through "trustees" and sometimes by bamboozling respectable businessmen into "fronting" for them. Virgil Peterson of the Chicago Crime Commission testified that "hundreds" of hoodlum-owned businesses are successfully camouflaged. He told us of having been consulted by a friend of his who had been offered a $25,000-a-year job to head a "new corporation." Peterson investigated for him and found that "the fellow who had contacted him was part and parcel of the Capone Syndicate."

There are other obvious dangers of having criminals in control of legitimate businesses. For one thing, a legitimate business is a very convenient front for a gambler or criminal: it can be used as a "cover" for the profits of his illegal operations, thus enabling him to defraud the government of taxes on many hundreds of thousands of dollars of income. Another drawback is the basic unwholesomeness of having gangsters in control of companies that perform vital services or distribute necessary commodities to the public. I am thinking particularly of instances we uncovered where men with criminal records own interests in transit and taxi companies, and where they sell and manufacture food products and even vital medicines. I, for one, do not like to think of food products necessary to the health of my children, or of medicine that can mean life or death to a great many people, coming from plants controlled by gangsters whose code of ethics is the dollar sign, and who do not care if that dollar sign is stained somewhat with blood. As one possible means of remedying the situation, I favor passage of legislation which would expose such operations by giving the Securities and Exchange Commission authority to require public listing of names of all large investors in corporations whose interstate operations affect the public welfare.

CHAPTER 10

KANSAS CITY:

LAW OF THE JUNGLE

WHEN the committee began its first hearings in Kansas City, Missouri, in July 1950 it was the second city in which we had staged a full-dress inquiry. Between Miami Beach and Kansas City, we had been assembling small pieces of the national crime mosaic which would fit later into the big picture. We had not been overwhelmed yet by the repetitious mass of evidence we were to accumulate all over the country, pointing to raw and brutal rule by criminals and utter prostitution of their oaths of office by some officials who were supposed to serve the public. Hence the Kansas City situation hit us with doubly powerful impact. The committee was gratified to report later that there has been considerable improvement since the combination of a vigorous federal grand jury probe and our hearings, which beamed some healthy rays of exposure on the mobster-politician combine that had operated in Kansas City. However, I shall never forget my first impression of the city as a place that was struggling out from under the rule of the law of the jungle.

When the committee went to Kansas City the disgraceful

1948 vote frauds in the Slaughter-Axtel congressional race, climaxed by the theft of ballots from the Jackson County courthouse, had already been investigated by the FBI and a federal grand jury. It was outside the province of the committee's primary authority to make legislative recommendations concerning election laws. However, we felt that our proposal for organization of a racket squad in the Justice Department and our endorsement of the Attorney General's suggestion for on-the-spot racket grand jury investigations can be useful in retarding future repetition of such deplorable scandals.

What the committee found in Kansas City was a staggering example of a prosperous city, blessed with many industries and inhabited by the same type of good citizens found everywhere in America, which, through indifference and civic inertia, had fallen under the influence of as vicious a bunch of criminals as existed anywhere. The Kansas City mob, led by men who were high up in Mafia, had milked the town.

It milked it well, too: the federal grand jury investigating crime in Kansas City found that the illegal gambling business in years past had grossed more than $34,000,000 a year. The mobsters could do this because they were able to "buy" many small and middle-sized officials, and to influence some big ones. We found honest and incorruptible officials who defied the Kansas City gang, but they were subjected to much pressure and harassment and in some instances even physical threats.

Actually the Kansas City Police Department was headed by a good chief and included some officers who made excellent impressions on the committee. The gangsters tried hard to supplant them. In the county, however, where Sheriff J. A. Purdome was the chief enforcement officer, it was a different story. The committee found Sheriff Purdome "notably lax in his enforcement of the liquor and gambling laws." One of the many fantastic facets of Purdome's administration was that he permitted a local racketeer, Wolf Riman, juke-box and pinball king, to hold a deputy sheriff's commission and to operate a car equipped with siren and red light. Riman later was murdered when he overextended his activities into the wholesale liquor field, and Sheriff Purdome has married Riman's widow.

No responsible person condones murder as an instrument of social justice, but there seemed to be a moral lesson in the violent end met by Charlie Binaggio, Kansas City's reigning evil genius of recent years. This conniving and not particularly courageous gangster, a fixer rather than a muscle man, was murdered in his political clubhouse, four bullet holes in his head. Dead beside him was his lieutenant and "enforcer," Charlie Gargotta. If ever a human being deserved the title of "mad dog" it was Gargotta. His record from 1919 to 1947 showed thirty-nine arrests on charges ranging from attempted burglary to murder. Once he was caught after killing a man in cold blood on the streets of Kansas City, but a corrupt police officer (who later went to the penitentiary for it) switched the identification tags on the murder weapon and Gargotta was able to beat the homicide charge. A determined former sheriff pressed felonious assault charges against Gargotta in connection with the same case; after twenty-seven postponements of his trial Gargotta finally was sent away for three years, but before he had served his whole term the Missouri Pardon Board, over objections of the Kansas City Police Department, recommended his pardon, which then was approved by former governor Forrest Donnell.

As noted in the earlier chapter on the Mafia, Binaggio, Gargotta, Tano Lococo, fat Tony Gizzo, and grizzled old Jim Balestrere, reputed Mafia chieftain in Kansas City, were known as "the Five Iron Men." Important among the lesser mobsters who were cut in for parts of their various illegal enterprises were Edward P. Osadchey, alias Eddie Spitz, and Morris (Snag) Klein. Binaggio and Gargotta now are dead; Lococo is in the penitentiary for income tax fraud; and Klein is in prison for his part in the Kansas City vote frauds. Osadchey, Balestrere, and Gizzo, at the time of this writing, at least, still were at liberty.

These Five Iron Men and their henchmen controlled most of the important gambling in Kansas City and the surrounding area. The pattern, developed in examination of witnesses by Counsel Halley, assisted by Max H. Goldschein, a Special Assistant to the United States Attorney General who had investigated the Kansas City 1948 vote frauds, followed an almost monotonous turn. Binaggio & Co. would spot a profitable gambling operation in the area and decide they ought to be "invited" in. If the operators were not smart enough to issue such an "invitation" their places of business would be bombed, robbed, or otherwise harassed until they got smarter. One gambler named Reneger, who was really stubborn, wound up with his head blown off.

Among other properties, Binaggio owned a one-fourth interest in Coates House, a large-scale bookie joint, which netted $100,000 profit in 1948. Gizzo and others were his partners in this operation. Another Binaggio property, in partnership with Gargotta, Lococo, Klein, and Osadchey, was the Last Chance Tavern; in fact on the night he was murdered Binaggio visited the Last Chance just before going to his political clubhouse to meet his mysterious death. The Last Chance was an intriguing establishment located on the border between Kansas and Missouri, with a thin wall right on the state line. When the cops from one state would come to "raid" it the gamblers with great hilarity would shift their equipment over to the other side and carry on without interruption. Cops from both states never seemed to arrive at the same time, so everybody had a lot of fun and Binaggio's gang made a lot of money. Senator Tobey did not think much of this operation. After we pried from Eddie Osadchey how the racket worked, Tobey exploded: "You know, Mr. Chairman, if I had been one of those cops, I would have gone across and brought them back and knocked them cold and said, 'Here they are in Kansas territory.'"

There was nothing glamorous about Binaggio and his crew. Gargotta was a thug—as ugly in appearance as he was in spirit. Binaggio, as we learned from Narcotics Agent Claude Follmer, who had gained his confidence to a degree, was a man with little stomach for his risky business. Just a few weeks before he was killed Binaggio told Follmer that he "planned to get out of politics altogether . . . too many headaches." He told the agent he planned to go to New Mexico to buy a share of a mining operation that was selling powdered pumice to the government.

Lococo was a mousy, insignificant, bespectacled little man whose appearance belied his reputation as another of Binaggio's "enforcers." He was often picked up by police for questioning after the murder of some non-Binaggio gambler, but nothing ever was proven against him. Lococo insisted he was no "muscle man" and said he never even carried a gun. "You can't give me a man in Kansas City who could ever say that I threatened him or said anything wrong to him or anywhere else," he replied with obvious agitation when Senator Tobey asked him about his ugly reputation.

Osadchey, known as Eddie Spitz, was a slick operator, not really tough himself but with the knack of making himself useful to the guys who were tough. Because he was quick on the brainwork Binaggio & Co. let Eddie have a twelve per cent share of the Last Chance. His function, Eddie said, was to "get customers." He was evasive about how much he drew from this gambling operation, but finally fixed the amount at approximately $4000 every couple of months.

I have already related, in Chapter 3, dealing with the wire service, how Osadchey, Gargotta, Lococo, and Klein muscled in on Simon Partnoy's profitable wire service in Kansas City after the Chicago-Capone Syndicate set out to take over the nationwide race news racket. Another time Osadchey and Klein, without putting up a dollar, moved across the state line into Iowa to "muscle" themselves fifty per cent of a gambling place in Council Bluffs called the Stork Club, in which the original owners had invested $90,000. Eddie, in an involved story, insisted that there really was no "muscle"; it was merely a case, he explained, where, after he and Snag offered to "buy" the whole club for $20,000, the owners countered with a proposition that they take half of it for nothing. Admitting that "it sounds a little fantastic," the little mobster insisted: "There are a lot of deals happen like that. If you find something you go to a fellow who has the money who is interested, you take a free ride." Senator Tobey, fascinated by this exposition of high finance among the gangsters, observed: "Very unusual. People who give a man an interest in a business of that sort and get nothing out of it—yes, very unusual! I wish you would tell me some place where I can go in and do it."

Osadchey was one of the first gangsters of his type to come before the committee, and Tobey, who always found these people incredible, tried valiantly to discover what made him tick. "You are a human being and so am I," Tobey reasoned. "Why in hell does a fellow who has as bright a mind as you have—and you have got a bright mind and could go places in business—what intrigues you about crooked business that makes you go into it?" Warming up, he asked Osadchey how his wife and nineteen-year-old son felt about him being a gangster. "What is there in it, dear friend? Tell us, will you, please?" he implored. Osadchey aggrievedly answered back: "I tell you, when I got out of the Army everybody was making a lot of money and had made a lot of money. My business went to the devil. Everybody who worked for me stole from me. I thought I could make some money that seemed legitimate to me." Senator Tobey sorrowfully shook his head and exhorted: "Where is Binaggio today? Where is Gargotta? They are gone. What do people say about them? A couple of rats, they call them. . . . You know in your heart how crooked and rotten these things are. You ought to hate yourself for being in them. . . ."

Jim Balestrere, the old Sicilian-born mobster, identified by Agent Follmer as one of the Kansas City Mafia leaders, was a different breed. He played dumb and represented himself to us as a poor old jobless fellow who lived on a little income from a piece of business property (once rented to a gambling house) and on a few dollars given him by his children. But he didn't impress us as dumb at all: as Special Assistant Attorney General Goldschein told us, people in Kansas City rackets used to say that "Balestrere has a piece of Binaggio."

Apparently the old gangster had a "piece" of many persons.

Balestrere himself told us how once when he "needed a job"—it was just after the end of prohibition, and he had gone out of the business of selling sugar to bootleggers—he sought help from the late Tom Pendergast, the Kansas City political boss later deposed by Binaggio. Pendergast, Balestrere related, fixed it up for him to get a cut of a keno gambling game run by some local racketeers. Halley asked:

Q. Did you pay any money to get into the keno?
A. No, no, Mr. Halley; no. He [Pendergast] said it was already up.
Q. Did you do any work in the keno or did you just get paid . . . ?
A. I just went up there every month and check up there and they give me a check, and I walk right out—all by checks.
Q. In other words, Tom Pendergast simply gave you a sort of gift?
A. Give me something to live.

The "something to live" gift from Pendergast, Balestrere explained further, usually came to $1000 a month.

Balestrere went on to explain how Charlie Binaggio—"I know Binaggio since he was a baby"—similarly gave him an outright gift once of a piece of a gambling joint known as Green Hills. He was just walking to the movies one day, Balestrere related, when he met Binaggio.

BALESTRERE: . . . He [Binaggio] said, "What are you doing?" I said, "I ain't doing nothing. I am trying to do something, to open me a little business or something like that." He said, "You know, I am getting a piece out at the Green Hills. Do you want any?" "Oh," I said, "I am not much in the gambling business. I don't know much about it."

He said, "Well, that is all right." I didn't see him no more. About thirty days later he came in and brought me some money. I said, "What is this?" He said, "We win, and here is your end." Okay, I took the money.

HALLEY: How much money did he bring you?

BALESTRERE: I don't remember how much it was, Mr. Halley, but in the period it was open I got $5000 out of it.

Halley, with tongue in cheek, asked what would have happened if Binaggio had come to him and said Balestrere had lost $500. With a great show of earnestness the reputed boss of the dread Mafia replied: "With the kid, I used to know him so well, I don't think he would tell me anything out of the way."

Of the whole crew, Gizzo, a boastful, noisy, beer barrel of a man, was the only one whose performance was a reasonable facsimile of how a gangster is supposed to act. When Senator Wiley questioned him about his reported habit of carrying large sums of money on his person Gizzo nonchalantly replied, "Do you want to see it?" He then pulled a thick roll from his pocket and counted off $2500 in hundred-dollar bills.

Binaggio probably was the outstanding example of political boss and undisguised gangster in the United States. In Kansas City he was the leader of the First Ward Democratic Club, and after he had supplanted old Boss Tom Pendergast he was top dog in politics in the area. As his surviving partner, mobster Tony Gizzo, told us, Charlie had become so immersed in politics that "every time you talked to the fellow he looked like he was out of his head. . . . He wouldn't know what you were talking to him about, so many things he had on his mind." Indeed, though his murder never has been solved, the committee felt there was good reason to deduce, on the evidence before us, that Binaggio may have met his violent end because he went too far in trying to mix his two specialties, crime and politics.

We delved thoroughly into the question of how—and through whom—Binaggio carried out his political machinations. The gangsters themselves, of course, did their part. Eddie Osadchey testified, "Charlie told me" to travel around the state and line up his "friends" for Governor Smith. Osadchey admitted he raised money for the campaign—"I would say two or three thousand, maybe." Any money he collected,

Osadchey said, he turned over to Binaggio. Osadchey also spent "at least" $2000 of his own money traveling and working for Smith. How much the gangsters actually raised was hard to determine because of what the committee's official report described as "certain irregularities in bookkeeping" on the part of the campaign committee. "Rumors were prevalent," the report also noted, that Binaggio had raised "sums as large as $150,000 to the Smith-for-Governor campaign," but we were unable to secure any tangible proof of large-scale contributions by Binaggio or his associates.

In the non-gangster field two of Binaggio's principal political lieutenants whom we interrogated were John K. (Pat) Noonan and Henry McKissick, Kansas City saloonkeeper and ex-magistrate. Noonan, indicted with Binaggio on a prohibition charge but acquitted in the thirties, covered the state for Smith by direction of Binaggio, whose political club paid most of his expenses. He also collected some money, he admitted, for the 1948 campaign, but squirmed—"No, I couldn't tell you," he said—when Halley asked him to name the contributors. On being pressed by Halley, however, he admitted receiving at least one "cash" contribution of $500 from a Kansas City policy racketeer named Bud Tralle, since deceased. Noonan also admitted taking an active part in Binaggio's efforts to juggle appointments in the Kansas City Police Department.

McKissick, one of the Kansas City politicians indicted and acquitted in connection with the notorious vote frauds, also admitted he "used to get a little campaign money from Bud Tralle" when he ran for magistrate. His philosophy was quite revealing as to what Binaggioism in its prime stood for in Kansas City. Speaking of conditions that had prevailed since Binaggio's death, the saloonkeeper piously deprecated the fact that police now were cracking down on gambling and other illegal enterprises. "I just think that has killed this town," he said. "This town is the deadest town in the country now. Your merchants and everybody else is noticing it. . . ." If he had his way, McKissick went on, he would open up more gambling places and even some red-light districts. He elucidated:

McKissick: It has got so a girl can't walk down the street. They raped three women out here the other night. If they had a little of that, I think, by gosh, we would be a little better off.

Goldschein: You think it would attract business.

McKissick: Yes. The girls brought a lot of people in this town. This town was built up for that reason, because it was a wide-open town.

At this point Senator Tobey broke in to observe dryly, "That is a unique argument for building up trade."

Before the committee ever went to Kansas City it had had a session in Washington with Roy McKittrick, of St. Louis, former state senator and attorney general of Missouri, concerning his knowledge of the alleged tie-up between the late Charlie Binaggio and Governor Forrest Smith. McKittrick, who also testified later in Kansas City, told us that Governor Smith, whom he had known politically for fifteen years, personally urged him to stay out of the 1948 governor's race. Smith told him, said McKittrick, "If you don't cause me any trouble, I can win it without much difficulty. . . . You stay out of this race, and I will support you in 1952 for the [U. S.] Senate."

McKittrick went on to quote Smith as saying, "I need some money to make this campaign on." In this connection the former attorney general testified that Smith asked him to help line up the political and financial support of Clarence (Gully) Owen, since deceased, an elderly, wealthy partner in Pioneer News Service, Continental Press's St. Louis distributor of horse-race news to bookies. McKittrick, after leaving the attorney general's office, had become legal counsel for Owen, who later was eased out of Pioneer by East St. Louis gangsters representing the Chicago-Capone Syndicate. But when he talked with Owen about Smith, McKittrick testified, the wire service man emphatically said he wouldn't support him because "he didn't think Smith would keep the gang from the East, as he called it, out of St. Louis."

In January 1948, McKittrick decided he would be a candidate against Forrest Smith. In fact, Gully Owen was one of those who "urged me to get in."

Q. Did you have any conversations with Charles Binaggio about your candidacy?
A. Yes, sir. . . . He wanted to discuss what he thought the chances to win were. It impressed me what he meant was the importance that he had to have a governor. He had been having a pretty rough time the last couple of years. The political game was very expensive to him. He just had to have a governor.
Q. Did he indicate specifically why he had to have a governor . . . ?
A. He discussed with me having to close up certain places which he owned and operated, and he didn't like to be underground all the time.
Q. What kind of places?
A. Gambling places.
Q. Handbooks?
A. Yes, regular gambling places, where they shoot dice and things like that.

Later, McKittrick continued, he saw Binaggio at a political dinner in Springfield, Missouri, and the Kansas City boss told him he ought to get out of the race; that "the East St. Louis fellows" weren't going to be with him. Still later, in St. Louis, McKittrick had another talk with Binaggio about the race and "we discussed it as a business proposition." McKittrick told us he said to Binaggio, "If you have made up your mind, I think the race is over right now because you are going to elect whoever you support for governor." Senator Hunt asked the witness why he placed such confidence in Binaggio's ability to dominate an election, and the witness replied:

McKittrick: He is the balance of power. He had a lot of friends and supporters in St. Louis, and he was the controlling factor in Kansas City. He had good alliances at St. Joe. He was very active. He was well supplied with money to operate with.

HUNT: What was his business?

A. He was in the gambling business.

HUNT: Any other business?

A. No, sir. He would tell anybody, "That is my business and everybody knows it is my business. It is just like the bank over there." He says, "I am in the gambling business. I don't want any chiselers, but I want to operate."

Finally the time came when Binaggio told him flatly, "I think I am going to have to go with Smith." Binaggio, McKittrick said, "had discussed with me at that meeting about slot machines and bookmaking places, and we just didn't agree." Soon after this Gully Owen came to McKittrick and said, "Well, the gang would like to get you out of this race, and they are willing to pay $35,000." The witness continued:

"I just laughed, and I said, 'Nobody would pay $35,000 to get me out of the race.' 'No,' Owen said, 'I am serious about it. They will. . . .' Subsequently, I had another conversation with him, and he said, 'They have raised that sum to $50,000. . . .'

"I said, 'I haven't changed my mind about it at all. I don't want to have anything to do with it.' "

Finally, just a few days before the deadline for filing as a candidate in the governor's race, Binaggio himself made him a proposition. He "insisted" that McKittrick withdraw from the governor's race and file for attorney general instead. Binaggio said, McKittrick testified, that the East St. Louis gang was "willing to pay all my expenses" in the attorney general's race at the rate of $1000 a month. This payment would run not only during the campaign but all throughout McKittrick's term of office. Binaggio also promised McKittrick "that Smith would agree to support me for the Democratic nomination for senator in 1952 and that they would pay the expenses. If I doubted his good faith in the matter, he would put up $25,000 in a bank that I would name to warrant the paying of my expenses for that campaign in 1952."

Turning down Binaggio's proposition, McKittrick testified that he asked the political gang leader, "Charlie, why do you want me to run for attorney general?" He said Binaggio replied:

"Well, to be just frank about it, there is some discussion about how much heat Smith will take. . . . We figure that if you are there you could brace him up and make him take more heat than he would otherwise. . . . You know he is kind of slippery at times."

Associate Counsel George Robinson asked:

Q. Before we get to the next conversation with Mr. Binaggio, would you state whether or not during the campaign you had any knowledge of the amount of money that was contributed to the Smith campaign fund?

A. It was generally understood—all of us fellows who would meet and everybody would discuss it—that $100,000 came from the east side, what they called the Capone crowd.

Came the election, and Smith, running with Binaggio's support, was victorious. McKittrick said he remained on good terms with Binaggio, and they had a number of conversations on how Binaggio and Governor Smith were getting along. Binaggio once told him, McKittrick testified, that the boys in St. Louis weren't "doing so good" and that he had "some things to straighten out." Binaggio's troubles apparently developed when Governor Smith appointed a tough, independent lumberman, Colonel William L. Holzhausen, as president of the St. Louis Board of Police Commissioners. Binaggio complained that "this fellow [Holzhausen] was too damned Dutch to be police commissioner."

Then came another conversation in which Binaggio, almost desperate, told McKittrick he was striving to get Holzhausen off the board.

Q. Your impression from what he stated was that he was in a difficult position?

McKITTRICK: That is right.

Q. Because he was unable to get the green light for gambling interests to open up. Is that right?

A. Yes. . . . It seemed likely they [the mob] thought he was to blame for it. . . .

A few days after that Binaggio was dead.

Through examination of two former police commissioners who had been independent of Binaggio the committee filled out the picture of the gangster's desperate flounderings to square himself with "the boys" and stay alive. The Kansas City police board was composed of four men, R. Robert Cohn and Colonel Hampton S. Chambers, both holdovers who had been appointed by a previous governor, and two Smith appointees, Jacob L. (Tuck) Milligan, a boyhood friend of Governor Smith's, and Sheridan E. Farrell, a Kansas City hotel man. It took three votes of the four-man board to effect any important policy or personnel changes. Cohn, of whom U. S. Attorney Sam Wear in Kansas City said, "He was doing a good job," told us in his testimony that Milligan, president of the board, and Farrell were "credited to the Charlie Binaggio group." Therefore it was necessary for the Binaggio interests to line up either Colonel Chambers or himself. Cohn testified that he was approached several times by Binaggio and other emissaries "who suggested that I be on their team and to follow through the program they had planned." But all efforts to bring either Cohn or Chambers into the Binaggio camp failed.

The last time he talked with Binaggio, the gangster had telephoned him one night "very much excited," and insisted on driving over to his home to talk with him. Cohn, who already had turned down all Binaggio's propositions, said there was no point in their talking, but Binaggio came anyway. Cohn testified:

"I went out and sat in the car with him. He appeared to be very much distressed. He said he was on the spot; that the boys were behind on their schedule and were making it hot for him. It seemed like I was the only one who could help him, because he couldn't do anything with Chambers. Governor Smith had been in . . . more than a half year . . . and nothing was moving. . . .

"He seemed very desperate, more so than I have ever seen him before. Like a bolt out of a clear sky, he pulled a roll of bills out of his pocket and threw them at me. . . ."

The roll of bills, Cohn said, was about two inches thick and held together by a rubber band, and the witness understood that Binaggio "was accustomed to carrying one-hundred-dollar bills."

"It took me by surprise," Cohn continued. "I just tossed it back to him like it was a hot rivet. He sat there for a few seconds, speechless, and then said to me, 'Bob, are you mad at me?'

"I said, 'No, but I am disappointed.' That was the last time. Then he tried to apologize and changed the subject, and so forth. He gave the appearance of a man who was drowning. . . . I don't think he intended to . . . but he did."

Cohn went to see Governor Smith the following month and said he told him the whole story of the pressure being put on him by Binaggio. He said he told the governor that "if he [Smith] subscribed to that program, of course, I just couldn't go along with it." Governor Smith, the former commissioner testified, "very vociferously" protested he knew nothing about Binaggio's activities and that he wanted Cohn to stay on the job.

Colonel Chambers told a somewhat similar story of pressure from Binaggio. The gangster, he said, was particularly insistent that Chambers agree to appoint a new chief of police and a new captain in one of the racket districts. When he told Binaggio to go peddle his papers, Chambers declared, the gangster cockily told him: "Well, the governor will be having you down before long to talk to you. . . . You had better get right." A few days later Chambers was, in fact, summoned to the state capitol to talk with Governor Smith. "I said to him, 'It looks like you have some leak in this office somewhere. . . . Your political friend in Kansas City called me on the phone two or three days ago and told me I was going to get this letter." The governor merely replied that he did not think there was any leak from his office, Chambers said.

Chambers declared that he, like Cohn, gave Governor Smith a frank report of the pressure to which he was being subjected, even telling him that Binaggio, in speaking of Governor Smith's appointee, Milligan, had said, "To hell with him [Milligan]. We will tell him what to do." Halley asked:

Q. What did the governor say when you told him these things?
A. That is all, just rubbed his hands together and looked down at the floor; not a word, not one word.

After that, Chambers went on, he began getting anonymous threatening calls once a week, telling him, "You had better be careful how you drive that car," and so forth.

Former Commissioner Milligan gave the impression of being a reputable man who was devoted to Governor Smith and who was willing therefore to "go along" to some extent, as the committee report noted, with Binaggio, who had supported his lifelong friend. Milligan conceded that he tried to give Binaggio some patronage on the police force but denied that the gangster influenced him unduly. Ex-Commissioner Farrell, who belonged to Binaggio's Fifteenth Street political club, spoke of the murdered mobster in surprisingly complimentary terms. Binaggio, he told us, "was very polite and pleasant to everybody." "I wouldn't call Binaggio a public enemy as much as I know about him," Farrell testified. "Never did really know anything wrong about the boy until after this all came out and then he was in everything. . . ." Farrell admitted that, as police commissioner, he favored an "open town . . . to a certain extent, of course." "We have no life in the town at night here. . . . I think it would help the city when people come to town. They don't come to town to go to bed," he said. "Mind you," Farrell added, "I am against anything crooked in any shape or form."

But Binaggio, Farrell went on, never tried to persuade him

that Kansas City should be an open town. "I will say this at this point," Farrell assured us. "He [Binaggio] did say that they wouldn't allow any gambling in this town. I will tell you why. He was figuring on running a pretty decent place because he really figured on getting into the city hall in the spring election. I think that was the idea of it. He didn't want any heat on his organization here...."

The pay-off for the entire police board came after the murder of Binaggio and Gargotta on April 5, 1950. The eyes of America were focused with disgust on Kansas City, and the decent citizens there did not like it. The Chamber of Commerce demanded a cleanup, and Governor Smith reacted by calling for the resignations of all the Kansas City police commissioners. Milligan and Farrell resigned, but Cohn and Chambers refused to do so, forcing the governor to "fire" them; that was their intention, they said, as they felt they were clean and did not want to be in a position of quitting under fire. The present Kansas City police board, our report noted, "is made up of four men of undoubted integrity," and the citizens of Kansas City have helped the drive for better law enforcement by forming a local crime commission.

As for Governor Smith, it seemed to the committee, after he had testified before us concerning the various allegations against him, that he was either a much lied-about person or a man of exceedingly bad memory. As he told it, he never asked McKittrick to stay out of the governor's race. On the contrary, he said, McKittrick "wanted me to run for governor" so that Smith could help him when McKittrick, in turn, ran for the Senate. He never asked, he said, for support from Gully Owen. His statement about Binaggio we also found hard to believe. Smith said he didn't even know the fellow by name until around November 1947 (though Binaggio's name by then was a byword in Missouri political circles); at that time, Smith explained, Binaggio just walked up to him in a Kansas City hotel lobby and said "he hoped I would run for governor, that he was going to support me." "When he told you those things," Counsel Halley inquired, "did you ask him who he was to

make such a statement?'"Governor Smith replied: "I did not.
I asked the young lady at the desk who that young fellow
was. . . . She told me."

The only other pre-election meetings with Binaggio were
equally casual, the governor insisted. Mostly they took place
in hotel lobbies. Even Binaggio's campaign henchman, Pat
Noonan, who also was Governor Smith's "old friend" from
World War I days, had it all wrong about the details of a
meeting in Smith's hotel room, the governor said. Noonan had
been asked:

THE CHAIRMAN: Smith was here [in a Kansas City hotel]
and you got hold of Binaggio and took him up here?
NOONAN: That is right. . . .
THE CHAIRMAN: Was it agreed that if Binaggio would put
his 30,000 or 35,000 votes in, Smith would remember him?
NOONAN: Well, yes.
THE CHAIRMAN: And recognize him over here as the leader?
NOONAN: Senator, I know you know a certain amount of poli-
tics. . . . That is it exactly, about what passed.

Smith, though admitting Binaggio had been up in his room
at the hotel along with other persons, insisted it had not been
by appointment arranged by Noonan and that the meeting
was not as described by his "old friend." "I have never talked
to Charlie Binaggio an hour in my whole life," the governor
declared, though he did recall that after his election Binaggio
visited him several times at the state capitol.

The first visit at the capitol, the governor explained, was
about a month after his inauguration when Binaggio dropped
by "with five or six other people." "What did he want?" asked
Halley, and Governor Smith replied: "He wanted to see what a
governor's office looked like. . . ." Another time Binaggio
called at the governor's office along with some other fellow who
had a "kind of unpronounceable name." That time, Governor
Smith related, "they asked me where would be a good place to
go fishing. They were going down on the lake." Then the gov-

ernor remembered a few other visits with Binaggio to discuss things such as cigarette and gasoline taxes.

"No, sir; no, sir," the governor assured us when Halley asked him if he had not known that there were two factions on the Kansas City police board, and that Binaggio was bringing pressure on the two commissioners who had not been Smith appointees. He flatly contradicted Cohn's testimony in which Cohn swore that he had told the governor all about the Binaggio situation. Cohn, the governor insisted, "said nothing about any friction on the board." Well, Halley asked him, what had been the purpose of Cohn's visit? "More or less a friendly call . . ." the governor answered. As for Colonel Chambers' visit, which Chambers had sworn was preceded by the threat from Binaggio, the governor insisted he merely "invited" Chambers to the capitol because "one of the senators" said Chambers was looking for "an excuse to come to Jefferson City . . . so I, trying to be a good fellow, I just wrote him a letter and told him to come down. . . ."

Of the connection between the late Charlie Binaggio and the Forrest Smith campaign, the committee, after sifting the mass of allegations and denials, concluded in its report to the Senate:

"It is abundantly clear that Binaggio did support Forrest Smith, and that his organization was active in the governor's campaign . . . but whatever Binaggio's expectations may have been as a result of his efforts in the campaign for Governor Smith, there is no substantial evidence that Governor Smith made any kind of commitment to Binaggio, or that Binaggio was successful in opening up the town.

"On the other hand, it is inconceivable that Governor Smith, being an experienced politician, could have failed to know of Binaggio's background, or that Binaggio expected a *quid pro quo* for his support. Smith's assertions under oath that he did not discuss politics with Binaggio, or discuss Binaggio's expectations, are simply not credible."

CHAPTER 11

THE ST. LOUIS AREA:
WHERE GAMBLING IS BIG BUSINESS

Bɪɢ business" is the descriptive phrase for crime in the St. Louis area, which takes in not only the large Midwestern metropolis but adjoining counties in Missouri and across the Mississippi River into Illinois. Criminal activities in the area now are centered mostly on illegal gambling, of both local and widely dispersed interstate nature. However, the committee found ample evidence that gambling is not merely the innocent, harmless "biological necessity . . . the quality that gives substance to . . . daydreams," that James Joseph Carroll, the cantankerous St. Louis bookmaker who did a multimillion-dollar annual business, described. In the past twenty years there have been sixty-four unsolved gang murders in the Missouri-southwest Illinois area of which St. Louis is the center. Twenty-five of the victims have been killed since 1940, when, as a published staff report noted, "the pattern of murders changed and it became obvious . . . that the murders from then on constituted a studied plan of assassinations to control all large-scale commercial gambling and vice. . . ."

During this period of many unsolved murders five gangs of major importance operated in St. Louis. These were the Hogan Gang, the Egan Rats, the Cuckoo Gang, the so-called Green Dagoes, composed largely of Sicilians, and a gang of Americans of Italian descent. The Cuckoos were mostly hoodlums of Syrian descent, and they co-operated with the American-born Italians in waging a war of extermination against the Green Dagoes. An offshoot of the Sicilian mob was the Pillow Gang, so named, our staff investigators noted, because its leader, Carmelo Fresina, "was once shot in the buttocks and thereafter carried a pillow with him to use when he sat." Eventually Fresina, an extortionist and bootlegger, was dispatched with two bullets in the head and no longer needed his pillow. In central and southern Illinois two major mobs—the Shelton Gang and the Birger Gang—operated. One of the Sheltons' principal lieutenants at one time was the notorious Frank (Buster) Wortman, an East St. Louis, Illinois, gangster whose gambling operations the committee traced in detail.

In St. Louis the committee heard from two law enforcement officers who, we felt, were doing a great deal to put the brakes on crime. One was Colonel Holzhausen, president of the St. Louis police board, whose independence, as related in the last chapter, caused the Kansas City gangster-politician, Charlie Binaggio, such anguish. The other official who attempted, through hard-fought court actions, to curb the gambling operations fostered by Pioneer News, the Continental Press's distributor in St. Louis, was J. E. (Buck) Taylor, attorney general of Missouri.

An indication of the magnitude of bookmaking operations was gleaned from the testimony of gambler J. J. Carroll, which, because of Carroll's antics about testifying in front of television cameras and microphones, the committee found it necessary to take in two sessions in St. Louis and Washington. The sixty-four-year-old Carroll told us he had been engaged in some form of horse-betting activities since he was twelve years old. He insisted that the Carroll-Mooney bookmaking operation, which maintained huge wire rooms in St. Louis, Missouri, and East

St. Louis, Illinois, really should not bear his name because it was run by his associates, John Mooney and Michael Grady. He finally admitted, however, that the business handles "in excess of $20,000,000" a year in bets, the bulk of which is "lay-off" betting by professional bookies to insure themselves against extravagant losses. The profits from this "handle," he said, come to approximately $750,000, and his own take is approximately $110,000 a year.

Despite the fact that he takes this huge sum annually out of the business, he quibbled outrageously with Senator Wiley and me over whether it could be stated accurately that he had an "interest" in the operation. "I would not use the word 'interest,' Senator," Carroll said. ". . . in my opinion . . . [it] is not an interest." Senator Wiley demanded:

WILEY: What do you do for it?
CARROLL: Well, oh, give advice, furnish financing——
WILEY: And take the returns?
CARROLL: That is correct.

The committee did not have much respect for Mr. Carroll. Psychologically, he seemed to have a characteristic in common with Frank Costello. Costello, a racketeer, wanted to pose as a businessman. Carroll, a gambler, glorified himself with the title of "Betting Commissioner." Though "this term was intended to signify some sort of respectability," as the committee noted in its report to the Senate, the committee found Carroll "to be an ordinary bookie operating clandestinely behind locked doors which had to be broken down, in order to gain entry to the premises in broad daylight, when many employees cringed behind the locked barrier."

It was Carroll who, in St. Louis, became the first witness to decline to testify before the television cameras. "The whole proceeding outrages my sense of propriety," said Mr. Carroll, walking out of the hearing room. We did not think much of this position; as I pointed out to Mr. Carroll, "We had a very good minister appear a while ago" who didn't seem to mind the television cameras. I had promised Carroll that I would recommend to the Senate "with all my vigor" that he be prosecuted for contempt. In order to avoid this, Carroll later came to Washington at his own expense to testify. We had more trouble with him there but managed to get it over with by keeping the cameras off his face, a concession we had made to Frank Costello in New York in the interim between Carroll's St. Louis and Washington appearances. In Washington this grown man, a person of wide experience, actually told Associate Counsel John Burling with a straight face:

CARROLL: . . . I have a little thing here. You see, you have injected the fright factor into this proceeding.
BURLING: The what?
CARROLL: Fright, f-r-i-g-h-t factor.
BURLING: In other words, you are in fright at the moment?
CARROLL: That is correct, sir. . . . I am speechless. The phenomenon of light fright and mike fright, and that is what I am subject to and I am speechless.

Carroll, of course, insists he has "retired" from bookmaking. As to this, we had a word from Captain Joseph A. Wren, the fearless and (in gang circles) feared head of the St. Louis Police Department's gambling squad. He told us how he had raided a new Carroll establishment in a St. Louis hotel only two days before the committee's arrival for hearings. Counsel remarked that Mr. Carroll was supposed to be "retired." Wren replied dryly that all gamblers say they are "going out of business" after a raid, but "they pop up the next day or three or four days afterward." The gamblers in the hearing room laughed with the rest of the audience at this one.

It was interesting to note that, six days after his appearance in Washington before the committee, Carroll was charged in Missouri, under an obscure and rarely invoked federal tax statute, with failing to report $52,688.15 in payments to bettors and agents during 1948 and 1949.

Another huge operation in St. Louis was C. J. Rich & Company, a clearinghouse for bets on major sports, which operates under the guise of a gold-bronzing company. We questioned two partners in this outfit, Charles J. (Kewpie) Rich and Sidney Wyman. Wyman was a dark, heavy-set man who put on a great show of scowling ferociously as he taxed his memory for answers to our questions. Rich, originally named Reich when he immigrated to the United States at the age of seven, was a pudgy, round-faced, unhappy-looking soul who in appearance lived up to his nickname of Kewpie. Neither Wyman nor Rich would quite admit they were in the gambling business, on grounds of incrimination, so we compromised by discussing their business as "Operation X." The company is less coy, however, when the partners are not testifying before a Senate committee; among other things we introduced as evidence a circular openly distributed by Rich & Company which said: "We do not restrict our transactions solely to racing. We would gladly handle wagers on all other sporting events, including baseball, football, fights and elections. . . ."

Wyman started off by telling us that "Operation X" grossed about $1,000,000 a year; after he left the stand he sent in word through his attorney that he was wrong and the correct figure would be $4,000,000 to $5,000,000. Rich admitted right off that the company handled between $3,500,000 and $4,000,000 a year.

As a sidelight on the psychology of these law violators, I asked Rich, who looked much older than his forty-six years, why he never had become an American citizen. He answered that he had applied "many a time" but had been turned down repeatedly. I asked him why, and he unhappily replied: "On account of the business I participate in."

THE CHAIRMAN: . . . [Do] you value the kind of business you are in higher than you do getting out of it so you can get to be an American citizen?
RICH: No, sir; I do not.
THE CHAIRMAN: Then why don't you get out?
RICH: I will.

One aspect of both the Rich-Wyman and Carroll-Mooney-Grady operations that gave the committee particular concern was the admitted involvement in these betting operations of the Western Union Telegraph Company, a vital instrument of communication in interstate commerce. We already had seen in the Continental Press investigation (see Chapter 3) how deeply Western Union was involved, and how the facilities of various subsidiaries of American Telephone and Telegraph Company were used in dissemination of racing news. In an earlier hearing, before ever coming to St. Louis, Prosecuting Attorney Stanley Wallach, of St. Louis County, had given us evidence of how a raid on a Rich & Company storehouse turned up a card index of between 100 and 150 names of Western Union agents throughout the United States who acted secretly as betting agents for Rich & Company. The records seized on this raid, we were told, disclosed that Rich & Company "probably operated in every state of the Union through the medium of Western Union." The Western Union employees were given "gratuities" —i.e., bribes—to handle and in some cases even solicit bets in their communities for the Rich firm. In some instances Western Union agents were even paid a percentage of Rich's winnings as a commission for their services. We learned of this through a letter furnished us by Prosecuting Attorney Wallach. Written by Rich & Company to a Western Union manager at Waterville, Maine, it stated: "We will be glad to make you what we feel is a good proposition. We will give you 25 per cent of the winnings at the end of each month after deducting the necessary expenses as wire charges and form sheets only." Even the literature distributed by Rich & Company made it abundantly clear that bets could be placed with the company through Western Union.

In St. Louis, Harry E. Vermillion, local Western Union manager, admitted that a "few" Western Union employees took such gifts of cash, whisky, perfume, and so forth from the gambling house. After the raid on the "gold-bronzing" company, Vermillion said, he called in Rich and Wyman for "investigation," and from what they told him he was able to single out "some seventy-one names" of Western Union employees who received bribes from Rich & Company. As Vermillion explained it, ". . . Mr. Rich tells me that he quite frequently bought a bottle of perfume or maybe a couple of bottles of whisky or threw a twenty-dollar bill on the counter and said, 'Split that up among the four people who work in that office.'"

Western Union, Vermillion went on, handled an average of $250,000 a month in money orders and messages for the Rich company. The betting concern, he said, had charge accounts in 168 Western Union offices around the country, and kept $25,000 posted in the St. Louis office to guarantee payment of accounts. What it boiled down to was that Western Union, through the medium of money orders, served as the transmitter of wagers to Rich & Company, and the paymaster to whichever party—more often the betting establishment than the better—won the wager. Western Union also transmitted a total of $3,275,000 to the Carroll-Mooney combination and returned $2,832,000 to betters.

Western Union, of course, found the gambling account highly lucrative, for Rich & Company alone received 500 to 1000 telegrams a day, and, in the month of May 1950 alone, Rich's telegraph bill was $26,700. The Carroll-Mooney-Grady operation was worth $77,749 to Western Union in 1950.

Though there was no evidence that Western Union's top officials sanctioned these practices, I personally found it rather frightening to learn that Western Union, a common carrier of communications, which is called on daily to handle for the public thousands of messages of the utmost secrecy—some dealing with private legitimate business enterprises; others even with matters of national defense and security—should be literally infested with agents who eagerly sought the opportunity of taking bribes and commissions from gamblers. I agreed wholeheartedly with the conclusions of the full committee that:

"It is quite clear that in the C. J. Rich Company operation, the Western Union aided and abetted the violation of the gambling laws of the state, because it was profitable to do so. Only when the C. J. Rich Company was raided on June 26, 1950, did the Western Union do anything to stop its participation in the bookmaking conspiracy. . . . One wonders whether the Western Union's obliviousness to its public responsibility not to permit its facilities to be used in violation of state law, was in part due to the fact William Molasky, of St. Louis, a well-known gambler, is one of its outstanding stockholders."

The committee learned a great deal about William Molasky, of St. Louis, the millionaire magazine distributor, whose finger was in many pies. Molasky, an ex-newsboy, became a lieutenant of the late M. L. Annenberg, who once controlled the country-wide race news service (see Chapter 3). Molasky was convicted of income tax evasion and in 1941 was fined $10,000 and sentenced to eighteen months in prison. Today, among other things, Mr. Molasky publishes a scratch sheet for horse players, and is a thirty-five per cent partner in *Pioneer News,* which has been fought over by gangsters ever since the trouble began between the late James Ragen and the Chicago-Capone Syndicate. Molasky and his family own 18,050 shares of stock in Western Union, valued at the time of his testimony at $783,000. Western Union furnishes tickers and other service to Molasky's *Pioneer News.* He vehemently insisted, however, that there was no connection between the two circumstances; that he made the heavy investments at a time when Western Union was earning no dividends, because the president of Western Union had taken him on a sight-seeing tour of the plant in New York City and Molasky was highly impressed by the modern equipment the company was installing.

Molasky first got into Pioneer as an associate of Annenberg at the time that the late Gully Owen was being subjected to pressure from the East St. Louis gang faction headed by Buster Wortman. Eventually, when Annenberg, on his way to jail, gave up all his gambling interests, he gave Molasky his [Annenberg's] 22½ shares of stock in Pioneer, valued at $45,000, for one dollar. Molasky insisted he does absolutely nothing for

Pioneer, of which he is vice-president, except to "countersign checks." For countersigning checks, Molasky, in 1949, drew $26,600 in salary and $40,000 in dividends.

When Molasky appeared before us both in Washington and in St. Louis he was accompanied by Morris A. Shenker, a St. Louis attorney who also appeared before the committee as counsel for others of the gambling fraternity, including Carroll; Joe Uvanni, an on-the-track agent for Carroll's associate, John Mooney; Wyman; Rich; and Molasky's own associate, William Brown. Our Missouri investigation revealed that Molasky had made a $2000 contribution to Governor Forrest Smith's campaign in 1948—with a certain string attached to it. According to John H. Hendren, who had been Governor Smith's campaign manager, Molasky wanted the privilege of recommending to Governor Smith that Morris Shenker, the attorney for the gamblers, be named to the St. Louis police board. Molasky admitted making the donation but insisted that "Shenker's name was never, never mentioned."

Molasky also insisted strenuously that Pioneer had no connections with gangsters, even though he admitted his late partner, Gully Owen, had told him "a certain mob is trying to muscle our corporation out." He said he never asked Owen who the mob was because "it was none of my business; didn't want to know." The committee established, however, through examination of forty-two-year-old William Brown, son of Owen's old partner, the late Paul (Bev) Brown, that there was a very definite hookup between Pioneer and the gangster-controlled Plaza Amusement Company, a juke-box corporation headed by three notorious gangsters, Buster Wortman, Elmer (Dutch) Dowling, and Louis C. (Red) Smith. In fact young Brown, now president and principal stockholder in Pioneer, used to work for Wortman.

The incredible young Brown insisted he "wouldn't have no knowledge" of the fact that Buster Wortman was a well-known racketeer, despite the fact that Wortman only recently had been released from Alcatraz penitentiary. Brown also displayed an astounding lack of knowledge about some of the financial affairs of his company. "Haven't you looked at the books of your own company?" Halley demanded. Young Brown floundered: "Well, I just—no, really I haven't." Brown did know, however, that his late father had made an arrangement with the Plaza Company for use of twenty-three telephone lines, which, instead of piping music to taverns, fanned out racing results from Pioneer to its bookie customers. This was accomplished by an illegal crossing of wires called a "jump-over." The committee concluded:

"The relation between Pioneer News Service, William Brown, and Buster Wortman's gang of racketeers is very close and indicates to the committee's satisfaction that the Pioneer News Service today, like the Harmony Publishing Company in Kansas City, is now under the domination and control of the Capone Syndicate."

No investigation of the St. Louis area would be complete without a look across the river into certain nearby Illinois counties. Particularly appalling were conditions of open vice and gambling in St. Clair County, where East St. Louis is located, and in Madison County. "Most shocking in Madison and St. Clair counties," the committee noted, "was the utter blindness of law enforcement officials and the evidence of their unexplained income. The testimony of John English, commissioner of public safety of East St. Louis, that he knew of no major law violations in his city, seemed to the committee to verge on incredible. He testified that he had never done anything to disturb the operations of Carroll and Mooney and did not know that they were among the biggest bookmakers in the country although this has been notorious on a nationwide basis for a long time."

We developed that Police Commissioner English, a former plumbing supply salesman, who at the time we questioned him was a candidate for re-election, had received $131,425 in "political contributions" from 1943 to 1949. He reported this as personal income and paid tax upon the amounts in his federal tax returns. English insisted he used the money for continuing campaign purposes and that, in paying the tax, he was only "protecting" himself on advice of his auditor. The committee commented on the "fortunate economic position" of Mr. English, who was able to acquire considerable business and real estate assets on a salary of $4500 to $6000. Our report noted: "The fact that the city was wide open for years and only two or three gambling arrests were made in 1950 may have some relation to the commissioner's wealth."

Two former sheriffs of St. Clair and of Madison counties also came off very poorly. Ex-Sheriff Adolph Fisher of St. Clair told us he knew nothing about the Rich or Carroll-Mooney operations in East St. Louis—although, as a matter of fact, the Carroll-Mooney operation had been described by Carroll himself in his published testimony before the McFarland Committee. Ex-Sheriff Harrell of Madison County at least gave us a frank answer as to why he didn't close certain open and notorious gambling establishments. He said: "If the mayor and the chief of police and the citizens of Madison, the city of Madison were satisfied with it, it suited me." Our report concluded: "There can be little doubt in the minds of the committee that 'wide-open' conditions flourish in Madison and St. Clair counties because of protection and 'pay-offs.'"

After some of the characters we encountered in our investigation of the St. Louis-southwest Illinois area, it was a refreshing change to meet Police Chief Gene Burnett of Granite City, Illinois. Granite City is in Madison County, an operating stronghold of Pioneer News and of the East St. Louis gang. Chief Burnett was an officer who gave every appearance of making a determined attempt to enforce the law. "I have recently closed gambling in Granite City," he told us. "I had quite a fight on my hands. . . . This didn't set so good with the local authorities . . . but nevertheless it was accomplished." The chief went on to tell us the details of how he put the bookies out of business and of the arguments he had with the local mayor about his activity. He summed up—and there seems a little sermon on political morality in his words—as follows:

"Since I have conducted raids on the bookies, my department and I have been more or less outcasts from the other officials of the county. . . . I am known as the renegade of the law enforcement profession on the east side."

Probably the saddest commentary on conditions in the area, however, was the testimony of Byron L. Connell, former State's Attorney of Pulaski County, Illinois. He told us of a certain situation in the river town of Cairo, seat of the neighboring Alexander County, which, he related, since the boisterous early days when the early rivermen used to come to town, has had a red-light district.

"Some years ago," Mr. Connell said, "with regard to this particular area of prostitution known as Thirteenth Street, the good people of one of the churches, I believe it was the Baptist faith, wanted to build a church in the neighborhood. After due deliberation, the city officials decided that the girls had a prior right to the locality, so the church people, if they wished to avoid that, would have to build somewhere else."

CHAPTER 12

LOUISIANA:

FANTASIA IN LAW ENFORCEMENT

AN ENORMOUSLY evil and dangerous situation was uncovered by the committee's investigation of crime in Louisiana. Our hearings were conducted in New Orleans, the fabulous city which is the center of the area from which much of the crime in the Bayou State emanates. Thus it was against a backdrop of sophistication and complacence, with undertones of venality and violence, that we developed a picture which both repelled and engrossed us, like the spectacle of a rattlesnake poised to strike.

What we found in Louisiana was a complete case history of infiltration by important representatives of the national crime syndicate who, through alliances with local racketeers, put gambling and other profitable rackets on a big-time basis. New Orleans, though it has been cleaned up steadily since Mayor De Lesseps S. Morrison took office in 1946, became one of the important provincial capitals of the East Coast Costello-Lansky-Adonis mob. As his proconsul in New Orleans, Frank Costello installed one of his most trusted lieutenants, Philip (Dandy Phil) Kastel, convicted swindler, and through Kastel controlled an important segment of the area's slot-machine and gambling casino rackets. A working partnership was effected by the New Yorkers with a vicious local criminal, Carlos Marcello, known locally as "the Little Big Man" and named in one of the committee's reports as "the reputed Mafia leader of Louisiana."

Carlos Marcello—born Caloreo Minicari, of Sicilian parentage in Tunis, Africa—came to this country as an infant forty-one years ago, and never has been naturalized as an American citizen. In my opinion Marcello is one of the most sinister criminals encountered by the committee anywhere, and, with some of his brothers and other relatives, he is building a criminal dynasty that one day may rival Al Capone's. Both Marcello and his brother Anthony steadfastly refused to give the committee any information other than their names and addresses, and were among the five New Orleans witnesses cited for contempt.

In every line of inquiry we pursued in New Orleans we found Marcello's trail. The Little Big Man with some of his brothers and lieutenants owned all or part of more than forty enterprises—all but a few of them illegal. These included pieces of four large gambling casinos in Jefferson Parish and various smaller dives; an interest in the local wire service, various horse parlors and bookie joints, and at least eight slot-machine companies. His known intimates and associates in New Orleans and elsewhere included some of the most notorious mobsters in the country. Among the many bars, restaurants, and inns in which he had an interest was one place known as Willswood Tavern, which the committee's report noted was "declared to be a hang-out for Mafia members."

From Thomas E. McGuire, head of the Federal Narcotics Bureau in New Orleans, we heard that New Orleans ranked in importance with other metropolitan port areas as a narcotics center. "It has been my experience," he testified, "that any place that is more or less open, a community that tolerates houses of prostitution, gambling, or any like condition, would be a perfect field for peddlers of narcotics." Out-of-state dope peddlers frequently slipped into New Orleans to purchase supplies for sales elsewhere, he said. The New Orleans bureau, which had state-wide jurisdiction, worked intensively on its investigations of participation by the Mafia in the dope traffic, McGuire said. I asked him if he had seen any "Mafia-type" operators testifying before the committee, and McGuire, without naming any names, answered: "I'll have to admit I have."

Our report stated: "The committee had information that Carlos [Marcello] and his brother, Anthony, owned a boat used in running narcotics into the port of New Orleans. Both, when questioned, refused to answer questions as to their narcotics activities. . . ." Carlos had been convicted in 1938 of narcotics peddling and had served time for it. Earlier he had served a sentence for assault and robbery in Louisiana but had been pardoned by a former Louisiana governor, which cleared his record on that count. However, his request for a presidential pardon on the narcotics conviction was rejected in 1948. Our present immigration laws provide that an alien narcotics peddler can be deported, but Marcello apparently has escaped deportation on the technical ground that his offense involved the handling of marijuana, and it was not until 1940 that the deportation laws were amended to include traffic in this particular drug as a deportable offense. The committee regards it as a great miscarriage of justice that Marcello has been allowed to remain in the United States, and I have recommended strongly to the Immigration and Naturalization Service that, even at this late date, it investigate to determine what can be done about it. In the meantime the committee has endorsed passage of a pending legislative proposal which would tighten up deportation proceedings for narcotics violators and under which retroactive action could be taken against Marcello and others like him.

Testifying as to the constant struggle to keep vice out of New Orleans, Mayor Morrison observed that the city once was so wide open that "you could walk the five-block stretch on St. Charles Street from Canal to City Hall and never miss the results of a single race from the loudspeakers which blared through the open doorways of the bookie parlors." A heartening feature of Mayor Morrison's testimony was his vigorous refutation of the old canard—one which the slot-machine kings and bookmakers themselves take great pains to keep alive—that a tourist town will suffer if gambling is eliminated. Said the mayor:

"There were many people back in 1946 who . . . thought that elimination of gambling in the city would destroy our tourist business. May I say how wrong the past five years have proven those people to be? Instead of decreasing, the tourist business in New Orleans has increased by leaps and bounds, and so has all the other general business in . . . [the] city limits. . . . My conclusion is that the elimination of gambling from our city limits has not lost us any tourists; but a healthier progressive law-abiding community, we believe, has brought us many more."

The interstate nature of the gambling operations (slot machines, casinos, and horse-race betting) and of the narcotics traffic which the committee investigated in New Orleans was highly evident. We also established beyond doubt that the out-of-state gangsters who came to Louisiana "depended in large measure on the negligence, the active support, or the participation of some local law enforcement officials, who . . . could nullify the efforts of diligent officials and public-spirited citizens in their own or nearby jurisdictions." In non-legalistic language, I might add that the conduct and the brazen acquiescence in gambling operations of some of the sheriffs and marshals we questioned in the New Orleans area was as outrageous as anything we found anywhere in the country. As a sample I quote the testimony of the late Sheriff Gilbert Ozenne of Iberia Parish, who naïvely declared that he did not know whether prostitution—organized prostitution had been carried on in his parish for years—was against the law. Ozenne later died of a heart attack near the climax of an Iberia Parish grand jury investigation which was studying his testimony before our committee.

It was the committee's judgment that "outright payments for protection were most clearly established" in the case of John J. Grosch, criminal sheriff of Orleans, the parish in which the city of New Orleans is located. Grosch has been sheriff since 1946, and, before that, chief of detectives in the New Orleans Police Department for sixteen years. On the day Grosch took office as sheriff one of the local newspapers ran a picture captioned "Just a Gift for Johnnie," which showed the new sheriff standing alongside a brand-new Cadillac limousine presented him by "unnamed friends." The article quoted a local coin-machine operator as stating that the Cadillac was the gift of "businessmen" friends of Sheriff Grosch. The sheriff's attorney also issued a statement that "there are no strings attached to the gift."

We heard testimony from the sheriff's divorced wife, Mrs. Viola Grosch,[1] a woman who held a responsible position at the Tulane University Hospital, that in the last six years of their married life together, ending in 1940 (the period in which he was chief of detectives), Grosch had accumulated $150,000 which he kept at home in a steel box. Mrs. Grosch said she bought the box for him and, acting on his instructions, used an assumed name and gave a false address when she made the purchase. She also testified she had seen him receive money weekly from a local slot-machine dealer, and that she herself received $39 every week in an envelope handed her by another slot-machine operator, who would tell her to "give it to Johnnie." Likewise, another character, who reputedly ran a house of prostitution, came by every Saturday "and brought all the food for the week."

Through testimony of an employee of the company where it was bought the committee corroborated Mrs. Grosch's account of the clandestine purchase of the steel box. Mrs. Grosch also produced two written agreements made at the time of her divorce, one for the record which ostensibly gave her a settlement of money and other assets worth $35,000. All this, as the committee's report pointed out, added up to the conclusion that "Sheriff Grosch's wealth ten years ago was far larger than could be explained by his salary of $186 a month."

Grosch himself was a belligerent witness who denied the

[1] Mrs. Grosch since has died of a heart attack.

allegations against him, insisted he never had a safety deposit box or safe in his home, and told us, "I didn't worry about gambling too much. I caught thieves." He since has been indicted for perjury by a local grand jury and at the time of this writing was awaiting trial.

As the committee noted in its report, Frank Costello, during his examination later in New York City, claimed that it was the late Huey Long who paved the way for entrance of the Costello slot-machine interests into Louisiana. Costello testified that Long sought out his advice on how much revenue the state could raise if it "legalized" slot machines. Costello, whose own slot-machine racket in New York was being hounded out of business by the late Mayor LaGuardia at the time, sent his partner, Dandy Phil Kastel, to New Orleans to make the survey. Senator Long was assassinated shortly after his discussion with Costello, and the state of Louisiana never got around to going into the slot-machine business, but Costello and Kastel did— illegally, of course. With Costello's brothers-in-law, Dudley and Harold Geigerman, and Jake Lansky, one of the notorious Lansky brothers, among the partners, and Carlos Marcello as the local satrap, they created what amounted to a slot-machine monopoly in New Orleans. Evidence before us indicated that only the machines of their syndicate were permitted to operate, and the profits of the illegal business ran into the millions. Costello and Kastel, in fact, were tried—but acquitted—in 1939 on charges of attempting to evade payment of $500,000 in federal income taxes on their 1936–37 income of nearly $3,000,-000 from the one-armed bandits. Mayor Morrison, however, like the late LaGuardia of New York, now has stymied the Costello-Kastel slot-machine empire.

Such organizations always need "characters" to help them operate. We questioned one such character in New Orleans— James Brocato, who calls himself Diamond Jim Moran. Brocato is an ex-pugilist who used to box at 122 pounds and now weighs 212. He runs a well-known restaurant in New Orleans and likes to bedeck himself with diamonds. The day he appeared before us he restrained himself to wearing one medium-sized sparkler

set into a ring. Ordinarily, however, as Brocato himself con-
fided to Investigator George Martin, he even had a diamond
pendant which he wore attached to the zipper of his trousers.

Brocato said he had been associated with Costello's slot-
machine enterprise from 1935 until Mayor Morrison put them
out of business. He told us with a straight face that his job was
to walk around and call on owners of slot-machine locations,
spreading "good will." If he found a machine "not looking
good" he would send word to headquarters to have someone
"brush it up." Describing the familiar one-armed bandits to
Associate Counsel Downey Rice, Brocato said the function of
the handle on the machine was to be pulled. "It's good exercise," he solemnly explained. Diamond Jim worked later as the
same sort of good-will representative for John J. Fogarty, the
local wire service magnate.

Fogarty and Joseph A. Poretto, a Marcello associate, along
with Dandy Phil Kastel and the two Marcellos, were the five
witnesses cited for contempt in New Orleans. It was with difficulty that the committee traced the outline of the tangled story
of the wire service in the New Orleans area. We came to the
conclusion that the New Orleans wire installation had been
"the object of a typical, successful, and mysterious attempt at
muscling in" by affiliates of the Chicago-Capone mob. For
nearly thirty years John J. Fogarty had operated the wire service
and published racing results and forms in New Orleans. In
later years his arrangement was with Continental Press. When
the Capone Syndicate (as described in Chapter 3) attempted to
take over the country-wide wire service, Joseph Poretto, a criminal whose definite connections with Capone mobsters were
traced by the committee, set up a rival service in New Orleans.
Poretto's associates in his "Southern News Publishing Company" included two of Marcello's brothers and the son of an
old Al Capone lieutenant.

In the meantime Mayor Morrison came into office and sent
police to raid both the Fogarty and the Poretto outfits. Within
a short time after the raids a new service called the Daily Sports
News, ostensibly owned by Fogarty and his son, was opened

in "liberal" Gretna. As our report noted, "Neither Fogarty nor Poretto would discuss what happened in the interval, nor would they admit any association." In fact both men on the witness stand refused even to admit knowing each other on the ground that they might incriminate themselves! But through Western Union records we established strong circumstantial evidence that a merger had taken place "and that when business was resumed . . . the Marcellos figured largely in the ownership."

Mayor Morrison had told us the city still licensed approximately 2000 "one-ball bandits." Ostensibly these devices were games of "skill," but obviously they were used for gambling. John Bosch, president of the local coin-machine operators' trade association, testified that there were at least 1000 additional unlicensed machines operating in New Orleans. Bosch also gave us an interesting but far from novel exposition on how people in his sort of business operate politically. When an election came along the pin-ball association raised a kitty and contributed to every candidate running. The candidate that the association thought most likely to be elected got the most money, but everybody got a little.

Outside of New Orleans, in the rural parishes, slot machines continued to operate as openly as if they had been stamp-vending machines in a United States post office. The wily sheriff of Jefferson Parish, white-haired Frank J. (King) Clancy, would not quarrel with our estimate of 5000 machines in his jurisdiction. We also heard from Sheriff C. F. (Dutch) Rowley, of St. Bernard Parish, another wide-open gambling center. "I don't snoop," Sheriff Rowley replied when asked if there were any slot machines operating in his parish, which was something like asking if there was any snow at the North Pole. His salary and expense allowance amounted to about $5200 a year, but he admitted that he had had a supplementary income of $6000 to $8000 over each of the past three years; also that he kept between $15,000 and $20,000 in a strongbox in his bedroom, and that he had approximately $12,500 in other cash, stocks, and bonds. When we asked the source of his funds the sheriff refused to answer on grounds of self-incrimination. Rowley complained that the committee was "just inviting burglars" to knock him off by asking questions about his strongbox.

An extremely odd story was related to the committee by a young man in Iberia Parish. The witness, Warren J. Moity, twenty-eight years old and a defeated candidate for mayor, told us he had been "shocked" to hear from friends that they were in the slot-machine business but could operate only if they would "pay a shakedown to the sheriff, Gilbert Ozenne, and Howard LaBauve, who was the city marshal." Moity, a real estate and insurance dealer, said he tried in every possible way to crusade against the slot machines, in the course of which, he said, his life has been threatened nine times and he has been shot at once. Finally, when all else failed, he decided to go into the slot-machine business himself to get the dope, he said, on what went on. The committee, of course, held a dubious opinion of the wisdom of this step by the young man.

Anyway, he went on to tell of his difficulties in securing good locations for his forty machines, as a cozy arrangement apparently existed, he testified, whereby all the strategic locations were held either by Sheriff Ozenne's son-in-law or by Marshal LaBauve's brother-in-law. Moity testified that LaBauve immediately summoned him to the marshal's office "to give me the third degree" and to tell him he would "crush every machine I had" unless Moity paid him $76 a year per machine. Moity said he was told the money would be "divided" between LeBauve and Sheriff Ozenne. Moity, who swore he made three such monthly payments, said LaBauve "did not have the guts to collect it himself" but sent a deputy marshal named Rodrique to collect it. LaBauve later coolly identified his deputy marshal as a "professional gambler" who made his living playing poker and repairing slot machines.

Moity said he finally stopped "paying the shakedown and things began to get hot." Not only he but the owners of locations where he placed his machines were threatened. When the experiment had "served its purpose," Moity said, he tried to get out of the business by selling his machines to a would-be purchaser from Florida. But the prospective purchaser, as our report noted, "couldn't come to terms with LaBauve and Ozenne and withdrew." Consequently, at the time he testified in New Orleans, Moity said he was still in the business, with twenty-five machines on location in public places, "paying off in cash strictly against the law." Before he testified, he said, he received another call from his anonymous threateners, who let him know that if he testified before the committee "the next time they won't miss."

THE CHAIRMAN: Are you scared?
MOITY: No, sir; not at all. I believe that, if it takes that to clean up, I am willing to die for it, and I am sincere.
THE CHAIRMAN: What makes you think it is so bad?
MOITY: Because I know it has involved killings. That is why you can't have decent government. I don't mean by that I am strictly a reformer, because I am not. I mean that it controls elections. Those boys contribute—they put up that cash to go out there and buy the poor fellows that don't understand how they should vote and why.

Both LaBauve and the late Sheriff Ozenne admitted that New Iberia, the parish seat, and Iberia Parish were wide open and had been for at least thirty years in so far as gambling and prostitution were concerned. Both denied that they took pay-offs from the gamblers. Ozenne was nervous, but LaBauve was a cool, poker-faced customer, who was not the least bit rattled by the questions which led to his admissions of law violations. LaBauve and his deputy marshal, Rodrique, since have been indicted by an Iberia Parish grand jury.

The Costello-Kastel-Lansky interests in Louisiana were not confined to slot machines. They acquired the luxurious Beverly Club gambling casino and night club just outside of New Orleans. Kastel became president and general manager, with Costello, Meyer Lansky, Marcello, and another local man named Rickefors as partners. Lansky later sold out his twenty per cent interest—"I guess the proposition was not making enough money to suit him," Kastel told us—for $100,000.

Another huge gambling casino operating wide open in Jefferson Parish was Club Forest, which ran dice, keno and card games, roulette wheels, slot machines, a football pool, and a horse-race book. The club owners, identified to us as Frank, Arthur, and Henry Mills, Edwin Litolf, Al Schorling, Gonzales Azcona, Lawrence Luke, and Vic Gallo, remained in hiding throughout our investigation.

Club Forest was a big operation; it reported assets at the end of the 1949 fiscal year as $718,904, and admitted gross receipts from gambling of $2,008,796. A former dice man and cashier at Club Forest, one Vernile Cavalier, gave the committee evidence of the practice, which we had long suspected, of "juggling of figures and keeping of books which did not accurately reflect the facts." As we noted, "the books and records of the Club Forest . . . were a model of bookkeeping practice, but Cavalier's story raised serious doubts as to the true situation." He admitted that on occasions when Sheriff Clancy's deputy, Paul Cassagne, entered the club one of the managers would instruct Cavalier to withdraw sums of more than $1000 to be charged, as the dice man put it, to "ice," which is the accepted term in the gambling trade for protection money. Our report summed up: "It was Cavalier's impression that the sum so drained off was merely taken off one of the dice tables as a loss, just as if one of the players had won the sum with a lucky streak. . . .

"Then, too, there was found the extremely questionable practice of charging off, as an expense for loss against the club's gross, the astronomical sum of $372,000 in one year with the explanation that this represented moneys lent to players and customers which was not repaid, or for bad debts resulting from 'rubber' checks tendered by customers. . . . Equally amazing sums have been charged off through the years without apparent action by the tax authorities to question or disallow."

The Rev. Dana Dawson, pastor of a Methodist church in the town of Metairie in Jefferson Parish, told the committee how attempts by citizens to curb these open gambling operations met with frustration. The Rev. Mr. Dawson organized a citizens' league in Jefferson Parish and brought padlock suits against both Clubs Beverly and Forest. Almost immediately the minister was approached by one Pete Perez, dice foreman at Club Forest, and was promised funds for a new Sunday school building if the suit was dropped. Perez subsequently made contributions of $50 and $75 monthly to the church, even though the padlock suit was pressed, the minister said.

On one visit the dice foreman was accompanied by the incredible Sheriff Clancy, who later, the minister testified, actually brought checks as contributions to the church which included not only Clancy's personal draft for $300 but others from several gambling houses in the parish, including a check from the Beverly Club signed by Dandy Phil Kastel. Associate Counsel Downey Rice asked:

Q. I take it, then, that Sheriff Clancy was a channel or a personally appointed collection agent from . . . several gambling joints for the benefit of the church?

REV. MR. DAWSON: That is true. . . .

Q. Did Sheriff Clancy ever tell you how many men he thought he had been instrumental in securing jobs in the gambling places?

REV. MR. DAWSON: I believe the figure was 2000. . . .

Q. Did Pete Perez ever tell you who the "satchel man" was, or how the "ice" was paid or who picked it up? . . .

A. . . . I am not sure whether Mr. Perez has told me that or not, but it is more or less common knowledge in the parish that a gentleman named Mr. Paul Cassagne——

Q. Yes. What is his function?

A. As I understand it, he is the "satchel man," as they say.

Q. The "ice" man? Is he the "ice" man?

A. He picks up the money and takes it wherever he takes it.

In any event the citizens got exactly nowhere with their padlock suit. Both the minister and the attorney for the citizens' group testified that the litigation, through some rather astounding legal actions by the court of the district in which the gambling clubs were located, had dragged on for four years and never got to trial.

The committee encountered some remarkable law enforcement officers in its peregrinations around the country, but none was more astounding than King Clancy, the virtual dictator of Jefferson Parish. In Clancy's kingdom not only Clubs Forest and Beverly but at least six other sizable casinos operated. Clancy, who had been sheriff for twenty-three consecutive years, was an old-style politician of the type that fortunately is becoming rarer. His face was florid and he wore a fixed smile that rarely changed, even when he was making the most damaging admissions against himself. In New Orleans, King Clancy, a graduate lawyer as well as sheriff, thought he would defy the committee by refusing to answer our questions on the ground that his answers might incriminate him—an incongruous reply for a so-called law enforcement officer to give a Senate committee. But King Clancy lost his nerve when the committee began to put in process a contempt citation against him which, if a conviction resulted, could send the "King" to jail. He sent us a telegram, begging the privilege of coming to Washington at his own expense to purge himself.

In Washington, Sheriff Clancy struck an attitude which, to the committee, reeked of pious hypocrisy: yes, he admitted, there was gambling in Jefferson Parish and it had gone on "for hundreds of years." A man who was opposed to gambling could not run for office in his parish and be elected, he said. However, the real reason that King Clancy condoned gambling was not because of "ice" or anything crude like that, but simply because the gambling casinos provided work for hundreds of "underprivileged and old people who could not get work any place else." In permitting gambling to flourish, he broke his oath of office, of course, King Clancy admitted, but he did so, he quavered, "for the sake of those old and unfortunate men. . . ." (Our investigators found few "old people" working in Jefferson Parish gambling dives.) But now, he went on ingenuously, the old order was over: times were getting better in so far as legitimate employment was concerned, and he was going to close up all those bad places.

Senator Tobey could hardly stay in his seat as King Clancy told his story. Staring at the hapless sheriff as if he were some rare insect, Senator Tobey thundered: "Why don't you resign and get out and put somebody in that can handle it—somebody who has got some guts? It seems to me that a man like you who stands before a committee of the Senate and admits that he has broken the law . . . is not worth a damn . . . don't you feel guilty as hell about these things?

". . . It is a revealing and disgusting thing . . . that a man like you can continue in office. . . . I simply cannot sit and listen to this type of what I call political vermin. . . ."

All King Clancy could do was listen with his frozen, sickly smile still on his face; he admitted that everything Senator Tobey said about him was true.

Clancy went so far as to admit to us that he personally had told Dandy Phil Kastel that if he wanted to run gambling at the Beverly Club "he would have to put men to work." "Kastel came to you and said, 'Can I open a gambling establishment here?' " Associate Counsel Rice asked. "That is right," Sheriff Clancy replied. "I said that as long as it will not interfere with the people there, if they don't object to it, it is all right with me, but you will have to put some men to work."

Q. In other words, what they say about King Clancy is true—they came to King Clancy and got the okay; is that a fair statement?

A. I would not put it in that term—"King" Clancy . . .

Q. And when Clancy lowers the boom and says close, they close; is that not right?

A. That is right; they close.

Deputy Sheriff Paul Cassagne, in fact, did collect money from the gambling clubs, Clancy admitted, but it was not for "ice," protection, politics, or anything like that, he explained. The money, he said, was "for all charitable organizations, the church organizations, USO, CYO, tubercular drive, and those various drives that they have." Cassagne also was the intermediary who approached the gambling houses to secure jobs for the poor old unfortunates whom Clancy wanted to help. At this, Senator Tobey erupted again: "You are the man supposed to enforce the law and admits he breaks it and disregards it, running an employment office to get jobs for the gambling houses which you under the law are charged to close up!" Clancy shook his head in painful assent and said, "That is right, Senator."

In the best tradition of sheriffs of his type, King Clancy also had managed to become a wealthy man, despite the fact that his sheriff's salary for the last twenty-three years had never exceeded $6000. His annual income was "$20,000 or better," Clancy told us. This was accomplished by many ventures and investments, and by judicious betting on the horses. In fact, the sheriff said, he profited $78,000 in the last four years by betting on the horses. He told us that his extraordinary good luck was the result of getting "some very good information" from stable boys and owners, as well as exercising remarkable personal restraint and betting only on the last two races. "You cannot play every race and win," he explained to us. "What is the difference between the first races and the last races?" I asked him. "Well," said Clancy, "if you play the first races, you stay there and get hooked and try to get out. If you play the last races, you get a winner, you go home."

One of Sheriff Clancy's little problems in law enforcement in his parish was the fact that the marshal of Gretna, principal town of the parish, was one Beauregard Miller, marshal since 1925 and pretty much of an institution himself. Beauregard Miller had once even given King Clancy a hot race for sheriff. There seemed to be a tacit agreement between them that Clancy would leave law enforcement up to the marshal in the incorporated town of Gretna, where the gambling clubs in operation at that time included the Bank Club, Billionaire Club, Clover Club, New Garden Club, Millionaire Café, and Blue Light Inn. J. J. Fogarty's wire service, the *Daily Sports*

News, also had its headquarters in Marshal Miller's town. As a matter of fact Sheriff Clancy's office in the courthouse on Huey P. Long Avenue was just across the street from the block where all these clubs and Fogarty's wire service were located; the sheriff could have stood on the courthouse steps and hit any one of these enterprises by throwing his junior-sized ten-gallon hat real hard.

When we asked Beauregard Miller what was the main business in his town of 14,000 population, he replied frankly: "The main business is the gambling business. . . . Without the gambling it would be a dead town." I asked:

THE CHAIRMAN: Do you have any connection with them [the gambling clubs] in so far as getting people located, getting them jobs, things of that sort?

MILLER: To be frank with you, very seldom I ever interceded for anyone to go to work in a gambling house. All the people that run it is my friends, and naturally they put my friends in there, so we don't have any trouble getting them in.

Before Sheriff Clancy left us in Washington, however, he gave the committee his word of honor that he would close up gambling in Jefferson Parish and break off his connections with the gamblers. He would even move in on Beauregard Miller's bailiwick in Gretna and, if Beauregard objected, "he will have to get an injunction against me," Clancy asserted. "I want to thank Senator Tobey for his remarks," Clancy said, "because I think it will help me to make Jefferson a better place." As a matter of historical fact, he actually telephoned his office from Washington at 3 P.M., and by 6 P.M. it was reported back to him that the Jefferson Parish dives were closed. Clancy had lowered the boom.[2]

[2]As this went to press, reports from Jefferson Parish indicated Clancy was keeping the dives closed.

CHAPTER 13

THE CLEVELAND AREA:
"MIDDLETOWN" OF CRIME

One of the nerve centers probed by the committee as it explored the interlocking pattern of organized criminal activities throughout the United States was Cleveland, Ohio, and the area surrounding it. Our investigation of this important and prosperous industrial and business center was a highly significant study, for Cleveland is a "Middletown" of crime, differing in many respects from other areas studied by the committee.

The Cleveland crime profile, as revealed by our investigation, is a powerful mixture of the good and the bad. Cleveland is a city that long has suffered from the tenacious grip of a shrewd and ruthless combine of public enemies. It has been a spawning ground for many activities of the nationwide crime network, as numerous alumni of the Cleveland underworld have moved on to important places in other big-city gangs. On the credit side, however, Cleveland offers a heartening and profitable example of how a well-intentioned local administration, backed up by a state government that is vigorously on the side of law enforcement, can harass hoodlums and lawbreakers and by such tactics take some of the profit out of crime.

The broad outlines of the Cleveland story—and the Cleveland story, of course, is the story of the city itself and surrounding counties, even other cities in Ohio, Kentucky, and West Virginia—follows the almost classic pattern of the rise of big-city crime in America. Alvin J. Sutton, Jr., the ex-FBI agent who is Cleveland's public safety director, testified:

"From the day the National Prohibition Act was passed . . . until its repeal, December 5, 1933, Cleveland went through an era of mob violence, gang slayings, hijackings, bootleg and racket wars. Out of the prohibition period came the same kind of city-wide, regional and even interstate gang organization that plagued other cities.

"Rival gangs fought for supremacy. They hijacked each other's liquor loads. Murder became a standard tool for all such illegal gangs as they fought for territories, for sources of supply, trucks, boats that ran the liquor blockade on the lakes, and for the upper hand among the hoodlums, gunmen, drivers, and customers."

Picking up the narrative, the committee's own report to the Senate noted that the Cleveland mob had followed the familiar course of transferring its activities from rumrunning to gambling after the repeal of prohibition. At the time of our investigation this was the situation:

"The Cleveland gambling syndicate consists primarily of the following individuals: Morris Kleinman, Samuel (Gameboy) Miller, Moe Dalitz (alias Davis), Louis Rothkopf (alias Rhody and Zarumba), Samuel Tucker, and Thomas J. McGinty. . . . This group has enjoyed close relationships and associations with certain gangsters and muscle men, who also participated in enterprises conducted by the gambling syndicate. Included in this latter group are the Polizzis, Alfred and Albert [Chuck], John and George Angersola (alias King), James Licavoli, Jerry Milano, Joseph Di Carlo, and others."

In the roll call of hoodlums and manipulators whose names were ticked off by Director Sutton, some curious phenomena of modern-day crime were stressed. Some of the strong-arm men of yesterday are quieter, tamer models today, though they are in crime for profit as much as ever. Some are heavily entrenched in legitimate businesses, which all too often they run with the ruthless "finesse" of their sub rosa illegitimate activities. Others have managed to operate through the years so slickly that they never have been convicted of any crime. "At the top of Cleveland's bootleggers," testified Sutton, "were Morris Kleinman, Lou Rothkopf, Moe Dalitz. . . . Ruthless beatings, unsolved murders and shakedowns, threats and bribery came to this community as a result of the gangster's rise to power. . . . A dozen . . . killings were strung out along the road to riches which took Kleinman up to a gross income in 1929 of approximately $931,000. Many of those killed along that road had been Kleinman's rivals, and some were his allies in the old bootleg wars."

Who are these men? Moe Kleinman, the retired rumrunner, is an ex-pug and whilom poultry dealer, one of whose claims to infamy is his sponsorship of Mickey Cohen, another onetime Cleveland pugilist whose nefarious activities in Los Angeles have made his name a national stench. The federal government finally tucked Kleinman away for income tax fraud; on leaving the penitentiary, he diverted his talents to less tumultuous activities of both illegal and legal nature. As Director Sutton testified, Kleinman today "is an individual . . . who is looked up to by a good many people in the upper part of the community"; he donates liberally to charitable causes and "will deny that he is connected with any gambling establishments and so forth"; yet evidence before the committee clearly stamped him as a partner in big gaming enterprises. Rothkopf is a small-scale version of Kleinman. He also was sentenced for tax fraud, has engaged since in gambling, and is a great personal pal of Mickey Cohen's. They were a pair who, when finally apprehended after hiding out from the committee for months, made a great show in Washington of refusing to testify before recognized media of public information. They carried their contempt to the point of refusing to look at Counsel when being interrogated and finally declining to voice even the stock refrain, "I refuse to answer." Kleinman, the committee thought, looked quite bad when he sat mute after Associate Counsel Joseph Nellis confronted him with a printed card which had come into our possession and which contained certain embarrassing information concerning the activities of the Beverly Hills Country Club, one of the Kleinman-Rothkopf gambling enterprises. The card read:

"Open Sunday, April 1 [Note: The Senate Crime Committee originally was scheduled to conclude operations on March 30], Beverly Hills Country Club, Southgate, Ky., Route 27. This card admits bearer to gaming room. This card has been mailed to only privileged customers. Keep it, and do not pass on. If you do not wish to use it, destroy it."

Dalitz never has been convicted of any offense. He owns several large laundries and a linen supply company in Cleveland and Detroit, and has other substantial investments. He told us his annual income "roughly" was $70,000 to $80,000 a year, but conceded it "could be $95,000." Dalitz also was instrumental in arranging for himself and his Cleveland associates to invest heavily in the Detroit Steel Corporation in 1944, a story that will be traced in the next chapter, dealing with Detroit. Yet his own accountant, testifying before us in Cleveland, identified this big businessman as a partner in various gambling casinos with Kleinman, Rothkopf, Gameboy Miller, Thomas Jefferson McGinty, and other police characters.

Dalitz and Sam Tucker were "on the duck," as Safety Director Sutton put it, when we sought to find them in Cleveland. Later both surrendered and were questioned in Los Angeles. It took the combined efforts of Associate Counsel Downey Rice, Chief Investigator Harold Robinson, and the chairman to secure from them roundabout admissions that their fortunes were founded during the rumrunning era on the Great Lakes in prohibition days.

With the end of prohibition, the Cleveland mob began setting itself up in various forms of gambling rackets. Swank casinos for the well to do blossomed in city and country; the iniquitous "one-armed bandit" slot machines sprang up in bars and cigar stores; horse parlors and numerous varieties of "numbers" games flooded the city. As a by-product of gambling, the extortion racket, with its macabre accompaniment of murders and mayhem, hit Cleveland and other Ohio cities. "It was the old sailors and truckers and the peddlers from the moonshine mobs who held control of all the numbers rackets," Sutton testified; with fists, bombs, and lethal weapons they made the gambling operators pay off—or else. The name of the so-called "Cleveland Gang" became infamous throughout the country, and the Mafia was extremely powerful in Cleveland.

Gradually, however, the vigorous efforts of honest, determined public officials—Governor Frank Lausche, Mayor Harold Burton, now a United States Supreme Court justice, Elliot Ness, who preceded Sutton as Cleveland's safety director, Mayor Thomas A. Burke, and numerous others—applied the brakes to organized crime in Cleveland. Governor Lausche himself took the witness chair to tell us a dramatic anecdote of what touched off his effective crime-smashing crusade; in the course of his testimony the governor also presented a highly useful formula that other officials interested in cracking down on mobsters might study.

It began when the governor was a young municipal court judge in Cleveland. A Polish butcher fell into the toils of a local gambling joint quaintly called the "Harvard Club"—since driven out of existence. The operators took the butcher for everything he had, and he engaged a lawyer to file suit for recovery of his losses.

"The day for the trial approached," Governor Lausche related, "and this butcher, who lost his life's savings and his two butchershops in the Harvard Club, was visited by a large, black sedan filled with men. They went upstairs in his house, and they said, 'If you love your wife and your child, you had better not appear in that courtroom and testify.'"

The case was continued, then set again for trial; the gangsters called again, and this time threatened the man's wife. So the victim dropped the suit. "To that Polish man," said the governor, "the question came, 'Were the courts more powerful than the gangsters?'"

But the "snapper" came, Governor Lausche indignantly continued, when the lawyer who had been engaged to file suit turned around and sued the victim of the gamblers for $2500 —the amount the lawyer said would have been his fee if his frightened client had not backed out! Since the gangsters had forced the butcher to take a few hundred dollars in "settlement" of the case, the court had to allow the lawyer—"It nauseated me to do it," the governor personally commented to me —a percentage of this nominal sum. Governor Lausche testified:

"When that case was concluded, there was only one conviction in my mind, and that is that the individual who commits a crime isn't the man to fear in our society. He stands by himself, and on the spur of the moment may commit an offense, but he is not a threat and a danger. The threat and danger to our society and our government is from the organized gangsters and racketeers."

From that day on, in the various public posts that he filled, Governor Lausche used every possible weapon to harass the syndicate. Gradually the wide-open gambling clubs were driven out of Cleveland. But the heads of the syndicate had already mapped their strategy: they took their illicit businesses into the counties outside of Cleveland where, as our report noted, "local sheriffs, prosecutors, and other persons charged with law enforcement were more susceptible to gangland influences." To make up for the inconvenience of locations and the loss of a ready "mass audience," the gamblers even arranged transportation for out-of-town and out-of-state participants, hauling would-be gamblers to the clubs from West Virginia, Michigan, Illinois, Indiana, Kentucky, and other states.

As an example of how the syndicate operated in the counties, stocky, triple-chinned T. J. McGinty, who looked for all the world like a movie version of an oldtime bartender, laconically told us that when he ran his Pettibone Club in Geauga County he made regular contributions, when solicited by the county clerk, to help the county buy fire engines, tractors, or whatever the clerk said was needed. McGinty's memory was bad on the amounts contributed, but he acknowledged "it might have been" about $10,000 in all. He also described his method for operating an illegal race track in the county without molestation: he ran under what he called "the contributions system," which he said he thought was "legal." He said he simply gave five per cent of the gate to each of two villages and another five per cent to the county, and nobody bothered him. "They took it as a tax," he explained.

When Governor Lausche moved into the state capitol he found four particularly flagrant gambling casinos, all under the domination of the Cleveland Gang, operating in rural counties. These were the Jungle Inn, Mounds Club, Colony Club, and McGinty's Pettibone Club. "I decided that we would close them, and that I would use every power in my command," the governor testified. Balked by spineless and often corrupt sheriffs, who would not obey his personal orders to shut them down, the governor summoned such prosaic arms of the state government as the Workmen's Compensation Department, the Unemployment Compensation Department, the fire marshal's office, the Building Code Department, the Department of Liquor Control, and told them to go to work on the gambling joints. By the time these agencies finished slapping violations—for everything but gambling—on these places the casinos were out of business.

Anthony A. Rutkowski, chief of the enforcement division of the Ohio Department of Liquor Control, to whom Governor Lausche assigned the job of co-ordinating the harassing attack on the gambling joints, followed the governor in the witness chair. Rutkowski, who carried out his assignment with bulldog tenacity, told a hair-raising story of what happened to him when he directed the "attack" on the particularly notorious Jungle Inn in Trumbull County near Cleveland, run by the Farah brothers, Mike and John, whom Rutkowski described as "the war lords of Trumbull County."

Rutkowski and his raiders—unarmed—arrived at 9 P.M. and promptly telephoned the local sheriff to come with assistance.

The sheriff did not arrive until 11:27 P.M. About all the sheriff did when he finally arrived, the governor's representative testified, was to interfere with an attempt by the state raiders to confiscate some eighty-three slot machines and other pieces of gambling paraphernalia.

"The sheriff told me in no uncertain terms that I couldn't touch them," Rutkowski testified. "I asked him who would stop me, and he said he would."

The Jungle Inn actually had a steel-armored gun turret inside the main gambling room, Rutkowski related. He discovered this fact in a disconcerting fashion. First, while his weaponless raiding party was attempting to hold some twenty prisoners, Mike Farah burst in, commenced "to use foul and indecent language against me, and attempted to incite a riot." After taking a poke at one of the state men, Mike dashed from the room.

At this point John Farah, "who gave all the orders and who was the kingpin in this place," began cursing, pointing, and shrieking, "Kill him, Goon—kill him, shoot him!" Rutkowski quickly looked in the direction to which Farah was pointing.

"That," he said, "is the first time I knew there was a gun turret there."

Fortunately for Rutkowski, "Goon" had been slow in obeying his master's orders. When there was no gunfire Farah himself ran to the turret, but one of Rutkowski's agents had got there before him. The agent grappled with the gunman, took away his shotgun, and thus was able to prevent Farah from shooting the chief raider.

At this point in his testimony Rutkowski dramatically tossed onto the witness table seven 12-gauge shotgun shells which the agent had confiscated in the gun turret.

Rutkowski also testified that, within half an hour after the raiders arrived at the Jungle Inn, between 100 and 200 hoodlums assembled outside and surrounded the place. "We were unarmed on the inside," he added; it was a very lonesome feeling. But state troopers arrived in time to quell the menace, and all turned out well: $11,000 was confiscated at the Jungle Inn;

the equipment eventually was seized, the building condemned by the fire marshal, and the place now is out of business.

After Governor Lausche made even the counties too hot for them the Cleveland syndicate moved its operations across the Ohio River into wide-open communities in Campbell and Kenton counties in northern Kentucky. Covington and Newport, just across the river from Cincinnati, became the big gambling centers. There the casinos were so unconcerned with the possibility of interference by the law that they advertised openly in Cincinnati newspapers and placed streamers on automobile windshields.

Eventually the Cleveland syndicate became so rich that when gambler Wilbur Clark needed more than $1,000,000 to complete his luxurious Desert Inn in Las Vegas he obtained the money from the Cleveland gamblers in a deal by which the syndicate acquired a sixty per cent interest in the Nevada gambling casino. Some members of the syndicate also branched out to Miami; Gameboy Miller, for one, was a substantial partner in Miami's swank Island Club.

At the time of his testimony, Director Sutton told us, Cleveland proper could boast "that it has stamped out almost all of the vestiges of the old gunmen; their dirty houses of ill fame; their bootlegging and their shakedown games. Many of the old gangsters have left to find easier pickings in cities which have looser ideas of law enforcement. . . . Racketeers still may make their headquarters here, but they have to set up shop somewhere else if they are going to make any money."

But here Sutton asked a question to which our committee also was seeking an answer. A few years ago, he observed, some of these gangsters were "a bunch of down-at-the-heel roughnecks, just out of prison or just out of court, with their shakedown system broken up." Now they "have become rich."

"We want to know why, and with whose help?" the safety director asked. "Mickey Cohen is one of these. The Angersolas, the Polizzis, and many more were not at all prosperous a few years ago. They are all launched in big business. We want to trace back the source of their wealth and power."

In search of the answer to Sutton's question, let us take up the case history of Alfred (Big Al) Polizzi, one of the Cleveland hoodlums who rose to wealth via the bootlegging and gambling route. Big Al, who came to the United States from Sicily at the age of nine, started out as one of Cleveland's rough-and-ready hoodlums. Rumrunning and gambling were the proven charges against him. Affable and a good mixer, Big Al was a well-liked member of criminal society—one of the "good fellows" of hoodlumdom. When he was married, none other than Pete Licavoli, the infamous Detroit racketeer, one of the most cold-blooded and contemptuous characters to appear before our committee, came over to serve as best man at Big Al's wedding.

Around 1940, Big Al decided it was time for him to become a gentleman. For one thing, his children were growing up and he "didn't like the bad publicity." Furthermore, he had a bank roll of, by his own admission, more than $300,000 tucked away. He had been dabbling in Florida real estate with Arthur (Mickey) McBride, the Cleveland millionaire whose activities as founder of Continental Press racing news service were described in Chapter 3; then, too, there was some money he had made in breweries and, of course, from his illegal activities. Anyhow, with loud and conveniently publicized declarations, Big Al let it be known that he was going straight.

In 1944, Big Al went straight—to the federal penitentiary for four months. There was a black market whisky deal he couldn't resist. When he got out he pulled up stakes in Cleveland and established himself in Miami Beach. There he became a partner in a highly successful construction company with one Forrest Thompson, a builder. Another associate in the business was a Polizzi pal from Cleveland days, Vincent (Doc) Mangine, ex-saloonkeeper. Big Al also became a partner in the operation of a luxurious resort hotel where gangsters habitually congregated.

Our committee had two rounds with Big Al. At the first round in Cleveland, Associate Counsel Nellis sought to question him concerning his past criminal record and his present

activities and associates. Polizzi appeared before us, a fine figure with a healthy tan, expensive clothing, and executive-type
horn-rimmed glasses with which he gestured impressively. His
voice was husky but well modulated; he sipped daintily from
a glass of water and said "pardon me" most politely when he
bent his head to confer with Counsel. "Well, goodness! I don't
know," he exclaimed at one point when I questioned him
about one of his past associations; another time he apologized
for using the word "hell" in quoting one of his associate's remarks.

The trouble at the Cleveland hearing was that Big Al, while
he told us some of the things we asked him—"I am trying to
be candid and frank," he assured us—would not answer other
questions about his criminal record. "Senator," he protested,
"I left [Cleveland] for one purpose, and that was to get away
from all this old stuff that has been throwed at me time and
time again, and I have had nothing else but heartache. . . . I
don't like to answer those questions; it just takes me back and
tears me apart." While my committee colleagues and I were
sympathetic to the aims of any criminal who honestly manifested a desire to go straight, there were so many associations
in Big Al's current operations that we were obliged to initiate
a contempt citation against him for refusing to answer legitimate questions.

So then Round Two began. Big Al got a new lawyer and requested the privilege of appearing before us again in Washington—at his own expense—to purge himself of contempt. This
time he was more frank, and an interesting picture emerged.
This time he admitted he had been a rumrunner in prohibition
days and had served time for it. He admitted he had been
picked up in Detroit on a fugitive warrant from Cleveland as a
suspect in connection with a double murder—there was no case
made against him, however—and that Joe Massei, notorious
Detroit gangster, was his associate at the time of this arrest. He
admitted committing perjury in 1926 in connection with his
application for citizenship papers. He admitted being a partner
for several years, until 1938, in the Buckeye Catering Company

of Cleveland, which dealt in illegal slot machines, and that John Angersola, mobster Chuck Polizzi, "a sort of cousin," and Nat Weisenberg, later murdered, were his partners.

He told us minutely, though with no apparent pleasure, about his hotel operations in Miami Beach in association with John Angersola and other police characters, which I reviewed in Chapter 7. He went on to admit that his construction company partner, Forrest Thompson, had agreed to sponsor the parole of James Licavoli, member of the infamous Licavoli clan, who was serving time for extortion. That occurred "before I even knew Thompson," Big Al protested. But further questioning developed that Thompson, to whom Licavoli had been a complete stranger, interceded for the convict at the request of Thompson's attorney, Nick Mangine, and that Nick Mangine was the brother of Big Al's partner, Doc Mangine; also that Licavoli never went to work for Thompson as he was supposed to do under the parole agreement, but went instead to live with Doc Mangine in Cleveland and to work in Doc Mangine's saloon, the Wagon Wheel. The surly Licavoli was interrogated as follows:

Q. Do you know whether or not there was a deal made whereby Thompson would be put in the building business with Mangine and Polizzi as a reward for his going sponsor on your parole?
A. No, sir.
Q. Thompson did go sponsor on your parole?
A. He did, but that ain't got nothing to do with Polizzi.

Big Al also admitted that he had met frequently with numerous hoodlums—mostly around his hotel—since he "went straight," and that he took a trip to New York with his old rumrunning associate, Moe Kleinman, "to see the fights." When asked why, if he was so concerned about burying his past, he plunged himself so deeply into business with an ex-convict like John Angersola, who had been arrested many times, Big Al protested in injured tones: "He hasn't been *convicted* since 1923. I have been arrested myself many times, and naturally I wouldn't think that was very kind to accuse somebody for the same things you have been accused for."

Pressed further, Big Al gave this revealing explanation, which would be interesting to a psychiatrist or a criminologist, for his continued associations with bad characters:

"I like people and people like me, and I like to be liked by everyone, and Mr. Kleinman asked me if I would like to go to the fights and I went with him, and I said I would, I mean . . . I am trying to get away from all of the publicity."

Associate Counsel Nellis asked:

Q. You are not concerned about the associations as long as there is no unfavorable publicity?

Polizzi replied:

A. As far as I am concerned, I don't butt into other people's business. They do whatever they please and I do likewise, and I am not so easily led that I can be led into anything that is wrong.

All in all, Alfred Polizzi—Big Al—presented a remarkable picture of a man who claimed to have disassociated himself with his past. As chairman of the committee, I felt constrained at the end to remark in open hearing:

"His answer is not satisfactory. I think we all will observe with a great deal of interest as to whether on the second try he is going to get out of business with these people who have known records and reputations, or whether he is going to continue to add to his acquaintanceship with people who are liable to get him in trouble again. I am afraid Mr. Polizzi is not making too good a start. . . ."

The Cleveland hearings also offered a significant case history of another aspect of criminal syndicate operations which the committee encountered elsewhere in the nation and which gave us considerable concern. Appearing before us as a witness was a well-known public accountant, Mr. Alvin E. Giesey, a veteran of two world wars and a person of standing in his community. Mr. Giesey was a man of excellent appearance; he gave an impression of prosperity and solidity. He was carefully groomed, and on the lapel of his brown suit coat he wore a diamond-studded emblem of a veterans' organization. Mr. Giesey, rather reluctantly under questioning, gave us a list of the properties and stocks he owned; he was a man of considerable worth.

As the story unfolded it developed that Mr. Giesey had started his professional career as an agent of the Internal Revenue Bureau. He was sent to Cleveland in 1921. He was a good agent—so good that he was assigned in 1931 to make an investigation of certain income tax frauds perpetrated by Morris Kleinman. One of the local newspapers referred to Giesey and his partner at that time as "a couple of fellows who get keen delight in tracing physical activities through involved bank records." He did in fact take such keen delight in tracing Kleinman's physical activities that before the case came up for disposition the mobster, who had been operating a chicken business as a front, ruefully told friends: "I shoulda stuck to poultry; there are fewer headaches in chickens."

In 1933, as a result of the sleuthing by Agent Giesey and his colleagues, racketeer Kleinman was sentenced to serve four years in the penitentiary and pay a $15,000 fine. In the local Internal Revenue office Giesey was regarded with admiration. But in 1934, Giesey decided to leave the bureau and set up his own accounting business. A couple of years later Kleinman got out of the penitentiary. He went straight to Giesey and asked the man who had sent him to the penitentiary if he now would work for him.

"He said," Giesey testified, "he had one thing in mind and that was to engage me for the purpose of seeing that from now on he didn't get in any more trouble with his income tax returns. . . . I have been making his tax returns out ever since."

Then we led Giesey through the list of "various people" whom he acquired as clients either directly through Kleinman or after the Giesey-Kleinman tie-up was effected. It was an interesting roster: Al Polizzi, John Angersola, Chuck Polizzi, Moe Dalitz, Lou Rothkopf, Sam Tucker, Jerry Milano, Mushy Wexler, the Cleveland wire service magnate, and a number of others whose names appeared in Safety Director Sutton's testimony. Soon Giesey and a partner he later acquired were handling returns for what Giesey acknowledged to be a number of gambling clubs.

At this stage of the examination Mr. Giesey began to get belligerently defensive. Associate Counsel Nellis probed him as to his estimated net worth, and the witness reluctantly answered, after a flurry of objections, "I can give an approximate figure of $50,000 or $60,000."

Q. Did you accumulate that from your practice as an accountant?

A. No place else in the world where I have ever got it. I have never been in any gambling enterprise. I have never been in anything connected with slot machines.

Q. You are sure about that, that you have never been in any gambling enterprise?

A. The only rackets I have ever been in are the two world wars, and the war criminals are working on me for a third!

But then Counsel, after tortuous questioning, drew from Giesey an admission that he was in fact secretary of two corporations set up by Kleinman, Dalitz, Rothkopf, and others in connection with the "restaurant" and "real estate" operations of the so-called "Beverly Hills Country Club." He also admitted holding a similar secretaryship for the restaurant and real estate operations of another Kleinman-Rothkopf-Dalitz gambling enterprise, the Lookout Club, near Covington.

Testifying in detail about the Beverly Hills operation, Giesey insisted "that the gambling part is set up as an entirely separate business; they have their own separate books and records," and that his appointment as secretary of the affiliated corporations was merely an "expeditious matter pertaining to signing tax returns and papers." He went on to admit that he knew the club was a gambling place; that in fact he had seen the dice, roulette, slot machines, and other gambling devices there, and that he had prepared the 1949 tax return showing gross receipts of $528,654 for the Beverly Hills Club. Chief Counsel Halley questioned him:

Q. Were you at all concerned about the possibility that you might be found to be aiding and abetting an illegal enterprise?

A. No, sir. I wasn't engaged in the gambling end.

Q. You were doing the accounting for the gambling end?

A. That is right.

Q. You certainly would be aiding and abetting in it.

A. Well, that's a legal question that I admit I hadn't thought of.

Q. Didn't it ever occur to you to check on whether or not you were apt to be prosecuted by the state of Kentucky?

A. No, sir, I never checked on it.

Counsel went on to probe as to what information the gamblers supplied Giesey when he made out the income tax returns. Giesey said they periodically gave him "a single sheet of paper" on which was written a few figures showing the purported "gross income" from various sources; then the deductible expenses. The gamblers later took these sheets back from him—"they wanted them in their possession and not mine," the accountant stated. Counsel asked, "Did you ever go down there as an accountant and try to make a test check of any of these sheets?" "No, sir," replied Giesey, "we did not." Halley continued:

Q. And you, as the accountant, filed the returns and haven't the faintest idea of whether you were getting a straight count or a bad count?

A. That is right. That is true of anybody. When we file an income tax return, we take their word from the figures they give us.

The examination shifted to the question of whether Giesey's gambler clients paid bribes to police and sheriffs for the privilege of operating. Giesey insisted he "wouldn't know," though he admitted "the average person would conclude that there must be such a situation." Counsel Halley asked him, "Have you made any effort to find out? Have you just point-blank asked your clients?" "No," said Giesey, "I don't think I would have the courage to ask them a question like that."

Finally, at the end of several harrowing hours, Counsel Halley drew the examination of the auditor to a close. "I am very curious," Counsel asked, "to know why you—a former agent of this government, with a background of which I presume you were proud, the man who had succeeded in putting Kleinman in jail—are willing to lend yourself to those illegal operations?" This question brought protests from Giesey's attorney, but Halley persisted: "What is the inducement to you? Why do you do these things?" To this, the accountant explosively replied:

"For the almighty dollar! The same as you are doing, the job you are doing right now——"

Personally, I found this answer a rather sad commentary. As our official report to the Senate summed up: "It was Giesey who gave the committee one of the clearest demonstrations of how the federal government may be defrauded of hundreds of thousands of dollars in taxes from the operations of gambling enterprises. . . ."

CHAPTER 14

DETROIT: WHERE UNDERWORLD
AND BUSINESS WORLD MERGE

STILL another alarming aspect of the picture of crime in America—the fact that certain manufacturers have entered deliberately into intimate business arrangements with racketeers as a means of controlling labor relationships—was spotlighted by the committee's hearings in Detroit. Senator O'Conor, serving as acting chairman in Detroit, aptly summed it up when he turned to William Dean Robinson, an industrialist who had just finished telling of a dubious contract with the son-in-law of an ex-convict, and forcefully declared:

"It is a pretty sorry state of affairs if American industry is brought to the point where it has to deal with hoodlums and . . . men with connections in the underworld and with criminal records in order to carry on its business."

In two days of public hearings in Detroit, prefaced, of course, by weeks of preparatory investigation by Associate Counsel John Burling, Investigator W. D. Amis, and Ben E. Caldwell of the committee staff, the committee traced four instances where large industrial concerns had awarded lucrative contracts to men who were either gangsters or had underworld connections. In one instance, definitely involving interstate links, the principal was the notorious Joe Adonis, mob leader of the New York-New Jersey area. The committee wanted to know why these characters of ill repute had been favored by respectable corporations, but in no instance did we get satisfactory explanations. The committee was greatly concerned as it realized that it must have exposed only a segment of the tie-up between crime and industry in this important city, often referred to as the arsenal of America. As the acting chairman remarked at the conclusion of the Detroit hearings: ". . . We feel that . . . a particularly serious situation . . . has been revealed here. Criminals with records which often have disentitled them to participation in legitimate business and in decent society have muscled in or forced their way into otherwise honest endeavors. . . . Men whose past records do not entitle them to any consideration, in our opinion, at the hands of decent people, have been allowed to make large amounts of money, live in comparative luxury and under circumstances which only those who have engaged in decent and legitimate enterprise ought to enjoy in our society. . . . That, we think, is noteworthy, because in certain key industries it is shown that public enemies have gained a foothold."

One of the cases into which the committee delved was the relationship of one Santo (Sam) Perrone with the Detroit-Michigan Stove Company, of which John A. Fry is president. The bespectacled, balding Perrone is a naturalized citizen whose criminal record includes a conviction and six-year sentence for violating the prohibition laws. Both Perrone and his brother, Espano Gaspar Perrone, admitted they had been arrested for questioning on murder charges, though later released, and there was another instance where three guns were found in a locker at the stove works shared by Santo, Gaspar, and Matthew, a third brother who worked for the plant. Ironically, at the time we questioned him, Perrone had a license to carry a revolver which was promptly revoked by Detroit authorities.

Santo Perrone, who testified he could barely read and write English, went to work more than forty years ago as a core-maker for the stove works, which is one of the largest non-automotive manufacturing plants in the Detroit area. The company also is perhaps the largest non-union plant in the area. Perrone, who was insistent that he had never even discussed labor problems with Mr. Fry, testified he never had heard of any labor difficulty or any physical violence at the plant.

Around 1934, however, there was a serious strike when a union made a strenuous effort to organize the stove works. President Fry was asked by Associate Counsel Burling:

Q. Was there any violence?
A. Not that I know of.
Q. You never heard of any violence in connection with labor disputes in your company?
A. No.

Then Burling produced a transcript of Fry's testimony given in 1946 before Circuit Judge George B. Murphy, sitting as a one-man grand jury in a labor rackets investigation. Fry, on that occasion, had testified that the union "threw a picket line around the place, pulled most of the men out, and we made up our mind we weren't going to co-operate on the basis they wanted, and we were not going out of business. . . ." Fry continued: ". . . I talked with some of the fellows in the plant, including the Perrones, and I wanted to know whether or not we could get some help to come in, and they said they thought they could." Burling then asked:

Q. Does that refresh your recollection that you asked the Perrones to recruit strikebreakers?
A. I think probably it does. I probably asked them to take a few people in who wanted to go along to work with the other employees we might have asked for.

Reading further from the grand jury transcript, Burling established that Mr. Fry, who in his testimony before the committee could not recall any violence during the strike, had been asked if there had not been considerable "rioting and bloodshed." Fry had replied: "There was some fights outside the gate on the part of the pickets attacking the men when they came in to lunch. I think after the first day we had seventy-five or eighty policemen around the plant guarding the employees working against any attacks on the part of strikers."

Shortly after this violent strike Santo Perrone, the coremaker, was given a contract to purchase and haul away the scrap from the stove works. The illiterate manual laborer thus acquired an income which in recent years has netted him between $40,000 and $65,000 a year. He lives in a luxurious mansion in the expensive Grosse Pointe area of Detroit, drives a costly car, and has been able to lend large sums of money to his various sons-in-law. One son-in-law got $50,000 to invest in a race track.

The company also had taken care of Santo's brother Gaspar, who had been helpful during the strike. It so arranged its operations that the coremaking department was changed to a subcontractorship and placed in charge of Gaspar. Using company materials and also the same company-owned equipment with which he had worked as an employee for more than twenty-five years, Gaspar theoretically became the contractor who supplied the stove works with sand cores. "Thus," as our report noted, "a manual laborer in one of the departments of the stove works became, through some legal machinations, a contractor, which, in turn, resulted in his receiving a very much higher income."

Soon after the scrap contract was put into effect Santo and his brother Gaspar each were sent to the penitentiary for illegally manufacturing whisky. The company kept Santo's scrap contract in effect for him while he was in prison.

Another part of the picture was filled in by Emil Mazey, secretary-treasurer of the United Auto Workers, CIO. Mazey testified that while the Perrone brothers were in prison the UAW, which previously had been kept out of the Detroit-Michigan Stove Company, was able to organize one of the plants. Burling asked:

Q. What happened when Mr. Perrone got out of jail?
A. The organization disappeared.

Still another significant facet was revealed in the testimony of Andrew Mosser, patrolman inspector in charge of the United States Immigration and Naturalization Service at Detroit. He told us that in the course of an investigation of aliens illegally in the United States he learned that twenty such immigration-law violators were working at the Detroit-Michigan Stove Company. Gaspar was questioned by the committee about a speedboat which he owns and operates on the Great Lakes between Michigan and Canada, but he denied that he ever smuggled in any aliens.

As the committee summed up in its report, "It is not the function of this committee to inquire into labor disputes, but the committee must point out the sinister relationship between the lucrative contracts granted to the gangster Perrones and the ability of the Detroit-Michigan Stove Works to keep labor unions out of its plant."

The Perrone-Stove Works case tied in squarely with what the committee termed "the more striking story" of a larger plant, Briggs Manufacturing Company, makers of auto bodies. President Fry of the Stove Works and President William Dean Robinson of Briggs are close personal friends. For approximately twenty years the Briggs Company had a contract with an established firm, Woodmere Scrap Iron and Metal Company, for removal of ferrous scrap from the Briggs plant. In April 1945, Santo Perrone's son-in-law, Carl Renda, then twenty-eight years old, suddenly applied to Briggs for the scrap contract. The contract was taken away from Woodmere and awarded to Renda, despite the facts that (1) he had no knowledge of the scrap business; (2) he had no loading machinery and no trucks; (3) no yard or railroad siding; and (4) not even a telephone or office where he could be called.

After being awarded the contract, Perrone's son-in-law turned around and made a subcontract with Woodmere, the old contractor, whereby Woodmere kept right on doing the work. The only difference was that Woodmere paid Renda $2.50 a ton more than it had paid Briggs for the scrap, thus giving the fortunate young man an income which since has ranged from $53,000 to $101,000 a year. As our report commented: "While it was not proved by judicially admissible evidence, the inference is inescapable that what Renda, the entirely unequipped college student, was being paid for was the service of his father-in-law, the 'muscle' man, Sam Perrone."

The Briggs plant, the committee developed further, has had a record of violence in labor matters going back at least to 1936 when, as he testified, Emil Mazey, the UAW-CIO official, "was bodily thrown out of the plant by four of the company thugs." Also, though President Robinson of Briggs insisted that "we do not and never have dealt with racketeers or gangsters" and that the contract with Renda was strictly a business proposition, our report took note of the fact that six prominent officials of the union in the Briggs plant "were beaten in a most inhuman fashion by unknown persons in the year that followed the granting of an otherwise inexplicable Renda contract." The report concluded: "It is the opinion of the committee that neither Fry nor Robinson testified frankly concerning their relationship to gangsters. This committee believes that these two presidents knew of the underworld relationships which their companies had entered into in connection with their labor relations."

Before ever coming to Detroit, the committee had explored as part of the early phase of its New York-New Jersey area investigation the tie-up between the Ford Motor Company and Joseph Doto, alias Joe Adonis. Adonis, we learned, is one of the principal stockholders of the corporation known as the Automotive Conveying Company of New Jersey, a licensed common carrier which transports automobiles away from the Ford plant at Edgewater, New Jersey. Because of the Adonis tie-up the committee looked with especial interest into possible relationships between Ford's plants in the Detroit area and other racketeers in the haul-away business. We found that the principal haul-away operator was the E. & L. transport company, in which one Anthony D'Anna was a fifty per cent stockholder. D'Anna drew a salary of $27,000 a year from E. & L. for which, so far as the committee was able to ascertain, he did nothing.

Though the Sicilian-born D'Anna, who now is a banker as well as a trucking official, actually wept on the witness stand and protested he was a good and patriotic citizen, his background was dubious. His father and two uncles had been killed in what appeared to the committee to be Mafia-type murders, and his father's slayer had been similarly rubbed out. D'Anna himself went to prison for attempted bribery of witnesses in connection with another Mafia-style slaying. He had been in the sugar business, with known bootleggers as his customers, and was an admitted associate of both Joe Massei and Pete Licavoli, two of the top racketeers in Detroit. Before acquiring his E. & L. stock, D'Anna, through negotiations with Harry Bennett, former labor boss for the late Henry Ford, Sr., had obtained a fifty per cent share of a profitable Ford agency in Wyandotte.

Bennett, now in retirement, was the man who, as the committee noted, "employed virtually a private army recruited from ex-convicts and criminals to engage in battles against labor and in other anti-social activities." He was subpoenaed from his California ranch to testify before the committee, and was a hostile and difficult witness; when we asked him about the gang factions in Detroit he snapped at Associate Counsel Burling: "Do you want me to get my head blown off?" The committee staff had been told by a former Ford security officer that burly hoodlum Pete Licavoli had recruited a special squad of about thirty strong-arm men for Bennett, but the informant would not back up his story on the witness stand. Bennett himself denied that he even knew Licavoli, while the gangster refused to tell us anything. Licavoli's replies were so contemptuous—in one instance the mobster himself laughed when he said it might "incriminate" him to tell how much he was asking for his luxurious Arizona dude ranch which he was attempting to sell—that the Senate cited him for prosecution. So far Licavoli has led almost a charmed life with the law; his record shows twenty-eight arrests on charges that include mur-

der (three arrests), kidnaping (two arrests), and attempted
extortion, but he has been convicted and fined only twice for
misdemeanors.

Another denial entered by Harry Bennett was that the
agency franchise given to D'Anna had any connection with
keeping peace among the gang elements which we heard had
fastened themselves on to the Ford plant when he was the
labor boss. As our report noted, however, Bennett "could give
the committee no satisfactory explanation" of the D'Anna deal.
Of the Joe Adonis connection, as we stated in our report, "Bennett testified, and the committee disbelieved him, that he had
no knowledge of the Edgewater negotiations and that some
official in New York must have attended to it."

Bennett also made the extraordinary statement that although
he was a key man in one of the largest plants in the world he
kept no files, records, or memoranda of any kind. Therefore, as
we noted, the question of "how D'Anna and Joe Adonis obtained such profitable relationships to Ford must therefore
remain shrouded in mystery." Still another question which remains unanswered is "why, nearly six years after Bennett was
removed from command of the Ford Motor Company, these
two mobsters remain in lucrative relationships with this organization."

Bennett, who has been a remarkable figure in American industrial history, gave a revealing insight as to his philosophy in
an exchange with Chief Counsel Halley, as follows:

HALLEY: Is it to the credit of the Ford Motor Company that
it hands over its agencies to people who have a criminal record
with no legitimate business, with no assets, and no experience
in the automobile business?

BENNETT: Yes; if they could cut down on the gangs that way,
I would give them all an agency.

HALLEY: Then you would recommend that in order to im-
prove criminal conditions, Ford give automobile agencies——

BENNETT: Give them all work or something to do.

"In fairness to Ford Motor Company," our report observed, "it should be noted that it is taking vigorous steps to disassociate itself from these racketeer-held contracts." We were advised that the Adonis connection is causing the Ford Company considerable embarrassment and that it now is attempting to terminate it by some legal means.

In the committee's opinion it was an extremely unhealthy situation for Joe Adonis' company to hold such a monopoly. We found it difficult to get all the facts, as Adonis refused to talk about it and a certain vagueness characterized the discussions by the other parties concerned. However, we did learn through John S. Bugas, now Ford's vice-president in charge of industrial relations, that Adonis' company had held this contract for at least fifteen years, and that, because his Automotive Conveying Company was the only motor carrier certificated by the Interstate Commerce Commission to haul automobiles in the areas involved in the contract, Ford contended it had "no alternative but to do business" with Adonis' company.

As to how the contract originally was obtained, Mr. Bugas said merely that the Ford representatives responsible for it "are not now employed by our company." The committee sought to discover at the Detroit hearings whether Adonis secured the contract as a reward for services he may possibly have rendered the Ford Company in labor disputes in years gone by, but we were unable to learn anything at all about the contract. Harry Bennett stood pat on his statement, "I don't know Joe Adonis," and that the haul-away contract was handled entirely by the Eastern branch manager. Senator O'Conor was keenly disappointed that Mr. Bugas failed to appear, as had been expected, at the Detroit hearings. The Ford official did write us, however, that "for some time" the Adonis tie-up "has been a matter of considerable concern to us" and that the company desired to terminate it "as soon as possible."

At a later hearing in Washington the committee pursued the subject further through interrogation of W. Y. Blanning, director of the Bureau of Motor Carriers, Interstate Commerce Commission, on the general problem of infiltration of the interstate motor carrier field by gangster elements. At this session Associate Counsel Burling stated for the record that Mr. Bugas, in a conference at the Crime Committee offices, had "suggested that perhaps no one had applied for a competing certificate [against Adonis' company] because it would not be healthy." The ICC bureau director—and the committee found it regrettable that he seemed lacking in any desire to initiate positive steps to clean up the situation—sparred with Counsel as follows:

BLANNING: Well, I don't quite get the point. You mean that the commission should force somebody to apply for it, or should do something to prevent it from being unhealthy?

BURLING: I submit, sir, that where a committee of the Senate is told by the vice-president of the Ford Motor Company that it must have its cars hauled away from its Edgewater, New Jersey, plant by Adonis' firm because you have certificated no other carrier, and where it appears you have certificated no other carrier, because Adonis has threatened gang force [we had heard evidence that other firms were afraid to compete against Adonis], that is something that might well occupy your attention.

The D'Anna episode, the Adonis case, and still another New Jersey instance in which we discovered that a racketeer and gambler named Gerald Catena, an associate of Joe Adonis, was a partner in the Peoples Express Company engaged in interstate trucking, led the committee to include in its recommendations the following:

". . . that the Interstate Commerce Commission be required by law to consider the moral fitness of applicants for certificates of necessity and convenience as one of the standards in acting upon applications for such certificates for transfers of certificates."

Also pointing out that legitimate truckers are apparently fearful of competing against gangster-permeated companies, we urged: "Every means should be used to weed out the criminals and prevent them from obtaining a further foothold." At the time of this writing the committee was giving further consideration to the problem of setting up legal machinery to revoke existing permits "where it has been shown to the Interstate Commerce Commission that the holders of such permits do not have the requisite moral fitness." We had the Adonis case directly in mind in this connection.

In Detroit the committee cleaned up the story, scraps of which had been gathered in Cleveland and elsewhere, of how certain members of the Cleveland gambling syndicate, described in the last chapter, had managed to acquire an important block of stock in a vital industry, the Detroit Steel Corporation. The missing details were secured through examination of Max J. Zivian, president of Detroit Steel. In 1944, he told us, Detroit Steel negotiated a merger with Reliance Steel Corporation, which then had its main offices in Cleveland. At the stage where the deal was to be closed, a disagreement arose as to whether Zivian, who had been vice-president of Detroit Steel, or the man who headed Reliance would become president of the merged company. It became necessary, if the deal was to be closed on the terms desired by the Detroit Steel group, that the Cleveland man be bought out. Zivian undertook to purchase the other man's stock for approximately $580,000. He said he had raised all the money except $100,000 and that he was in Cleveland, attempting to close the deal, when gambler-businessman Morris Dalitz, whom he had known slightly, "bumped into me in the street." Dalitz inquired what Zivian was doing in Cleveland, and Zivian said he told him that he was attempting to close a big deal but was short $100,000. Dalitz casually remarked, "I think I can arrange to get it for you," and contrived a meeting at his attorney's office within the hour. They met in the office of Samuel T. Haas, attorney for many of the gambling syndicate's operations, and Dalitz, without even looking at a balance sheet, arranged a bank loan for the necessary money. The Cleveland group acquired 10,000 shares of Detroit Steel stock, which Zivian said subsequently

were divided among Dalitz, Haas, Morris Kleinman, Lou Rothkopf, and Sam Tucker. Alvin Giesey, accountant for the Cleveland gambling syndicate, later followed suit by buying Detroit
Steel stock on the market.

The steel company president subsequently became friendly
with the Cleveland gambler. He took a trip on Dalitz' yacht on
one occasion, and at a later date Zivian loaned Dalitz $75,000
to help in a real estate deal. Dalitz himself, when he surrendered to us and was questioned in Los Angeles, said the
Cleveland group actually put up only $66,666 for the stock
which, at the time he testified, he said was valued at more than
$230,000.

One of the most shocking instances or weakness in the enforcement of our deportation laws by the Immigration and
Naturalization Service was uncovered in Detroit through examination of fifty-one-year-old Nono Minaudo, a native of
Sicily, now owner of a $40,000 bowling alley in the industrial
city. Minaudo, known at various times as Giuseppe Mangio-
pani, Tony Palaria, and other aliases, admitted he had come
into the United States by jumping ship in New Orleans in
1924. He has been arrested in Detroit numerous times, but,
rather astonishingly in the committee's viewpoint, has been
able to have his record removed from police files by a court
order. Subsequently, when he applied for a beer distributing
license, he stated under oath he had never been arrested. The
serious issue against Minaudo, as Senator O'Conor stated for
the record, was that official records of the Immigration and
Naturalization Service, based on information transmitted to the
State Department by the Italian government, indicated that
Minaudo "was sentenced in absentia to life imprisonment on
December 28, 1925, in Italy for murder," and that two other
sentences were passed against him in Italy on heinous charges.
Minaudo insisted that this information was a mistake.

In any event, when the Immigration and Naturalization
Service moved some years ago to deport Minaudo, he stalled
deportation on one occasion by posing under the name of an-

other Italian immigrant who had entered this country legally. A second time he told still another story about his entry into the United States. The central office of the Immigration and Naturalization Service recommended that further investigation be made to determine whether Minaudo could be deported. However, according to the testimony of Patrolman Inspector Mosser in Detroit, "it appears from the file that the alien was not further questioned . . . and said file was marked 'Closed.' "

At present Minaudo is managing to remain in the United States under a technicality of a law passed by Congress which provides that anyone who entered this country prior to July 1, 1924, is not deportable; he has even filed an application for United States citizenship, which he is pressing through an attorney. Patrolman Inspector Mosser commented: "The file discloses that this man is not deportable under any law of the United States at the present time." With considerable heat, Acting Chairman O'Conor commented: ". . . This certainly seems to be not only a miscarriage of justice but a glaring instance of how our immigration laws have been flouted. It certainly is a sad commentary, it seems to me, that a man can come into this country illegally, can remain here twenty-seven years, be arrested on a number of occasions and virtually be a public enemy, and still be allowed to be here and to enjoy all the privileges of American citizenship. . . ."

CHAPTER 15

PHILADELPHIA: POLICE TACTICS
IN THE CITY OF BROTHERLY LOVE

Two days of executive hearings in Philadelphia in October 1950, followed by additional public hearings in Washington at which two of the Pennsylvania city's notorious racketeers were questioned, convinced the committee that one of the nation's largest and most efficiently organized numbers rackets flourishes in Philadelphia, operating through "a politico-gambler police tie-up that makes it impossible for any intruder to edge his way in from the outside." A paralyzing attitude of *laissez faire* seems to hang like an ether mist over the administration of the Philadelphia Police Department. One local judge who agitated—finally with some degree of success—for stiffer action against the numbers racketeers told us frankly that the "big fry" just didn't seem to get caught.

The evidence before us indicated that Philadelphia is organized by the numbers operators into various geographical territories, each with its own "numbers bank." Public Safety Director Samuel H. Rosenberg told us that this was his understanding of the way the racketeers operated.

The safety director, a former secretary to Mayor Bernard Samuel, was questioned by Associate Counsel Klein:

Q. Are you aware that it is common knowledge, in connection with that gambling operation, that payments are made to police officers?

ROSENBERG: I have never been able to prove that. . . . We have asked for proof, and have never been able to obtain it.

Later, however, in response to a question from Chief Counsel Halley, Rosenberg acknowledged, "I would be very naïve if I sat here and told you that every member of the Philadelphia Police Department was absolutely honest and wouldn't take a nickel."

One of his worst handicaps in administering the Police Department, the safety director stated, was Philadelphia's peculiar civil service regulations, which he described as "originally intended to be on the merit basis, but which have put us in an absolute strait jacket." He said: "It is absolutely impossible for me to demote a man unless I can prove a case that would stand up in court, and in police matters that is very difficult. . . . Nor have I authority to promote a man, strangely enough. I must take them from civil service lists. . . ."

On this point, to digress briefly, the Philadelphia civil service system, as every serious student of municipal government in America knows, has been a farce. It is not civil service in the true sense at all, but is merely a convenient method for ward heelers to keep their fingers on the patronage pork barrel. On the credit side of our committee's accomplishments, I was tremendously pleased, some months after our Philadelphia hearings, to hear from Chairman Donald C. Rubel of the Committee of Seventy, which has been struggling for nearly half a century to achieve better government in Philadelphia, that a long-desired city charter reform had been voted by the citizens. The victory was achieved despite the opposition of the incumbent administration and, among other things, will set up machinery to take civil service out of politics. Mr. Rubel stated that our committee's hearings provided valuable ammunition to use against the entrenched opposition.

To resume with Safety Director Rosenberg's testimony, he told us frankly that he lacked confidence in four high-ranking police officials, not because he had any evidence that they had violated their trust, but because he believed they had failed to demonstrate what he called "sufficient aggressiveness" in going after the lawbreakers. The highest official in whom he said he lacked confidence was George F. Richardson, then the assistant superintendent of police in charge of detectives, who was a key witness in certain phases of our hearings, but whose testimony indicated no lack of aggressiveness in his dealings with the gangsters.

The principal racket character whom we questioned was Harry Stromberg, alias Nig Rosen. Stromberg was a stocky, swarthy, balding character with intensely dark eyes and an annoying habit of repeating almost every question before giving an answer. We had two sessions with him: one in Philadelphia, where he was faced with the possibility of a contempt citation for refusing to answer certain questions which the committee considered legitimate; the second in Washington, where he came to purge himself of contempt by clearing the record of the unanswered questions.

Stromberg immigrated to the United States from Russia as a child and grew up in New York City, where at the age of nine he was sent to a protectory as a juvenile delinquent. He has been arrested numerous times since, and has served time in a New York State penitentiary for attempted burglary. He admitted to us that he had been a bootlegger during prohibition and more recently a numbers operator and bookmaker in Philadelphia. It was evident from the testimony Stromberg grudgingly gave us that he had been the kingpin of rackets in the City of Brotherly Love. At the present time, Stromberg said, he was engaged in the dress manufacturing business in New York City, and he insisted he had no connection with the rackets.

We also questioned, in both Philadelphia and Washington,

Willie Weisberg, one of Stromberg's chief followers. Weisberg was a scared little man whose lips and limbs trembled as he answered our questions about his association with Stromberg and other Philadelphia hoodlums. He told us he made a mean living by following the race tracks. He insisted he made only legal bets at the tracks and never patronized bookies. "My business is very undesirable," Weisberg explained. "I play the horses to show and no bookmaker will take them."

The nemesis of Stromberg and Weisberg in Philadelphia was the assistant superintendent of police, George Richardson, one of the officials in whom Safety Director Rosenberg said he lacked full confidence. The white-haired Richardson, who heaped vilification upon Stromberg, Weisberg, and another Stromberg associate, Herman (Mugsy) Taylor, asserted Stromberg had run his part of the Philadelphia numbers rackets by remote control from New York, after leaving Philadelphia around 1934.

Though his testimony was not entirely clear because of his extreme wordiness, the detective chief seemed to think that Stromberg, alias Rosen, still had a hand in Philadelphia rackets. As recently as eight months before he testified before the committee, Richardson had written the director of the Greater Miami Crime Commission as follows: "Rosen has connections with the underworld throughout the entire nation. So far as the local mob is concerned, he is their undisputed leader and is commonly known as 'The Mahoff.' Among his followers his word is law, and an unfortunate accident is likely to befall any member who flaunts his authority."

Though somewhat on the wane, the numbers racket still is active in Philadelphia today, Richardson testified. He was insistent, however, that he had never even heard rumors of pay-offs to policemen. Halley asked:

Q. There have been persistent rumors that the people in the numbers racket pay off policemen. Had you heard such rumors?

RICHARDSON: No, I never heard any rumors. . . .

Q. In all honesty, mustn't you say that at least at the very lowest levels in your Police Department, you were bound to have some dishonest cops?

A. I think we have a pretty good Police Department here, Counselor. . . . I wouldn't say any cops are taking any dough off anybody; no.

Chief Richardson further accused Stromberg and Mugsy Taylor of having muscled in on the gambling club of the late Jimmy LaFontaine in Prince Georges County, Maryland, just across the line from Washington, D.C., after LaFontaine was kidnaped in the early thirties and allegedly had to pay a $10,000 ransom. The police official's enmity toward Stromberg, Weisberg, and Taylor was undisguised. He admitted he had threatened them with physical violence, had slapped them around and intended to do it again if he caught them in Philadelphia. "I laid down a policy that these men were not to be permitted the freedom of the streets or night clubs or any sporting event. . . . Anywhere they were seen, they were supposed to be stood up and given rough treatment and put on their way," he told us. ". . . Any time I ever seen them anywhere, they were given a rough time." Weisberg, in fact, told us almost tearfully that he had been in fear of Richardson since the detective chief had threatened to split his head open.

While testifying in Washington, Stromberg stolidly related that at one period he had entertained Assistant Superintendent Richardson a good deal and had given him gifts of ties, custom-made shirts, and a $150 clock. Next day Richardson was down in Washington, heatedly denying that Stromberg had ever treated him or given him anything. "That bum couldn't get near me let alone give me any shirts!" he exclaimed. "He never gave me anything. He was never permitted to talk to me, only when I was standing him up. . . . He couldn't get near me even with a million dollars!" He went on to term Stromberg and Weisberg "two of the yellowest curs you ever laid your eyes on," and when I asked him why the mobster should have claimed he gave him gifts, Richardson replied: "He is a desperate man, Senator. He is getting chased around the country. Wherever he goes, I tell them who he is and what he does. He would probably scheme up anything to get a crack at me."

Since testifying before us, Chief Richardson has been suspended from duty, not in connection with Stromberg or Weisberg, but on a charge that he had been overzealous in forcing the "confession" of a man who had been sent to the penitentiary for homicide. After spending twelve years in prison, the victim was found to be innocent and released.

Judge Joseph Sloane of the Common Pleas Court told us without equivocation that many of his colleagues on the bench were content merely to impose small fines and no jail sentences on persons pleading guilty of gambling offenses, which included horse books as well as numbers. In five years prior to 1950, we learned, out of thousands of gambling arrests, only two defendants had actually gone to jail. This "cavalier outlook," Judge Sloane asserted, led to "demoralization" of both the police and "minor judiciary." However, as our report summed up: "There has been a change in this attitude on the part of judges since the committee held its hearings in Philadelphia. More and more jail sentences are beginning to be imposed and it is a fact reported by municipal authorities, that the numbers game is no longer as easy to carry on in Philadelphia. . . ."

Another interesting highlight on Philadelphia justice was given us by William A. Gray, veteran attorney who is recognized as the leader of Philadelphia's criminal bar. Mr. Gray, who represented Stromberg and Weisberg, told us he tried to reason with Chief Richardson several years ago when the latter had threatened violence against Weisberg. All Richardson would say, Gray testified, was, "I am going to personally split his head wide open . . . and when he gets out of the hospital I will lock him up." Thereupon the attorney went over Richardson's head, but, instead of protesting to the assistant superintendent's superior, he went to see a judge, the late Harry S. McDevitt, who had the general reputation, as Attorney Gray stated, of having "a very decided influence over the police force" and over Richardson in particular. The lawyer said he told the judge: "If you don't see Richardson and have him stop this, I am going to take some steps in the matter which won't be pleasant for a lot of people in the city of Philadelphia." After this, Richardson laid off Weisberg for a while, but later resumed his harassment.

Touching on still another phase of Philadelphia police administration, the committee's report to the Senate took note of a local *cause célèbre,* which we regarded as "indicative of the tie-up of gamblers, politicians, and police." Michael McDonald, a Philadelphia policeman, had arrested a numbers writer named Jack Rogers. While Rogers was being booked, McDonald said, one Mike Caserta, "who had been named by Rogers as his backer," came into the station house.

McDonald, who swore that Rogers had offered him $100 not to arrest him, went on to testify that Caserta offered him $200 if he would only modify the charge against Rogers to disorderly conduct. McDonald testified: "I refused the offer. As he turned away he said, 'I will frame you good, you son of a bitch.' When he said that, I grabbed hold of him and placed him under arrest."

At that point, McDonald continued, a police captain named Vincent Elwell appeared and "wanted to know who locked up 'Mike.' He addressed him as 'Mike.'"

That night, McDonald said, he was called in to Captain Elwell's office, was reprimanded by him for stepping out of line, and was ordered to alter his report on Caserta. "I have known Mike since he was a little boy," McDonald said the captain told him. McDonald claimed he retorted, "I wouldn't brag about knowing that thug!" and refused to change his report. Captain Elwell then told him, "Stick around. I want to talk to you a little while," McDonald testified. In about ten minutes Captain Elwell walked to the door and asked, "Who is hollering out there?" (McDonald claimed he had heard no disturbance.) A sergeant promptly stepped in—"He had been standing there all the time; I could see his reflection on the wall," McDonald said—and dutifully announced: "A man is complaining about being short some money out here." Thereupon, on Captain Elwell's orders, the numbers writer, Rogers, was brought in and complained he was short about $123. McDonald was accused of turning in less money than he had taken from Rogers at the station house when he brought him in, and Captain Elwell immediately suspended him.

"McDonald gave a picture of the operations of the politico-gambler-police triumvirate," our report continued. He named a policeman who, he said, was known as the "collector" for Captain Elwell—he would come into the station house with his pockets "bulging," McDonald testified. He also named a ward boss who frequently conferred with Captain Elwell at the station house. McDonald estimated that protection money paid to police alone in Philadelphia, exclusive of "payment to the higher-ups," totaled at least $152,000 a month. As we noted: "The general picture . . . given by McDonald indicated that there is a tie-up between the three elements in Philadelphia which permits these operations to continue with the token 'convenience arrests' [i.e., periodic arrests of underlings, but never the big operators, to make the record look good] that are characteristic of the same kind of operations in other cities."

Captain Elwell was given a chance to tell his side of the story. He denied all of McDonald's charges and insisted the patrolman had acted improperly the night he booked Rogers. He said he had "heard the rumor" that some officers under his command took bribes from numbers writers but that he knew nothing about it.

Captain Elwell had a presumably embarrassing moment during his cross-examination by our sharp-eyed Chief Counsel Halley. Counsel asked:

HALLEY: Captain, do you mind if I ask a personal question? Do you have a scar on the pinkie of your left hand or do you habitually wear a ring there?
ELWELL: This hand?
HALLEY: Yes.
ELWELL: Yes; I wear a ring.

HALLEY: Do you have a reason for not wearing it today?

ELWELL: Yes; I had a sore finger. . . . I forgot it. I washed my hands and left it off.

HALLEY: I was just wondering, because apparently you wear it customarily. There is a very noticeable ring mark on your left finger.

McDonald, incidentally, since he testified before us, was given a retrial by the civil service board, was cleared and reinstated. He thereupon resigned and entered the United States Army.

Moving from the police field, the committee inquired into an instance of underworld penetration of a Philadelphia steel fabricating concern, which we concluded had been accomplished through "political influence." A numbers racketeer named Louis Crusco had bought his way into the Strunk Steel Company by virtue, the committee inferred, "of his close association with the son of Philadelphia's mayor." Crusco was an old friend and neighbor of Richard Russell Samuel, Sr., son of Mayor Samuel. The numbers man bought his interest in the company under extraordinary circumstances whereby he carried the purchase price, $34,000, in currency, contained in a satchel, to a stockholders' meeting. Richard Samuel, Jr., nineteen-year-old grandson of the mayor, accompanied Crusco to this meeting, and, according to the testimony of one of the stockholders who was selling out, "apparently was the mouthpiece for Mr. Crusco." Richard Samuel, Sr., was the Republican leader of the Thirty-ninth Ward in Philadelphia, and held two jobs, one as a solicitor of legal advertising for a Philadelphia newspaper, and the other as a personal property assessor for the city, an appointive position under his father.

"Until Crusco came along," our report to the Senate summed up, "the company had never been able to get any business from the city of Philadelphia but, while Crusco was negotiating his stock purchase in the company, it received a contract from the Philadelphia Transit Company, a local public utility, on which there were no competitive bids. The president of the company testified that this deal had been suggested to him by the mayor's grandson, who, coincidentally, was placed on the company's pay roll as part of the Crusco stock deal."

William M. Strunk, former president of the now bankrupt company, told us he had understood that Samuel, Sr., also would attempt to procure business for the company. The mayor's son acknowledged that "maybe Mr. Strunk had that idea in telling my boy he wanted him to come with him, thinking he could use whatever influence he had to sell things to people by using the name." However, he denied ever promising or implying that he would become a business procurer for the company, or that he had had any connection with the transit company order. He also denied that he had ever had any business dealings with Crusco.

In so far as the state of Pennsylvania was concerned, the committee had an abortive brush with the State Board of Pardons and the office of former Attorney General Charles J. Margiotti when we sent a representative to the state capital to examine records pertaining to pardons of certain Philadelphia convicts associated with the boxing game. One was Frank (Blinky) Palermo, for whom the late Judge McDevitt had interceded with the pardons board. Our representative reported back to the committee that he was told by the secretary of the pardons board that, "on advice of the attorney general," the information would be withheld until former Attorney General Margiotti "had checked certain constitutional questions which he thinks might affect the necessity of producing these papers." We let the state officials know that the committee would not hesitate to exercise the subpoena powers vested in it by the United States Senate. A little talk with Mr. Margiotti produced a change of viewpoint, and the pardons board secretary came in with the desired records.

The committee, frankly, did not probe as deeply into corruption in Philadelphia as it did in some other cities. Certain observers have surmised, with complete lack of logic, that the reason for this was because I, as chairman and a Democrat, did not want to examine the apparent symptoms of muncipal rottenness in a city which had a Republican administration. This, of course, was plain silly. There was a sound reason for our decision to postpone further hearings in Philadelphia. It so happened that shortly before our hearings were conducted in Philadelphia a federal grand jury was convened to investigate organized criminal operations in the entire eastern district of Pennsylvania. This grand jury was under the able direction of Special Assistant Attorney General Max Goldschein, who had conducted the Kansas City vote fraud and rackets investigation and had given our committee valuable assistance in its probe of the gangster-dominated Missouri city. We decided that further investigations and hearings in Pennsylvania would be postponed pending outcome of the federal grand jury investigation so as to avoid any conflict or hindrance. We felt Mr. Goldschein and his grand jury would do a thorough and effective job, which, after all, was the end result that the committee desired—not the smearing or glorification of any local administration, be it Republican or Democrat. Also, at that time the life of the Senate Committee was scheduled to expire on March 31, 1951, and we had much ground left to cover which was not being touched by other investigative bodies. Since our hearings, the investigations of the federal grand jury are being augmented, in so far as Philadelphia itself is concerned, by a local grand jury inquiry. Our committee has offered both bodies all the information it collected on the Philadelphia area. The transcript of our executive sessions since has been made public along with transmission of our third interim report to the Senate. There was no politics, no fear, and no favor in our handling of the Philadelphia story.

CHAPTER 16

NEVADA: A CASE AGAINST
LEGALIZED GAMBLING

THE Senate Crime Investigating Committee went to Nevada, the only state in the Union which presently legalizes gambling on an all-out scale, to make an on-the-spot study as to whether, in the committee's opinion, it would be a deterrent to organized crime to legalize gambling on a nationwide basis; also, of course, to study interstate crime connections. After hearings in Las Vegas our conclusion was: "As a case history of legalized gambling, Nevada speaks eloquently in the negative."

The committee found itself completely in accord with numerous competent studies which have been made from time to time, indicating that, both morally and financially, legalized gambling in Nevada is a failure. It is true that revenue derived from state and local levies on the gambling dives is welcome, for Nevada is a sparsely settled state with limited financial resources. However, the amount the state receives is only a pitiful fraction of the millions of dollars that the gamblers themselves drain from the pockets of the public—not all of whom are out-of-state tourists, either. Furthermore, Las Vegas, Reno, and other Nevada gambling centers have become headquarters for some of the nation's worst mobsters. As our report noted, the state of Nevada has found it necessary to increase police surveillance substantially (an expensive proposition) as a result of the legalization of gambling and "the accompanying influx of hoodlums, racketeers, and the other inevitable parasites who spring up like weeds wherever gambling operations are carried on." A sample of the type of "citizens" Nevada attracted as a result of its legalization of gambling was the late Bugsy Siegel, formerly a director of New York's Murder, Inc., who became the gambling boss of Las Vegas until he was murdered in his mistress' home in California in 1947.

Another example of the type of hoodlum attracted to Nevada by legalized gambling is Lester (Benny) Binion (currently alive), who in 1936 was run out of Dallas, Texas, where he was boss of a $1,000,000-a-year policy racket. Binion still has a hand in running the Texas racket by remote control from his Nevada refuge, according to Lieutenant George Butler of the Dallas Police Department.

Lieutenant Butler, who assisted the committee as a special investigator, brought out details of the lurid feud between Binion and Dallas gambler Harold Noble, who had been shot at so many times (nine at the time Butler testified) that he was known in the underworld as "The Cat" or "The Clay Pigeon." After Noble's wife was blown up in a dynamite explosion obviously intended to kill the gambler, Binion sent an emissary from Las Vegas to Dallas to assure Noble that Binion was not behind the killings. Butler, a shrewd sleuth, got wind of the meeting and he and colleagues secreted a recording instrument in the tourist cabin where the conference took place. Thus we learned that Binion and the Nevada mob were unhappy over the bad publicity which was having the indirect effect of hurting business in Nevada gambling casinos. Binion wanted to make peace with Noble, and his emissary assured The Cat that Benny had learned who was pulling the rough stuff and, if Noble said so, was ready to have them bumped off—even though one of the alleged dynamiters since had been convicted of another crime and was in the penitentiary. During the course of the tourist cabin conference a long-distance call was placed to Binion, and the talk ended on a conciliatory note. Apparently Binion's promises have come to naught, for there since have been two more attempts—making eleven in all at this counting—to kill the unfortunate Mr. Noble.

Studying the effects, not only in Nevada but throughout the country, of what happens when a state or community is "Siegelized" or "Binionized," my personal opposition to legalized gambling has become firm. It is my opinion that big-time gambling is amoral—I refer to the casino type of operation, which is more often crooked than not—and that legalizing it will not make it less so. Gambling produces nothing and adds nothing to the economy or society of our nation. America will be in a bad way if we ever have to resort to taxing crime and immorality for the purpose of raising revenue to operate our institutions. The fascination of gambling to many people is so strong that, in my opinion, it would be complete folly to make the facilities more available than they presently are.

Pages could be filled with examples heard by the committee of the old, familiar story of how fine citizens and family men became paupers, embezzlers, and worse because of the enticements of the gambling tables. As an example of how legalized gambling can be an economic blight, we learned in Nevada that employees of a certain magnesium plant near Las Vegas were paid extremely high wages and should have been prosperous. Yet when the plant had to be moved several hundred miles, many of the employees simply did not have the money to move their families to the new locations; their earnings had gone into the convenient slot machines and gambling dens. No, I can shed no tears over the fact that experiments being conducted at the new atomic bomb testing range near Las Vegas are rattling the windows of the gambling dives and making the sharpers nervous.

There is more than an abundance of evidence that wherever gambling is allowed to exist, legally or illegally, money is taken out of the normal and legitimate channels of commerce, and

that when gambling is minimized legitimate business flourishes. Senator Hunt, a member of the committee, told us of his
experience as governor of Wyoming. When gambling was out-
lawed in his state business increased tremendously and sales
tax revenues to the state immediately soared.

Nevada's gambling laws have been subject to periodic altera-
tions. One of the latest changes took effect in 1949. It is now
required that persons engaging in gambling operations, including operations of handbooks, must be licensed by the state as
well as by the county or city in which they operate. Such license
power is vested in the Nevada State Tax Commission, which is
authorized to conduct hearings and to grant and revoke licenses
on the basis of the individual applicant's qualifications. It
struck the committee as ironic that the Tax Commission member appointed to "represent business" is a man named William
J. Moore, who himself is engaged in a gambling operation as
part owner of the hotel known as the Last Frontier. The lanky,
drawling Commissioner Moore, who addressed everyone—even
the dignified Senator Tobey of New Hampshire—as "fellow"
explained to us that his particular function on the commission is to deal with licensees engaged in bookmaking and gambling operations.

As part of the same "reform" in Nevada's gambling laws
there is supposed to be an "impartial" distribution to all licensed bookmakers of the race-news wire service, which is the
lifeblood of gambling. The Tax Commission is authorized to
fix rates for this service and, in general, supervise the operation
of the wire service. The same Mr. Moore told the committee
that he recently made a deal for wire service for his own hotel
at a rate which, in the expressed opinion of the committee,
"gives him a considerable financial advantage over his competitors." He explained that the reason for the comparatively
low rate was the newness of his operation, but we found at least
one other new operation in Las Vegas "which had not been
given the same low rate." As our report noted: "The conditions
above described are not healthful."

The driving force behind the 1948 "reforms" which gave

licensing power to the Tax Commission was the frightening fact that the out-of-state hoodlums and killers who have invaded Nevada had become so greedy and violent that an outbreak of gang warfare was feared. By "licensing" them, and particularly by ordaining that the rule-of-gun monopoly established over the race-news wire service by the late Bugsy Siegel was to be broken up, the state hoped to stabilize the industry. Yet—and the committee found it a fantastic situation—the Tax Commission promptly granted licenses to the same hoodlums who had been established in Nevada, including several with felony convictions. This, as the dual-roled Mr. Moore explained to us, was a sort of "granddaddy clause" to protect the people who were in the business when the law was passed. "Are you going to throw out a man with a $3,500,000 investment?" Moore protested. ". . . You can't correct overnight a situation that existed prior to your enactment of a new law." When Counsel Halley asked him how the Tax Commission could possibly have licensed a certain Detroit gambler named Wertheimer, who had a flagrant record for illegal operations in other states, Moore replied: "Sure, but . . . that is no sign that he shouldn't have a license in a state where it is legal." Halley incredulously asked: "It makes no difference to you whether he gambles in a state where it is not legal?" "No," drawled Moore, "how was he going to learn the business?"

We also were captivated by the unique role of Clifford Aaron Jones, attorney at law in Las Vegas, lieutenant governor of the state of Nevada, and also a partner in the Pioneer Club, the Golden Nugget, and the Thunderbird Hotel, all of which were gambling operations. Lieutenant Governor Jones's two and a half per cent interest in the Pioneer Club, which he purchased for $5000, has yielded him approximately $14,000 a year, and his one per cent interest in the Golden Nugget, for which he paid $23,310, pays about $12,000. His sizable percentage of the Thunderbird, a new enterprise, had not yet been profitable.

The lieutenant governor affably agreed with my statement that the Tax Commission licensing law had "blanketed in a lot of racketeers who were already doing business." "You can't legislate them out of business," Jones, like Moore, explained. All this, of course, was strictly legal, but the example of the lieutenant governor and the tax commissioner of the state engaged in the gambling business struck the committee as decidedly incongruous. In our report to the Senate we commented:

"The profits which have been taken from gambling operations are far greater than those which can be earned quickly in any other business. The availability of huge sums of cash and the incentive to control political action result in gamblers and racketeers too often taking part in government.

"In states where gambling is illegal, this alliance of gamblers, gangsters, and government will yield to the spotlight of publicity and the pressure of public opinion, but where gambling receives a cloak of respectability through legalization, there is no weapon which can be used to keep the gamblers and their money out of politics."

The move which placed the Nevada Tax Commission in the business of licensing gamblers, as a matter of fact, was precipitated by Robert E. Jones, district attorney of the county in which Las Vegas is located and a law partner—though no relation—of Lieutenant Governor Jones. He wrote the Tax Commission that the gangsters were getting too quarrelsome since Siegel's assassination and that warfare might break out at any time. Siegel, an associate of Lucky Luciano, Frank Costello, Joe Adonis, Meyer Lansky, and other rulers of the Eastern mob, moved into Las Vegas around 1942 and established the Flamingo Hotel, one of the plushest gambling places in the country. Working with Moe Sedway, ex-convict and long-time gambler and racketeer, and others, Siegel was the indisputable czar of the Nevada wire service. Actually he was believed to have muscled in as a silent partner of every bookmaker to whom he sold the wire service, and he would refuse service to any bookie who would not stand still for the "muscle." During the Trans-American-Continental Press fight over control of the wire service (see Chapter 3), Siegel represented the interests of the Capone Syndicate's Trans-American service. He was shot to death in the home he was leasing for Virginia Hill in Beverly Hills, California, a few days after Trans-American folded. There are two theories for his assassination, and it is possible he was killed because of a combination of both: (1) he attempted to carry his "muscle" tactics too far; and/or (2) his East Coast and Chicago mob backers were displeased with the way he had managed their Western interests.

None of Siegel's underworld intimates would speculate on why he met his violent death. When we asked the nervous and ailing Sedway in Las Vegas why Siegel was killed, he replied: "I don't know. I wouldn't know if he was killed in connection with the wire service or any other reasons." In California, Allen Smiley, alias Aaron Smehoff, who was sitting next to Bugsy when the shotgun blast ended Siegel's life, had no theories to offer. He did tell us, however, "I relinquished my interest" in Bugsy's Flamingo within thirty days after the murder because "it was a terrible shock to me and I didn't care if the hotel burned up."

Law enforcement officers were less reticent. Police Chief Clinton H. Anderson of Beverly Hills told us that the Fischetti brothers of the Chicago-Capone Syndicate, the Frank Costello-Frank Erickson interests in New York, and certain members of the Detroit mob had invested heavily in Bugsy's Flamingo, which reputedly cost between $4,000,000 and $5,000,000. They were said to be displeased with Bugsy's management of the expensive property. Chief Anderson, who happened to be in New York on official business when Bugsy was killed, testified: "I had a conference with a certain law enforcement official just the day before. At that time he predicted that Siegel was to be eliminated because he was in the bad graces of Mr. Costello and Mr. Erickson. He said there was a lot of bad feeling about the way he was spending money at the Flamingo. . . . I was rather surprised the following day when I received a telegram that he actually had been killed."

The police chief further testified: "Virginia Hill is alleged to have been familiar with the entire operation and the trouble between some of the individuals involved. It is reported that she was aware that the killing was to happen and she was out of the United States at the time." In New York later, Virginia Hill furiously disclaimed such knowledge; professing her devotion to the late Mr. Siegel, she exclaimed: "If I knew anything about it, believe me, I would be the first one to talk. . . . I have asked people and they don't know anything. Nobody seems to know anything."

Anyway, after Siegel's murder the Flamingo's operation was taken over by Sanford Adler, a gambler with a long record of arrests; he was supposed to control operation of the hotel, although Morris Rosen, Moe Sedway, and a man who controlled the wire service in Phoenix, Arizona, Gus Greenbaum, held the controlling number of shares in the hotel. Adler and Greenbaum fell out and Adler retired, leaving the other three in charge. Sedway and Rosen attempted to carry on the late Bugsy's race wire monopoly but weren't tough enough. Soon the Stearns brothers, operators of the Santa Anita Club, which adjoined the Sedway-Rosen Frontier Club, were tapping the Frontier Club's race wire. It was then that the district attorney became afraid that shooting would break out, and the licensing arrangement, which has led to dubious peace among the gamblers in Nevada, was set up.

In Las Vegas and Reno the committee traced connections of the Nevada gamblers with the New York, New Jersey, Michigan, Texas, and Ohio mobs. It was clear to us, and we so reported to the Senate, that "the gambling operations in Nevada are inexplicably tied to interstate commerce." This is not only by the connections with out-of-state racketeers but through bets placed daily by out-of-state sources with Nevada bookmakers. In reverse, the Nevada bookies also protect themselves by laying off their biggest bets with out-of-state operators. Our judgment on the legalized gambling experiment in Nevada was summed up as follows:

"It seems clear to the committee that too many of the men running gambling operations in Nevada are either members of existing out-of-state gambling syndicates or have had histories of close association with the underworld characters who operate those syndicates. The licensing system which is in effect in this state has not resulted in excluding the undesirables from the state but has merely served to give their activities a seeming cloak of respectability."

On the general subject of legalizing gambling as a nation-wide proposition, the committee rejected the premises advanced "by many well-meaning and conscientious individuals" that such a measure would remove the crooks from the field and remove temptations from corrupt public officials who play along with the gamblers. To the contrary, we felt it was not the illegality but the huge profits that made gambling attractive to gangsters and hoodlums. No plan for legalized gambling that was proposed to us seemed to carry any guarantee of success. On the contrary, we noted, "much of the propaganda for legalized gambling can be traced to organized and professional gamblers." Every plan that was suggested, when subjected to impartial analysis, seemed to play right into the hands of the Siegels, Costellos, Sedways, Binions, and others, large and small, of their ilk.

CHAPTER 17

CALIFORNIA: WHERE LOBBYISTS
GROW BIG AND MOBSTERS THRIVE

CRIME, vice, and corruption in California had a special flavor—exotic, overripe, and a little sickening. The rackets there, like the state itself, were big and colorful. We waded through unpleasant disclosures of venality and, to put it politely, "ineptness" by some local law enforcement officers and public officials—countered, of course, by the heartening examples of a number of good officials. We listened unhappily to the story of how a few federal internal revenue agents disgraced their service by participating in obvious shakedowns—one agent even enclosing a government-franked envelope in his letter demanding money from the madam of a house of prostitution. We explored the dim and dirty world of the contemptible little mobster, Mickey Cohen, and the other gang-world denizens who practiced the art of strong-arm and blackmail in the Golden State. And finally, in our concluding interrogation, we met the smooth and slippery Arthur H. Samish, portly superlobbyist for the brewing industry, who, over the past six years, has had a $1,000,000 fund to play with and who is credited with boasting, "I am the governor of the legislature. To hell with the governor of the state."

Senators Tobey, Wiley, and I first went to Los Angeles and San Francisco to conduct seven days of marathon executive sessions, stretching from early morning until nearly midnight. Additional details were filled in through voluminous evidence taken in Washington, and then I returned, as a subcommittee of one, to conduct four days of public hearings in the two cities. Our able investigators, Harold Robinson, now a deputy assistant to the California attorney general, Herbert Van Brunt, former FBI agent, and William D. Amis, formerly with the Internal Revenue Bureau, felt we could have held hearings in California for two months without exhausting avenues for investigation. I shall set forth in this chapter the highlights of our findings:

OF "JUICE" AND CERTAIN OFFICERS. For years, parts of California have been literally infested with every conceivable kind of gambling racket: bookie parlors, "bridgo-bingo," slot machines, dice, poker parlors, off-the-coast gambling ships, and so forth. The "take" runs into the millions.

Some effective action against the big-scale gamblers resulted after Governor Earl Warren in 1947 appointed a California Commission on Organized Crime. Warren Olney, former counsel to the commission, testified that one of the evils exposed by the state group was the fact that, as was noted in our second interim report to the Senate, "representatives of the attorney general's office, with the apparent blessing of Fred Howser, then attorney general, attempted to organize a state-wide system of protection for slot-machine operations and for the distribution of punchboards." The voters since have retired Howser from office.

Healthy results were also produced in Los Angeles by Mayor Fletcher Bowron's effective anti-crime crusade, which the racket elements tried unsuccessfully to counter by a brazen attempt to force the mayor's recall. In general, times now are more difficult for California gamblers. We found that some even were reduced to resorting to use of collapsible crap tables which could be loaded into the back of an automobile and used for "sneak" games.

One of the biggest gambling rackets broken up in Los Angeles after the California Crime Commission went into business was the so-called Guarantee Finance Company, which posed as a legitimate loan agency but actually was a front for a $6,000,000 bookmaking combine. When the combine's books finally were seized, examination disclosed recorded payments totaling $108,000 for the service known as "juice," which is the California gambling profession's euphemism (in Florida the term is "ice") for "protection" money. Since Guarantee operated as a "fifty-fifty book," with participating bookies sharing equally in the expenses, a pay-off of $216,000 thus was indicated.

The Los Angeles City Police Department was headed by a determined officer, Chief William H. Parker, who made life hard for the gamblers and gangsters. The committee, however, was not impressed by the Los Angeles County sheriff's office, particularly after hearing the remarkably uninformed Under-Sheriff Arthur C. Jewell testify: "I never knew the Guarantee Finance was in existence, nor neither did the sheriff, until the state come and took it over." When Chief Counsel Halley asked Jewell if he could tell the committee of any illegal activities of which Mickey Cohen was suspected, the under-sheriff replied: "Personally, I cannot, sir; that is honest and sincere."

Guarantee had shrewdly located its main headquarters in a peculiar geographic setup, an "island" inside Los Angeles proper known as "Sunset Strip." This was county territory and accordingly was not subject to the jurisdiction of the tougher Los Angeles city police. One of Chief Parker's aggressive officers, Lieutenant James Fiske, finally became so incensed by the sheriff's inactivity that he entered Sunset Strip and came down through a skylight into the huge telephone room of the bookmaking operation. Because he was out of his jurisdiction he was unable to make any arrests, but he did give the bookies a bad time by methodically tearing up all of their markers so they were at a loss as to how to settle their bets for that particular day. As a result of that foray, Lieutenant Fiske advised one of our investigators, a stern letter was received by the Police Department from one Al Guasti, then a captain in the sheriff's office, demanding that city police officers stay out of county territory. Guasti, since retired and, at the time of his second appearance before us in Los Angeles, under indictment in connection with the Guarantee case, denied he ever wrote such a letter. The elderly Sheriff Eugene Biscailuz, who had not retired Guasti at the time of our first hearings, told us: "I have never seen that letter and I have had denial after denial from Guasti himself."

MURDER OF A "MOUTHPIECE." One of the strange avenues explored in Los Angeles was the murder of Samuel Rummel, lawyer for Mickey Cohen and other Los Angeles gangsters. In November 1950, when we first went to Los Angeles, Police Chief Parker told us it was his opinion that Rummel was the brains behind Mickey Cohen. At the same time a Los Angeles County grand jury was probing vigorously into the question of pay-offs to law enforcement officers by the so-called Guarantee Finance Company. When we returned to Los Angeles the following February we heard from Carey S. Hill, foreman of this grand jury, how the Rummel murder was linked with the investigation.

About three weeks after our committee's first hearings in Los Angeles, Foreman Hill and four other county officials, including a representative of the district attorney's office, held a highly secret meeting to determine a plan of action for the probe. The only other persons let in on the plans were the two process servers who were to serve subpoenas on the prospective witnesses. The very next day, Foreman Hill testified, someone "leaked" the plans to Sammy Rummel, and "our witnesses scattered." "Here was clear demonstration," a special grand jury report later asserted, "of the power of the underworld. Their successful infiltration into law enforcement agencies was clearly demonstrated by the smooth operation of their intelligence system."

The secret meeting had been on a Wednesday. On the following Sunday a series of incredible events took place. First, Rummel arranged a clandestine rendezvous with Captain Guasti. Guasti, in turn, arranged for the "mouthpiece" to meet that night with Captain Carl Pearson, then head of Sheriff Biscailuz' vice squad, and Sergeant Lawrence Schaffer, also of the vice squad. At this meeting, Guasti said, Sergeant Schaffer actually exhibited to Rummel the confidential files from the sheriff's office, dealing with the Guarantee case.

His mouth twitching noticeably as we questioned him, Guasti was unable to give us any logical explanation for the strange Sunday meeting between the criminal lawyer and the officers who were supposed to be on the other side of the fence. Guasti told us that he, Pearson, and Rummel first met and drove around in Rummel's car while talking; then arranged to pick up Schaffer and examine the confidential files. Guasti said he dropped out before Schaffer was picked up, but testified he knew the three of them later went to Rummel's office with the files on the Guarantee case. Thus the captain and the sergeant—and they have admitted that they met with Rummel in his office—were the last people known to have been with the lawyer that Sunday night. Next morning Rummel was found dead—killed by a close-range shotgun blast as he walked from his garage to the front door of his home. The "mouthpiece" was silenced forever.

"Doesn't it seem to be a strange coincidence," I asked, "that he . . . went over the files with you and, apparently, he was going to give you some information or blow the lid off . . . or get something fixed up with you officers? When he got home that night or early the next morning, he got killed. Do you think that is a strange coincidence?" His voice barely audible, Guasti murmured: "Strange, yes."

Pursuing the possible motive for the murder, Associate Counsel Rice inquired of Grand Jury Foreman Hill:

Q. Do you associate the Rummel shooting with . . . the leak to Rummel or the anticipated action of the grand jury?

HILL: I think it is a very plausible theory and I haven't heard a better one. . . . Rummel, at least, had his foot in the gambling business. . . . Undoubtedly he knew about the Guarantee's "slush fund" and he may have threatened someone to move over.

At the time Foreman Hill testified, indictments had been returned by his grand jury against Captain Pearson, ex-Captain Guasti, and Sergeant Schaffer.

THE INTERNAL REVENUE BUREAU SCANDALS. We found a particularly sordid mess in the practices of a few internal revenue agents in northern California and Nevada. Into our record was placed repeated evidence of shakedowns of taxpayers and of other reprehensible practices.

Credit for originally breaking the internal revenue scandals, involving employees of the offices of the Collectors of Internal Revenue for northern California and for Nevada must go to William Burkett, a young and diligent former special agent of the Treasury Department's intelligence unit in the northern California district. The shame of it is that neither the district office nor the Internal Revenue Bureau in Washington acted promptly on Burkett's disclosures. Eventually the young agent resigned in disgust, after he had been reprimanded by his immediate superiors for incurring the expense of making a long-distance call to New York to secure vital information on one aspect of the investigation. The call involved a matter of about six dollars, where as the government was being deprived of hundreds of thousands of dollars. Furthermore, we heard from the agent in charge of Burkett's unit that when Burkett talked about quitting the older hands urged, "Let him go; he is a troublemaker." Truly, the ways of bureaucracy sometimes are wonderful to behold!

Out of the facts uncovered by the "troublemaker," however, we learned that Patrick Mooney, former chief field deputy in the internal revenue office at Reno, had a scheme whereby he sold stock in his obviously worthless Mountain City Consolidated Copper Company to individuals (including some lawbreakers) whose tax cases were under investigation. Some of Mooney's customers were Gertrude Jenkins, convicted abortionist, and Elmer (Bones) Remmer, big-time California-Nevada gambler, who at the time of our hearings had a tax deficiency claim of approximately $910,000 against him.

"I had been after Bones Remmer for about two years to buy some stock," Mooney himself told us. He was a pathetic old man of eighty-one who obviously once had believed in his copper mines. "He has been chasing these 'glory holes' for fifty years," his son, who appeared with him, told us. "He still has faith that he is going to pull one of them through." When Mooney called on the gambler in 1946 with a tax warrant calling for immediate payment of about $7000, the old agent related, Remmer told him, "If you can stand me off for a little while on my income tax . . . I'll buy that stock today." Thereupon the deal was made and Remmer wrote him a check for $2400 worth of the valueless stock. The crowning insult was that Remmer tore up the $7000 check he had ready to pay the government on his tax bill and wrote a new check for $2400 less.

After that, Mooney related, the agent used to travel from Reno to San Francisco—out of his district—to make out Remmer's income tax returns for him. It was during these years—1942–47—that the gambler, according to the government's claims, fell more than $900,000 behind. Mooney said Remmer paid him nothing for these services except "my expenses." "He is stingy that way," the old man told us in a faraway voice.

Mooney admitted he was aided in his operations by one Martin Hartmann, a convicted "blue sky" operator who became a salesman for Mooney after the internal revenue agent had assisted in obtaining Hartmann's parole. Hartmann, according to the evidence, was the contact between Mooney and the Jenkins woman.

Also mentioned in connection with the Mooney-Hartmann-Jenkins transaction and other matters was Ernest (Mike) Schino, former chief field deputy in the northern California collector's office. The Jenkins woman, in an affidavit given Burkett, swore that Hartmann approached her and told her that if she went to Reno and handed $5000 to Mooney a $50,000 tax case against her "would be reduced substantially" and that she would be protected from criminal prosecution for tax fraud. "Hartmann had told me," her affidavit stated, "that Mooney would give me some worthless mining stock and the $5000 I paid Mooney was because Mooney knew Schino . . . and other Bureau of Internal Revenue officials. . . ." She went to Reno, taking along her son-in-law as a witness, and paid $5000 to Mooney for which she was supposed to receive 10,000 shares of his stock. Mooney admitted he used this money and that he never got around to issuing the stock to Mrs. Jenkins but said, "It is available any time she wants it." He also admitted he went to San Francisco to talk with Schino about the Jenkins case, but said, "I backed away from it right away" when Schino told him the fraud squad had the case. Mooney further testified, "Mr. Hartmann suggested that I give 5000 shares [of the worthless mine stock] to Mike Schino" after the Jenkins transaction. "I says, 'It wouldn't be right to put it in Mike's name,'" Mooney related, so the gift was registered in the name of Schino's sister.

Schino later testified it was a "difficult thing" to understand why Mooney should issue stock to his sister. He said he appreciated "Mr. Mooney's good thought and generosity, but I don't care for any of the stock."

The committee came close to a serious clash with the Treasury Department when an assistant internal revenue commissioner in Washington ordered Holden Sanford, special agent in charge of the internal revenue office at Fresno, California, not to testify before our open hearing. Sanford is an agent whose record has been good but who obviously used poor judgment in certain transactions; personally, I hope he has learned his lesson and will not place himself again in such a precarious position.

We were seeking Sanford's explanation of trips he made to Palm Springs, the fashionable California resort, in company with John Prunty, a businessman whose tax case was under investigation by Sanford's office. The same individual was directly involved in a dispute with another businessman whose affairs were being investigated personally by Sanford. Advising Mr. Sanford he would be held in contempt if he defied a committee of the Senate, I commented: "Whenever we reach a point where somebody in the executive department can tell a witness, a federal employee, he can testify or not testify, then the power of Congress to investigate has been dealt a death blow."

Fortunately for Sanford, who was being made the hapless victim of an ill-advised decision, higher Treasury Department officials reversed the assistant commissioner's indefensible ruling and permitted the agent to give his side of the story. We had already heard the testimony of John Prunty, the businessman involved in the case, and of Rex Blom, a former internal revenue agent. Prunty told us his taxes were being investigated in 1947 and that he hired Blom, who had become a private tax consultant after leaving the bureau, to represent him. Eventually Prunty, without going to court, was allowed to settle his case for approximately $16,000, which included interest on the government's claim but no fraud penalties. He admitted he paid Blom a fee of $4000 for his services. That amount, I remarked, seemed "a pretty good fee" for handling a $16,000 case. The $4000, incidentally, was paid Blom in cash, and Blom, though a tax man, gave his client no receipt.

During the course of the Prunty investigation, Agent Sanford made three trips to the fashionable California resort, Palm Springs. Two of the trips, he told us, were for "business," for the purpose of interviewing witnesses "who were located in the vicinity." On the first trip Sanford and the agent who was handling Prunty's case, James Coe, who since has left the service, went in company with Prunty. They rode in Prunty's car, stayed at Prunty's club, and Prunty paid the bill. This was because it was a private club where Prunty was accustomed to signing the bills, Sanford said, insisting that he later reimbursed the taxpayer. On the next trip Rex Blom, who testified, "I talked to both Mr. Coe and Mr. Sanford" about Prunty's tax problem, went along with the two agents. This time Blom picked up the check, stating he was paying it out of money he'd won at "gambling." "The way it looks now," Sanford conceded, "I made a mistake in allowing him to pay the bill."

Then there was a third visit to the resort. This time it was purely a pleasure jaunt on which Mr. and Mrs. Sanford went along with Mr. and Mrs. Prunty. "I paid every penny of my own expense on that trip," said Sanford.

The final—and perhaps the strangest—link in the network of these relationships was Prunty's testimony that he met Agent Sanford once by appointment in Salinas, California, where Sanford introduced him to Anna (Tugboat Annie) Schultz, also known as "Dixie," a notorious brothel keeper. Prunty testified under oath that Sanford suggested to him that he lend Tugboat Annie $12,500 to help her lease a hotel near a military installation, and that Prunty would receive fifty per cent of the profits. Prunty went through with the deal but it was a bad investment inasmuch as the authorities within one month closed up Tugboat Annie's establishment. "They claimed that she was running a house of prostitution," the businessman testified in an embarrassed voice. Sanford admitted he had casually introduced Prunty to Tugboat Annie, whom he was questioning about another matter, but denied that he induced Prunty to invest in her business.

The business Sanford was questioning Tugboat Annie about was still another story. Former Agent Burkett, whose curiosity touched off the Mooney and Schino investigations, in checking on Schino's actions, had discovered through an office file that was gathering dust that one W. D. Malloy, deputy in charge of the Salinas office, had been dunning Tugboat Annie for funds. Malloy made the mistake on June 25, 1946, of writing a letter to "Dear Dixie" on Treasury Department stationery. "I am most grateful for everything you did for me and I am wondering if you could let me have another $75 or $100 to complete my repair and painting job," the agent wrote the brothel keeper. ". . . Please use the enclosed envelope, which requires no postage, at your earliest convenience. Also come in and let me fix up your social security tax and withholding papers before August 1."

Senators Tobey, Wiley, and I, who heard Burkett's original testimony, called in the internal revenue collector for the district, James Smythe, to ask him about the Malloy case and the other matters. Smythe said that, although he thought it was a "reprehensible, stupid thing" for Malloy to do, he had recommended to Washington that "in view of the fact that this man had had some fourteen years of service and a good enough record in the bureau, that the commissioner show leniency. So the commissioner ordered us to retain him on our staff and he placed him on probation for a year." At this, Senator Tobey exploded: "Here he was playing with this madam here, a footy-footy deal . . . and all you did was to slap his wrist!"

"He didn't do anything dishonest; just stupid," Smythe protested.

"Oh, no!" Senator Tobey exclaimed. "He didn't do anything dishonest; he merely held her up for money and more money and more money. . . . My God! What has come over you here that you are not able to get sore about this thing and kick him out and knock him down the stairs, too? . . . Don't you have some sense of character in these things, you public servants?"

"I admit the punishment was lenient," Smythe mumbled, and Tobey thundered back: "It isn't any punishment at all! After getting off like that, he could get out in the street and sing a *Te Deum* to God. He could have a royal thanksgiving on this thing. Lenient! My God!"

The epilogue has been that Schino, Mooney, and Hartmann, Mooney's stock salesman, have been indicted on a charge of conspiring to defraud the government, in connection with the Jenkins case. At the time of this writing they were awaiting trial. Agent Malloy was dismissed from the service two weeks before our public hearings in California were scheduled to start—nearly five years after he wrote the letter to Tugboat Annie. Schino was not discharged from the service until after our second California hearings, and four days before the indictment against him was returned.

In justice to the internal revenue service in California and Nevada, I feel I should point out that these few employees were not typical of the many thousands of workers in the two offices. To the credit of the Treasury Department in Washington, it should be said that, though it was hard to convince the department originally that things were as bad as reported, it has acted with commendable firmness once action was started. The Treasury also has been one of the outstanding departments in taking positive steps, since the committee submitted its report, to put the brakes on the organized crime syndicates.

THE GANG WORLD OF MICKEY COHEN & CO. At one point in our discussion with Police Chief Parker, the tough Los Angeles cop who has made life miserable for Mickey Cohen in recent years, Senator Tobey inquired:

TOBEY: Is he [Cohen] nimble-witted?
PARKER: No; I would say he is essentially stupid. He is heavy-set and heavy-browed and quite ignorant. The private conversations we have been able to pick up do not indicate he is an intelligent or educated man.

Nevertheless, the chief continued, the Los Angeles Police Department does not go along with the theory that the little ex-pug has slipped and now is a second-rater in the crime world. Mickey, as a gambler and bookmaker, with far-flung interstate connections, an extortionist and all-round rackets boy, is decidedly important. Cohen's "business interests" invade many spheres, including prostitution, Chief Parker said. "We do know that the hotel . . . where his satellites are prone to gather has shown up in some of the call-girl operations," he testified. "I have some information that they must pay tribute, in order to carry on their business, to Cohen and his group, and failure to do so will lead to physical punishment."

Cohen, a simian figure, with a pendulous lower lip, thinning hair, and spreading paunch, appeared before us dressed in "sharp" clothing, including a suit coat of exaggerated length, excessively padded in the shoulders, and a hat with a ludicrously broad brim. We traced the story of his activities in recent years. Apart from the police harassment, Mickey's troubles—there have been at least five attempts to assassinate him—have been due to his falling out with the Sicilian-controlled Mafia element on the West Coast: this was the period of Mickey's $16,000 bulletproof Cadillac.

Mickey, in the parlance of the underworld, now is regarded as "an outlaw," we were told by Barney Ruditsky, a private sleuth. He is "not with the syndicate" and is fair game for poaching activities by any hoodlum. At one time, however, Cohen apparently had a working arrangement with mobster Jack Dragna, alias Antonio Rizzotti, once regarded by the California Crime Commission as "the Capone of Los Angeles" and described in our report as "a leader of the Mafia in California." Our report recounted how, in 1946, Cohen and Joe Sica, "undoubtedly acting on behalf of Jack I. Dragna, a leader of the Mafia in California," paid a call on Russell Brophy, son-in-law of the late James Ragen and local representative of Continental Press. Sica beat Brophy with his fists, while Mickey ripped the telephone from the wall and got in a few blows of his own. Later Dragna, after Ragen's murder, in Chicago, became a $500-a-week "employee" for a Continental Press dummy. Both Cohen and Sica, when we questioned them, admitted having slapped Brophy but each chivalrously claimed he didn't remember what the other had done with his fists. When Counsel Halley remarked to Cohen, "The Court apparently did think you both hit him; you were fined $100 and [Sica] was fined $200," Cohen gave us a sample of a mobster's brand of humor. "Then I must have hit him less," he said.

The gang situation in Los Angeles and the Hollywood area has changed since the aging Dragna has begun to lose his power. The up-and-coming gangster is Joe Sica. Sica, his brother, and others were under indictment in an important narcotics case, but the key witness, Abraham Davidian, was murdered, and the indictment against Sica and his codefendants had to be dropped. The Sica faction now is believed to be operating independently of Dragna, though Chief Parker's intelligence aide, Captain James Hamilton, told us that the Sica mob still was cutting in Dragna "for a certain share." Dragna is running out of money and complaining bitterly about it. After our concluding hearings in California he was picked up by police on a morals charge, and there is a possibility that immigration authorities may be able to deport him on grounds of moral turpitude.

Captain Hamilton, in describing Mickey, had told us: "He is a very excitable fellow. Under questioning he is very much inclined to blow his top. I talked to him on the telephone, and he was just screaming." When he testified before us Mickey started off calmly enough, but some time later our poker-faced Mr. Halley had brought him to the state described by the Los Angeles police officer. "I object to the way the man is questioning me," Mickey howled almost hysterically. ". . . He is asking me questions like that is the truth!"

"I have never been a strong-arm man for nobody," Cohen told us. "I have never bulldozed anybody in my life." His own testimony, however, was a series of contradictions of this remarkable statement. There was the time that one Max Shaman entered Mickey's "paint shop" (Mickey always seemed to have either a paint shop, a jewelry store, or a haberdashery on his string and some investigators are unkind enough to believe that he used these businesses as a front for his bookmaking operations). Mickey had had a fist fight with Shaman's brother, and Shaman "came in with his gun," Mickey related, to kill him. Mickey pulled his pistol out of the desk at which he was sitting, killed Shaman first, and was acquitted, he told us, on his plea of self-defense.

There was at least one other arrest on suspicion of murder, and an assortment of beatings which Cohen admitted he had administered to various characters. One victim, for example, was Hymie Miller, a rival bookie. Some years after the beating, which was precipitated by "harsh words," Cohen borrowed

$5000 from Hymie and has not repaid it. When he calls Mickey about it, Hymie told us, "he says he hasn't got it."

Mickey painted us a lugubrious picture of his financial situation. All the money he had in the world was in his pocket, he said; after reaching in his pocket and checking his roll—a stunt already performed for us in Kansas City by gangster Tony Gizzo—Mickey sadly told us it came to only $286. However, in the past four years Cohen had "borrowed" approximately $300,000, he said, from various sources. Most remarkable of all his loans was the $35,000 he said he had been able to borrow from the president of a Hollywood bank, without giving a note or paying any interest. This $35,000, Cohen said, was the banker's "personal money," not bank funds. "He is a very fine man," Mickey explained. "He just happens to like me." The Hollywood bank president, incidentally, has been disassociated from his bank.

"What do you do for them," I inquired, "that makes them so generous with you?" Cohen replied: "I can't answer that; they must just like me." At this Senator Tobey murmured: "In the days when they used to have those old-fashioned writing books with the copperplate on top, there was something on them that said: 'Character is the basis of credit'!"

Finally we questioned Mickey about the activities of a man who had been described to us by police as one of his closest lieutenants and strong-arm men, twenty-five-year-old Johnnie Stompanato, whom Mickey described as "a nice fellow . . . a good boy." Halley asked:

Q. . . . Was he [Stompanato] a man of wealth?
A. I don't know that. I know he was able to get some money someplace. . . .
Q. He borrowed very large sums of money from a rich man; did he not?
A. That is right; yes.
Q. Isn't it a fact that the government is now charging that he got that money by extortion?
A. I don't think so; I think it is not a fact.

Then Halley read into the record an official statement by an internal revenue agent who had conducted an examination of Stompanato. The form, which had been subpoenaed from Cohen's own accountant, stated:

"The Government intends to try to make a showing Mr. Stompanato, that Mr. Blank is a very wealthy man without too much business experience. That in 1948 and 1949 he was blackmailed by various persons for amounts in excess of $65,000."

"That is a very funny question," Cohen mused. "He [Stompanato] just had dinner with the fellow three nights ago. I don't think he would have had dinner with the fellow three nights ago if he blackmailed him. It don't seem possible. On what grounds would Stompanato blackmail anybody?"

Halley said, "I am trying to find out how you and Stompanato succeeded in persuading people to loan you large sums of money."

"I can only answer for myself," Mickey replied coldly. "If you want Stompanato you can ask him."

In exploring the financial operations of the little gangster, the committee had uncovered some interesting facts on Mickey's method of reporting income to the government. It consisted of supplying a few unsubstantiated and undocumented figures to his accountant, Harry Sackman, of Beverly Hills. Some items as large as $10,000 were described merely as receipts from "Various Commissions." "Do you get away with that?" Halley asked the auditor. Sackman replied: "I always ask him each year to give me the detail on it. I tell him the law. But he says, 'Well, here is the figure and this is the only thing I can present to you.' Therefore, on that basis I file the return with the government."

These financial operations interested the Internal Revenue Bureau, too, and a month after our final hearings Cohen and his blond wife Lavonne were indicted for alleged income tax evasion over a period of three years. Instead of paying taxes on approximately $318,500 income, they reported and paid on only $87,500, the government contends. If convicted, Mickey can be fined $40,000 and sentenced to jail for a maximum of twenty years.

THE $1,000,000 WORLD OF LOBBYIST SAMISH. The *pièce de résistance* of our West Coast investigation was the appearance of that incredible character, Arthur H. Samish, the $1,000,000 lobbyist. The people of California have had snatches of the squalid story told them before, but never in quite such detail direct from the lips of the master lobbyist himself. The question now is: will they continue to stand for it?

In both personality and physique Samish is a remarkable figure. Physically, he stands over six feet two inches in height and must weigh better than three hundred pounds. He is bald with a monk's tonsure of gray fringe, and his face has the bland innocence of an *enfant terrible* about to light a giant firecracker under his nurse's chair. In manner, he is a combination of Falstaff, Little Boy Blue, and Machiavelli, crossed with an eel. He gesticulates freely in the grand style, sometimes stabbing the air with his horn-rimmed glasses, sometimes fiddling with his watch chain, a heavy affair of white gold or platinum, made up of large links which form and repeat his initials— A H S. He speaks magniloquently: "I am here to co-operate" and "Just let me help you a little further," he would boom at us—all the while, of course, failing to produce canceled checks from his lobbying account that we sought. He could be cute too: "May I explain that away, please?" he would wheedle in what I surmised was supposed to be a winning manner.

He didn't win me or any of the committee staff, however. I kept thinking of the tough, hard side of the boss political lobbyist, who also had his links with the underworld. We kept hearing of connections and coincidences involving Samish and Mickey Cohen. Samish himself admitted he regularly took the baths at Hot Springs, Arkansas, one of the gangster-favored resorts, where, on his last trip, he met the East Coast gangster, Joe Adonis. "Have you ever met Adonis any place outside of Hot Springs?" asked Associate Counsel Rice, and Samish, now peevish instead of arch, snapped back: "Oh, I might have seen

J ACOB (Greasy Thumb) G UZIK, reputed money handler for the late Al Capone. Refused to answer questions "on grounds it might tend"—etc. Had no lawyer but said he had heard the phrase "on the television"

Louis (Little New York) Campagna (*left*) and Paul (The Waiter) Ricca stand in show-up line for questioning after death of ex-policeman William Drury

ANTHONY J. (Tony) **ACCARDO**, heir to Al Capone's Chicago mob, refused to talk

Photo by Morris Gordon

(ABOVE) A "horse room." The photographer had to take it on the run after making this picture. (BELOW) Giant binoculars, used to get race results from Santa Anita at distance of one mile from the track, are examined by an investigator

Acme

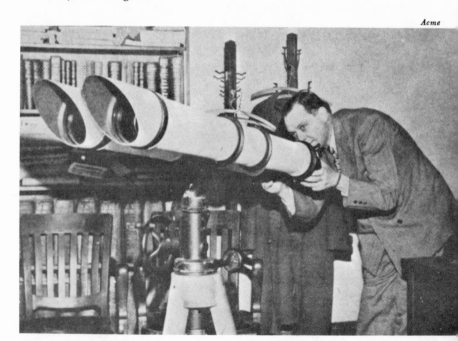

RUDOLPH HALLEY, chief counsel, explains underworld chart to Senators Kefauver (*seated*) and Wiley, of the committee

Myron Ehrlich, Washington attorney, presents paid bills for a racing news service operated by Tano Lococo (*left*) and Eddie (Spitz) Osadchey

FINANCE

Tony Gizzo, friend of the late Charles Binaggio, counts out $2500 when Senator Wiley asks him how much money he is carrying at the moment

Mobster Mickey Cohen looks bored as he waits to explain his income to the committee in California

(*Left*) Carlos Marcello, branded "one of the leading criminals in the United States," at the hearings in New Orleans. There is considerable competition for the title. (*Right*) Nono Minaudo testifies before the committee in Detroit

him around New York." While in Hot Springs he also put in a long-distance call to gambler Dandy Phil Kastel, who looks after Frank Costello's interests in New Orleans.

Before we ever encountered Samish in San Francisco we knew a good deal about him. Our investigators had prepared a thorough and impressive dossier. At the hearing Samish finally yielded some of his personal—though few of his business—records. From his 1949 tax return we knew his gross reported income had been $143,697.09, which shrunk, after his liberal deductions, to $86,923.90. Of this income, $90,999.94 represented fees from his "public relations" clients. The principal contributor was the California State Brewers' Institute, which provided a modest $30,000 in salary and expenses, plus control of a $153,000-a-year slush fund. Schenley Distillers of New York also paid him $36,000 a year, for which sum Samish said he was "callable." The rest of his income came from other clients, dividends, and miscellaneous holdings.

We also had heard in Los Angeles from Howard R. Philbrick, former investigator for a California legislative committee, who in 1938 submitted a report to a former governor of California tracing in great detail, with names, dates, and places, how Samish had operated with California legislators. Said the Philbrick report: "The principal source of corruption has been money pressure. . . . The principal offender among lobbyists has been Arthur H. Samish. . . ." It then went on to trace Samish's cash contributions to various legislators. It was the Philbrick report which quoted and credited to Samish the famous declaration that he was "the governor of the legislature" and "to hell with the governor of the state."

In so far as practical results were concerned, however, nothing came of the Philbrick report. The document itself has become something of a collector's item, since all the copies printed for sale to the public by the state printer "suddenly and rather mysteriously disappeared." The report also was expunged from the official journal of the California Senate so that the record for that day does not carry the text of the study on Samish.

Our committee's hearings added an up-to-date incident to the Philbrick report's record when we developed the details of how Samish enabled an influential state senator, Ralph Swing, to buy for $500 a twenty per cent interest in a new liquor distributorship that was being formed by Alfred Hart, one of Samish's friends. Between 1943 and 1947, when he finally disposed of his interests, Senator Swing, in addition to dividends paid over the years, received the sum of $40,000. "It was very pleasing to Mr. Samish to have some participation in getting Mr. Swing a good business deal like that?" I asked the attorney for the distributorship who told us of the transaction. "Well," he replied, "I think it is fair to say that it was a feather in his cap."

Samish was called up three times in our two days of public hearings in San Francisco. He was the first and the last witness to take the chair. This was because Investigator Amis, our specialist in tracing tangled figures, had been unable to get hold of Samish previously to require him to produce his records in response to the committee's subpoena. With the press photographers' flash bulbs popping, Samish made a great show of turning over a mass of papers which were supposed to contain, as Samish sonorously intoned, "everything complete for the last ten years."

While Amis combed over the papers we got on with our interrogation of James G. Hamilton, secretary of the California State Brewers' Institute, an association representing eleven of the fourteen California brewing companies. The State Brewers' Institute's charter says one of its purposes is "to educate and elevate the minds of men." Hamilton told us of the financial arrangements the institute has set up to achieve this noble purpose. The association, which is a non-profit organization, has two funds. One is an "operating expense" fund, raised by taxing the member brewers a sliding-scale levy ranging from 3 to 4 cents on each barrel of beer produced by the member. (For purpose of simplicity we called this the "4-cent fund" throughout our examination.) Over a period of six years the total of this fund came to more than $500,000, and, for tax purposes, the eleven individual brewers deducted the entire amount of their contributions. The institute, of course, as a non-profit organization, paid no tax either. Digging away with Secretary Hamilton in the attempt to discover how the institute proceeded "to educate and elevate the minds of men" with the aid of this tax-free fund, we learned that a great deal of the money had been spent in 1948, to mention just one example, on opposing a local option prohibition referendum.

Then there was the special so-called "5-cent fund," set up under terms of a 1935 contract between Samish and the brewers. For every barrel of beer produced the brewers paid 5 cents into a fund which Samish spent as he saw fit. The individual members also charged off fifty per cent of this contribution as a deductible business expense. This was on the theory, as expounded by Secretary Hamilton, that, though funds collected "for so-called political purposes" are not deductible, money spent "to establish good will or protect the industry" is an allowable tax deduction. Associate Counsel Rice asked:

Q. . . . Do you know how the fifty-fifty ratio was arrived at?
HAMILTON: I don't know how it was arrived at. No, sir; I don't know.

Into the 5-cent "Samish fund," over a period of six years, as of December 31, 1950, a total of $953,943.19 has flowed. As of the date mentioned, all but $43,913.29 of the $935,000 had been spent by sole and exclusive direction of Samish. Some of it, he admitted under intensive examination, went to pay his own personal hotel expenses when he presumably was engaged in business for the institute. Yet in his own tax returns there was no mention of any part of this huge sum.

That Samish was the dictator over the "5-cent fund" was indisputable. The lobbyist himself told us that "checks are drawn against that fund at my request." Hamilton explained that three officers of the institute were required to sign the checks in the amounts requested by Samish, but that "for practical purposes" Samish was in complete control of the account.

One of the brewers, William P. Baker, whose signature was required on the "Samish fund" checks, said he never questioned any checks which were presented him for signature. Of the other two men whose signatures were required on the checks, Joseph Goldie was reported sick and "ordered by his doctor not to leave the house," and Karl Schuster, president of the institute, was off somewhere and simply couldn't be found.

The fireworks began after Investigator Amis had gone over the books and records which Samish had turned over with flourishes. It developed that Samish's personal records and books were in understandable shape, but there were no records concerning the "Samish fund" of nearly $1,000,000. We summoned Samish's accountant, one H. T. Hoertkorn, to ask him about it and got the astonishing reply: "I'm not aware that there are any books and records on that particular account. I have not seen any books and records." What happened, I asked, to the canceled checks? "At the end of every month," the accountant said, "the checks are given to Mr. Samish, and at that time he destroys them." "How about the check stubs?" I pursued. "Don't they have a book to write stubs out on?" "That," said Hoertkorn, "I don't know."

The accountant's ingenuous explanation for all this was a classic: in the contract between the institute and Samish, he related, it is specified that Samish's "total compensation, including expenses," shall be $2500 a month. Samish reported this amount in his tax return; therefore there was no need for Samish to keep any records on the $1,000,000 account!

With this, we put out a call for a Miss Ready and a Miss Martinell who worked in Samish's office, a repeat call for Secretary Hamilton of the Brewers' Institute, and a request for the presence of Oscar Koehn, bookkeeper for the institute, who worked directly in Hamilton's office. They all were to appear on the next day, the second day of the hearing, which, it so happened, fell on a Saturday. When Saturday came Hamilton appeared to tell us that Koehn was out of town. In the colloquy Samish popped up to "explain" that we had come at a difficult time, since "we have a 40-hour week" and everybody left on Friday.

Holding back my exasperation, I ordered a subpoena issued for the missing bookkeeper; then inquired:

THE CHAIRMAN: Who keeps these check stubs, Mr. Hamilton? That is what I want to know.

HAMILTON: If anybody does it would be Koehn—if there are any.

THE CHAIRMAN: "If there are any?"

HAMILTON: I have no knowledge of that account whatsoever, sir. . . .

THE CHAIRMAN: Does Mr. Koehn work in your office?

HAMILTON: He works in my office, yes.

THE CHAIRMAN: This is the strangest thing I ever saw. How about Miss Ready? Is she out of town, Mr. Samish?

SAMISH (*standing up*): On vacation.

THE CHAIRMAN: Where is she?

SAMISH: That I couldn't tell you, Senator. But she wouldn't know as much about that as I would.

THE CHAIRMAN: Let's see if there is any possibility of locating Miss Ready. And how about Miss Martinell?

SAMISH: Well, she doesn't know anything about that.

THE CHAIRMAN: Where is Miss Martinell?

SAMISH: I couldn't tell you.

THE CHAIRMAN: Does she live here in town?

SAMISH: Yes, sir; I guess so. That I don't know.

We had Samish, though, and we asked him what happened to the checks and stubs. "It seems fantastic," I told him, "that there are no check stubs kept of checks written on this fund. Also, I can't understand why the checks should be thrown away when they come back and why something isn't kept in a little book. . . . The Internal Revenue law requires it, Mr. Samish." Samish, of course, knew nothing about the check-books containing the stubs, because the missing Mr. Koehn handled those, but, as for the canceled checks, he knew where they went and he enlightened us:

"At the end of month, the bank statement, reconciled, is mailed to my office [by the Brewers' Institute] together with canceled checks. I sometimes look at them and sometimes I don't. And I destroy them by throwing them in the wastebasket."

Later that day, after the gambits of the missing checkbooks and the week-ending witnesses had been played out fully, we finally put Samish in the witness chair for his detailed interrogation. In retrospect I think of his performance as a struggle between deep-sea anglers and some monster game fish. The bulky Samish fought us tenaciously and with the shrewdness of vast experience. He would take the line, pull furiously against it, then double back in an attempt to foul it or get off the hook. In the end, however, we had him all but landed. He was almost entirely "in the boat"—perhaps the nets of the Internal Revenue Bureau and the state of California will be used to complete the job of landing him.

The list of clients for which Samish did legislative lobbying and other services over the years was impressive. At the time he appeared before us his main interests were the Brewers' Institute, the Motor Carriers' Association, Schenley spirits, Philip Morris cigarettes, Yellow Cab, and a Los Angeles restaurant. As one example of how he worked, Samish disclosed that, before the 1950 election, he had written a memorandum which went to all of California's 43,000 retail liquor licensees. In it he urged them not to make any political contributions or commitments to "any candidate" until they had received the recommendations of "an industry-wide committee." This committee, in effect, was dominated by Samish.

For a man who didn't clutter up his files with things such as canceled checks, bank statements, or anything else that would show how he spent nearly $1,000,000 in six years, Samish had been remarkably meticulous about preserving commendatory letters written him by various organizations. For almost an hour he treated us to what amounted to a filibuster while he read into the record these letters and other material attesting what a fine man Arthur Samish was. I gave him his head on this point, letting him read his testimonials to his heart's content. When he was all through I said, "Now then, tell us about how the California Brewers' Institute operates."

We were not entirely without information on which to question Samish concerning his expenditures. Earlier, when we had been hammering at him to produce some records pertaining to the $1,000,000 fund, he finally relinquished to us, through his accountant, Hoertkorn, a typewritten "analysis" of the status of the "Samish fund" from September 30, 1949, to the end of February 1951. The document, we were told by Hoertkorn, had been prepared from a work sheet handwritten by Koehn, the missing accountant for the Brewers' Institute. The papers, Hoertkorn said, had been handed him only that morning by Samish.

It wasn't much of an "analysis," because it merely showed that most of the big checks—in amounts ranging from $10,000 to $40,000—were made out to "cash" or "contributions." But with this evidence we secured Samish's admission that " 'cash' and 'contributions' are the same thing," and that these items in most cases meant that money was distributed by him personally to "good, honest, outstanding officials that subscribed to the temperate use of beer, wine, and spirits. . . ." Earlier he had told us: "I make the decisions."

He further said it had been his practice to give the money to the candidates in cash and that he demanded no receipts from them. I commented that he might have been better off to get the legislator's names on a canceled check just in case "one of these legislators tried to jump the corner," but he demurred:

SAMISH: We don't do it that way. As long as we know that a man who is elected to office is more or less temperate in his thinking and is a good, honest, and outstanding official, we don't——

THE CHAIRMAN: And a little wet?

SAMISH: And a little wet.

THE CHAIRMAN: . . . And a little willing to listen to Arthur
Samish on legislation?

SAMISH: No; wait a minute. I can explain that. . . .

Samish couldn't explain it very well, however. What it boiled
down to was that the lion's share of the money paid into the
"Samish fund" by the Brewers' Institute, on which the brewers
took a fifty per cent income tax deduction, had been parceled
out by Samish in the form of cash to politicians, with no records
kept. He admitted that he played both sides of the street and
made contributions to candidates of both major parties, but he
couldn't seem to remember to whom he gave the money. For
instance:

Q. (*By Rice.*) . . . We are trying to find out where the money
went, physically; whose hands it got into.
SAMISH: Well, it comes into mine.
Q. And then where does it go from yours?
A. It is given in contributions.
Q. To whom?
A. To different campaigns.
Q. Name one.
A. Well, I don't keep a record of that. I would be glad to see
if—to see if I can find it for you.

After this had gone on for a while I remarked to Mr. Samish
that I doubted that these practices could be justified under
the Federal Corrupt Practices Act in instances where any part
of the money went to candidates for federal office. I also told
him I did not see how the corporations comprising the Brewers' Institute, which are prohibited by law from making political contributions, could get away with putting the money
in a so-called trust fund and letting Samish, as their agent,
"pay it out for political purposes." "Suppose the internal revenue people come along?" I asked him. "How are you going to
be able to tell them what this money has been used for?"
"Well," Samish boomed, "when that time comes, I think the

only thing I can do is to be as honest and factual as I am trying to be with you."

Samish's personal deductions also presented some problems. He admitted that his $2500 monthly check from the brewers included "expenses"; that, on top of this, some of his hotel bills at least were paid out of the big fund. And that certain entertainment expenses were taken care of by both the 5-cent fund and the 4-cent fund of the Brewers' Institute. Yet in 1949 he claimed $13,899.35 as a personal deduction for "entertaining." Rice asked:

Q. What is that for?
SAMISH: Oh, I can't give you any details. . . .
Q. In general, who is entertained $13,000 worth?
A. I can't tell you. If you want to ask or inquire about those things, I think our tax consultant . . . will explain things to your satisfaction.
Q. Is he the one who spends the money?
A. It isn't a question of that. . . . I just don't know, Mr. Rice.

The examination closed with Samish elaborately assuring us that henceforth everything was going to be done by check and that full records would be kept. He promised us at least a dozen times—and the spectators in the hearing room and the vast television audience heard him—that he would make up for the missing records by going to the bank and "reconstructing" where every check had gone over the past decade. The committee left Investigator Amis in California to work with Samish on this promise. Nothing at all resulted. It was impossible, of course, as we had anticipated, to reconstruct the expenditures record, as the particular bank where the Brewers' Institute kept the $1,000,000 account had no microfilm records of the checks.

Was Samish clever in fencing with the committee as he did? Undoubtedly there was a certain advantage to him in withholding information from us that could have been damaging to him. Yet before the bar of public opinion I think he con-

victed himself. The checkbooks "filed in the wastebasket" . . .
the missing secretaries, accountants, and directors . . . it simply
did not look good.

The committee has recommended to the Commissioner of
Internal Revenue and to the Attorney General of the United
States that a thorough examination of the practices of the California State Brewers' Institute and the individual members be
conducted. We proposed that the deductions of nearly
$2,000,000 which the brewers have taken for their contributions
to the two funds expended principally by Samish be disallowed,
and that steps be taken to recover the taxes due, plus interest.

What will be done by the government and by the state of
California in regard to Samish personally remains to be seen.
In March 1951 a California legislative committee did leave the
name of Arthur Samish off its list of approved lobbyists.

The Senate Crime Committee has been specific in its recommendations to the appropriate federal authorities that a double-
barreled investigation of Samish should be undertaken. First,
the Attorney General has been asked to investigate the possibility that the lobbyist may have violated the Federal Corrupt
Practices Act. Second, it has been suggested to the Internal
Revenue Commissioner that Samish be assessed for $935,943.19,
the admitted six-year total of the "Samish fund," as additional
income, and that he be taxed for this amount, with interest,
"unless he is able to show that the money was expended for
properly deductible purposes."

It was the opinion of the committee, duly expressed to the
United States Senate, that: ". . . From the record it could be
said that the money went into Samish's own pocket . . ." But
so labyrinthine were Mr. Samish's operations, and so scarce the
documentary evidences of them, that whether the money
stopped there or went further the committee was unable to
determine.

CHAPTER 18

HOW THE LAWS ARE ENFORCED
IN UPSTATE NEW YORK

S THE Senate Crime Committee followed the trail of the national crime syndicate across the country, evidence in every city where we conducted investigations pointed in some fashion to New York City. By the time we came to New York for open hearings in March 1951 we knew that the big city and surrounding area ranked with Chicago as one of the two hubs on which the national crime axis revolved. America's largest metropolis, nerve center of much of the financial and industrial life of this great nation, also was a nerve center of the underworld. Crimewise, it was the capital of the so-called "prime minister" of the underworld, Frank Costello, and of other malevolent proconsuls of hoodlumdom, such as Joe Adonis, Albert Anastasia, Frank Erickson, Meyer Lansky, and their host of ruthless lieutenants. At the time of our New York hearings the city was in the throes of various political upheavals and investigations aimed at rooting out the unhealthy links between organized crime and politics.

The public hearings in New York City, conducted just a few

weeks before we were scheduled to submit our final report to the Senate, prior to the decision to extend the life of the committee, focused greater attention on our work than anything that had gone before. Our New York investigation, however, was not confined to the metropolis itself; nor was it limited to the eight days that took the nation by storm via the television channels. Months earlier we had conducted closed sessions in Manhattan at which we probed the workings of a vicious New York-New Jersey gambling ring which, operating across state lines, had been fleecing the public on a multimillion-dollar scale. Also we directed our attention upstate to Saratoga Springs, turning the spotlight of exposure on the flagrant operation of gambling establishments, in which both New York City and out-of-state hoodlums had a hand. The evidence left little doubt that these had the acquiescence of Saratoga police, and we extracted admissions from the high brass of the New York State Police that they had known about it. One result of the Saratoga exposures was that Governor Thomas E. Dewey, whose abstention from co-operation with the committee was, to say the least, disappointing, convened a special grand jury to investigate the conditions to which we called attention.

The Senate Crime Committee which I had the honor to head by no means claims that all the avenues it explored in the New York area were our discoveries. Investigations of such scope are tedious, painstaking propositions that sometimes require years to develop. While our own investigators turned up many fresh leads, we were given invaluable assistance in many instances by local authorities. In behalf of the whole committee, I express particular thanks to District Attorney Frank Hogan of New York County, who, with his diligent staff, has been hammering away for years at criminal and political corruption. The same grateful and unstinted acknowledgment goes to District Attorney Miles McDonald of Kings County, who was pushing ahead courageously and effectively with a grand jury probe of links between bookmaking and police corruption in Brooklyn. Both of these outstanding officials unselfishly assisted our committee, and they and many others who aided us, including Judge Samuel S. Leibowitz, deserve full credit. At the same time I believe that our Senate Committee performed a function that will be of unique and considerable aid to these and other conscientious public officials. With our broad latitude of inquiry, our carefully assembled blueprint of the mob's nationwide methods of operation, and the deadly anti-gangster weapon President Truman placed in our hands when he permitted us, through Executive Order, to examine income tax returns of lawbreakers, the committee placed on the record a mass of information that will be a big stick, indeed, to any public official or prosecutor who wants to use it against political criminals and criminal politicians. Also the force of public opinion which the committee marshaled against continued complacence toward politico-criminal corruption was a tremendous and, to me, inspiring thing.

In our closed hearings in New York in October 1950 we examined the details of a gigantic gambling ring in Bergen County, New Jersey, just across the Hudson River from New York City. These gambling operations had become so open and notorious that there finally had been a partial crackdown by the authorities. At the time of our hearings only one of the operators, Anthony Guarini, who seemed to have been the front man for the ring, had been sent to jail. Some three months after our hearings, however, gambling indictments were returned against Joe Adonis, Salvatore Moretti (alias Solly Moore), Arthur Longano, James (Piggy) Lynch, and Guarini. Evidence turned up by the Senate Crime Committee was an important factor in the cases against Adonis and his henchmen. In May 1951 the five of them entered pleas of "non vult"—a legal procedure meaning they admitted no guilt but would not defend themselves. They were fined $15,000 each and sentenced to jail. Adonis was ordered to serve a term of two to three years. It was the first time in the career of this archracketeer that prison doors ever closed on him.

The utter viciousness of the gambling racket as practiced by the professionals—and the hopelessness of winning against it—

is best told in the testimony of one of the numerous "suckers" questioned by the committee. He was a highly nervous $46,000-a-year secretary-treasurer of a reputable firm which, he said, has 23,000 clients. In addition to the sizable sum he lost, he was afraid of the effect that disclosure of his folly—"I don't want these corporations to know that I go in and gamble"—might have on his customers. Out of consideration for the man, who already had suffered considerably, I will refrain from mentioning his name here.

The story of how the sucker and his money were parted was unfolded by Counsel Halley as follows:

HALLEY: In the year 1948 did you lose certain moneys gambling?

VICTIM: I did.

Q. Was the total of that $19,700?

A. I wouldn't say that was the total. It might have been in checks, but I took back some cash—maybe $4500 in cash.

Q. Where did you lose this money?

A. In a place over in Jersey.

Q. Do you know where the place is?

A. No. All I know is that I was taken in an automobile . . . over the George Washington Bridge. You ride for about three quarters of an hour, and then there is a place where they have secondhand automobile cars, and they take you through a driveway into a dark spot. There was some man with a little service light that opens the door and lets you in. There was a party of five of us including my wife.

Q. How did you arrange to go?

A. While I was sitting in the lobby [of his hotel], to my sorrow, a fellow who was in the fur business said he heard of a gambling place over in Jersey where you can get a nice steak dinner free. They serve a wonderful meal, he said. . . . I said to my wife, "Do you want to go over to a gambling place in Jersey?" I said, "We will lose a couple of hundred dollars and come back." Instead of losing a couple of hundred dollars, we lost $800.

So the sucker went back on three occasions after that to "re-coup his losses." Before they were through with him he had lost more than $14,000. "I was just a damned fool," he told us.

Describing the place, which we learned was in Lodi, New Jersey, he said there were two to three hundred people playing dice, roulette, and chemin de fer every time he went there. There was at least $2000 on the dice table at every play, with people standing "three abreast and everybody fighting to get in to the table."

The irony of the situation was emphasized when Halley inquired if the victim ever got the free dinner. "Free dinner! By golly, it was the most expensive dinner I ever ate in my life!" the victim exploded. "Listen," he went on, "I wish to God that you would stop all that gambling throughout the United States, and if I could help you, I would be the first one to come to the front for you." Truly, this was the voice of experience.

From testimony of a Newark, New Jersey, certified public accountant, I. George Goldstein, we began to fill out the picture of the New Jersey gambling operations. He acknowledged that for some years he has handled tax returns for "the New Jersey gambling partnerships." He said he first was brought into this work in 1945 by Anthony Guarini, the convicted gambler. The first work was done for an outfit known as G & R Trading Company, which actually was a gambling partnership. Then there was work for other outfits known as L & C, B & T, Pal Trading Company, and General Trading Company. Profits from one or more of these various companies, Goldstein testified, were shared by Guarini James Rutkin, Joe Adonis, Gerald Catena, Salvatore Moretti, and James Lynch. It was big business. Actually there is no way of telling exactly how much the casinos did take in, as Goldstein admitted he made out the tax returns merely from figures brought in by Guarini, which were not based on any real audit. But G & R Trading Company, for example, admitted itself to gross receipts of $488,698 in its 1945-46 tax return. After deductions for "overhead" there remained an admitted net profit of $255,271, which was divided between the G & R partners as follows: Adonis, $76,581; Rutkin, $51,054; Catena, $51,054; Guarini, $38,290; and Moretti, $38,290.

We learned that Goldstein's tax work also branched out to other gambling operations in Saratoga, Miami, and New Orleans, in which, in addition to some of the above-mentioned gamblers, interests were held by such underworld characters as Meyer Lansky, Frank Costello, and Dandy Phil Kastel. Goldstein also said he handled some of Longie Zwillman's "legitimate" business.

The auditor particularly aroused Senator Tobey's wrath when he told how there were "no bank accounts" for the New Jersey operations. "You weren't suspicious of that kind of vermin?" Senator Tobey demanded. ". . . I want to know the ethics about it. . . . Don't you know that . . . a man who was concealing money in cigar boxes is trying to conceal the facts? You were aiding and abetting him." But the auditor merely answered that in his opinion there was "no concealment."

Still another businesslike facet of the gambling casino operation was their method of converting into cash the sizable checks taken from their victims. There was a man named Max Stark—since sent to jail by District Attorney Hogan—who was the "check cashier" for the North Jersey gambling mob. Daily he would bring to the Merchants Bank of New York City, a small institution, some sixty to seventy checks that had been given by losers at the gambling casinos. Over a period of about six months the checks brought in by Stark came to approximately $5,000,000. Stark, conveniently, had become a stockholder in the bank that he utilized to collect the checks for him; he owned 2000 shares, which was ten per cent of the bank's stock. The vice-president of the bank told us that he asked Stark where he got the checks, and Stark replied he was "cashing them for some person, that he has acquired them from some games in Jersey."

Q. (*By Halley.*) Did he elaborate whether he meant gambling games?

A. I don't remember whether he elaborated gambling games or not.

Q. You didn't think it was tennis or ping-pong, did you?

A. No.

Q. What did you think?

A. Some kind of games.

Another New Jersey operator examined by the committee was Willie Moretti, born Guarino Moretti, alias Willie Moore. The fifty-six-year-old Moretti, older brother of Salvatore Moretti, was—and is—a big-time gambler, and, more lately, an official and one-seventh owner of a big laundry and linen supply company. Willie, ravaged in appearance and garrulous in manner, let slip a great many scraps of information about the East Coast mob; and I suspect he could have told us a great deal more had he been completely frank.

We questioned Willie in Washington because, at the time we wanted him in New York, his physician and his attorney both advised us Willie was ill—a continuation of an old nervous disorder. Even in Washington, when Willie seemed in fine shape, his attorney kept interrupting at intervals to caution us that Willie was a sick man who frequently got "confused" and talked a lot. Concern over Willie's talkativeness, apparently, was not an isolated phenomenon. When rackets boss Frank Costello was testifying months later Counsel Halley taxed him with ordering Moretti to go to California in 1943 and "keep his mouth shut." When Costello indignantly denied it Halley quoted transcripts of telephone wire taps, legally obtained by court order, which showed that Moretti called Costello "Chief," and that Costello at various times told him: ". . . Rest and don't call me so much." . . . "Stay away from the telephone." . . . "Don't talk too much; you know. . . ." Costello insisted he was just giving a little friendly health advice to a sick friend.

Excerpts from Moretti's rambling testimony are worth quoting, both for the information revealed and for the psychological study conveyed of a typical boastful racketeer. Willie, who was born and grew up in the Harlem district, started off with the old refrain we heard from dozens of racketeers: that the numerous arrests and the scattering of convictions in his unsavory career were due to misunderstandings. The first time Willie was misunderstood was in 1913 when he was sent up for five years for second-degree assault; that one happened because "some barber said I tried to hit him and take money off him so they charged me with robbery; it was no more robbery than sitting here." Next time he just happened to be standing on a street corner in Harlem minding his business, when he heard "some shooting." There was a fellow lying on the sidewalk, so Willie toted him to the hospital. "While they were taking the clothes off him a gun fell out of his pocket, so I took the gun and put it in my pocket," said Willie. "I come out of the hospital to give it to the Police Department. I got caught coming out of the hospital with a gun in my pocket." The same judge who had sent him up for assault gave him a two-year suspended sentence, warning him, "Next time you hear shooting, turn the other way and don't take any guns out of people's pockets."

It was always like that, Willie went on. When he went over to live in New Jersey in the thirties the "politicians" got a misguided idea that Willie was a "numbers" king, so they "put ten disorderly house charges against me." Willie didn't like the sound of that. "I had three daughters going to school," he explained, and he didn't want people thinking he was mixed up with "ill-famed houses." So he made a deal with the prosecutor, he said, to have the charge changed to "conspiracy," to which he pleaded guilty. However, as he told us, "they found out through records themselves that I was innocent," so they let him off with a suspended sentence again.

"Why," asked Halley, "did you plead guilty?" "Just because I wanted to get it over with," Moretti, in the manner of a tolerant father explaining things to a backward child, informed him. "Everybody else went to the can." But Halley pressed on:

Q. What was your business in 1934?
A. I had no business.
Q. You were a gambler?
A. Yes, sir.

There were other similar "misunderstandings," Willie went on—a highway robbery charge in Philadelphia; a murder charge in New Jersey, and so on. Willie admitted that he knew Tony Guarini—"I stood up for him when he got married"—and the other principals in the northern New Jersey gambling ring, including, of course, Willie's brother Salvatore, but he insisted he had no piece of the business himself. We also took him through a list of most of the leading gangsters of America, and with only a few exceptions, Willie knew them all.

HALLEY: Aren't these people we have been talking about . . . what you would call rackets boys?
MORETTI: Jeez, everything is a racket today. (*Laughter.*) . . .
HALLEY: These people come from a great many different cities around the country. . . . How do you get to meet all of these people . . . ?
MORETTI: Well, you go to race tracks and you go to Florida, and you meet them; and the man that is well known meets everybody; you know that.

But how, for instance, Halley persisted, had Willie come to meet, say, the late Al Capone? (Willie had testified he had known Al "very well.") Displaying a little impatience, Willie said he'd met Capone, naturally, "at a race track."

Q. Who introduced you?
A. Listen, well-charactered people, you don't need introductions; you just meet automatically.

After Moretti said he also had a lot of politician friends Halley asked him if he belonged to any political clubs. "I don't belong to any; I am a bipartisan," Moretti answered. Enjoying his own joke, the incredible gambler went on to boast that he didn't "operate politically"; that, if he did, he might have become a member of Congress—"maybe sitting where you are."

We then took up the story of how Moretti moved into the laundry business. It came about through three of his fellow defendants—Johnny Welsh and Ben and Mark Golden—in the 1934 "numbers" prosecution. They were less fortunate than Willie, for they were sentenced to serve six months each, he said. "When they come out . . . they had a proposition of a linen business," Moretti went on. "Being I'm well known by everybody, they took me in with them. . . . They made me president of the firm. We called it the U. S. Linen Supply business."

HALLEY: Were you made president because you were a well-known character?

MORETTI: Just because a lot of people know me and I can get business, that's all. . . .

Halley went on to ask Willie about some old charges filed with a grand jury by a long-established competitor in the same Jersey area that Moretti was taking business away from them by "strong-arm" methods. It was all a lie, Willie said; he did business in "a polite way," and he increased the earnings of his outfit, now set up in two companies known as U. S. Linen Supply and U. S. Linen Laundry Service, from $1800 to $13,500 a week. Even the firm that had complained about him now has merged with his company. "Fortunately, God helped me," he explained; the president of the rival outfit "went horseback riding, fell off the horse, got kicked in the head . . . and died, so his company became my partners." Moretti said he had been offered $850,000 for the business—one seventh of which is his —but that he refused to sell.

We were interested in how Willie apparently had been able to get the inside track on buying a block-long plant in Paterson, New Jersey, on a tax sale; it was worth $400,000, he said, but he got it for $10,000. He also told us he got one of his New Jersey houses—the one he calls "The Moretti Estate"—on a foreclosure for $16,250, and that it is worth $250,000. His other home is just a modest place he built in 1947 for $45,000.

Willie was able to tell us that he keeps $30,000 in cash lying somewhere around the house; that he and his family stay in a $75-a-day suite when they go to Miami Beach; and that there are two Cadillacs and a Lincoln in the family. He was not able, however, to tell us the $64 question—what his net worth is today. He insisted he has no bank accounts, and when we asked him how he keeps his financial records he came up with a ludicrous single sheet of paper with some notations on it.

Moretti also wins considerable money gambling at the race tracks, anywhere from $20,000 to $40,000 a year. He also bets successfully on elections. For income tax purposes he keeps a record of his winnings either "in my mind" or on odd slips of paper.

Our examination of Moretti ended on a friendly note—with an invitation, in fact. He showed us a postal card which he had had made of "The Moretti Estate" on the Jersey shore. "Six acres of land there, too," Moretti pridefully said. "I have a lake there." Expansively, he told his attorney to give me the postal card. "Let him look at it," Moretti said. "Maybe he wants to come down for dinner sometime." And as he left he urged, "Don't forget my home in Deal if you are down the shore. You are invited."

Turning to the Saratoga picture, it was difficult for those of us who listened to the evidence—Senator O'Conor, Senator Tobey, and myself—to understand how a state such as New York, which, on the state level, prides itself on respect for law and order, could wink, as it did, at the open flouting of the law in Saratoga Springs.

The situation we uncovered in Saratoga Springs was this: in August 1947, Superintendent John A. Gaffney of the New York State Police instructed Chief Inspector Francis S. McGarvey to have a survey made of gambling conditions in Saratoga

Springs. Chief Inspector McGarvey passed on the order to Inspector Charles LaForge. With no difficulty at all LaForge established that six wide-open gambling casinos were in operation: Smith's Interlaken, the Piping Rock Club, Newman's Lake House, Delmonico's, the Chicago Club, and the Arrowhead Club. The last-named, at the time, was backed by William Bischoff, alias Lefty Clark, notorious Detroit gambler, and Joe Adonis, of New York City. There was a seventh casino, Outhwaite's, which operated as a private club with $100 membership cards.

LaForge dutifully transmitted all this information to Chief Inspector McGarvey, who in turn passed it on to Superintendent of Police Gaffney. Gaffney put it in his "Confidential File," and that was that. Nothing at all was done about it until 1950, when, because of newspaper exposés and bad publicity resulting from the alleged trimming of a customer at one of the casinos, orders went out to put the lid on, and the gambling was throttled down.

The excuse given us in many hundreds of words for the existence of this situation was, in effect, simply this: gambling had been going on at Saratoga Springs for some time. (It was, however, everyone conceded, a violation of the law.) True, the State Police were supposed to enforce the law. But there was a "policy," it was explained, that the State Police enforce the law in "rural areas," not in cities that had regularly organized police departments. Of course if a "complaint" was made about law violations in cities, or if the local police department should ask for help, the State Police would step in. But no complaints or requests emanated from Saratoga Springs between 1947 and the end of the gambling season in 1949, so, despite the complete report in Superintendent Gaffney's Confidential File, nothing at all was done.

None of us on the committee had any respect for this type of convenient legal sophistry. The New England conscience of Senator Tobey was particularly outraged by such deviousness, and the three State Police representatives—particularly the superintendent—were treated by Senator Tobey to scathing denunciations such as he usually reserved for the worst of law-breakers. "You discovered those hellholes out there, didn't you?" he thundered at LaForge. ". . . And then as you went along in your work as a policeman and a citizen, you found out that there was not a damn thing done about it? . . . Why didn't you as a public-spirited citizen and policeman say, 'I will go to the governor about it'?"

"We just don't do those things," the inspector said.

"Why not?" demanded Tobey.

There was no answer.

His greatest ire, however, was reserved for the thoroughly unhappy Superintendent Gaffney. I quote from the record:

TOBEY: Well, if you saw Tom Dewey and said, "This is a rotten condition, what shall I do, Mr. Governor?" what do you suppose he would say?

GAFFNEY: "Go in and clean it up."

TOBEY: Didn't you hate it yourself? Didn't you feel a sense of outraged dignity seeing these things going on?

GAFFNEY: Yes. . . .

TOBEY: Well, what good are you, if you have a report showing illegality before you and you pay no attention to it and just put it away in cold storage?

GAFFNEY: That is not my responsibility.

TOBEY: Of course it is your responsibility.

GAFFNEY: That is your opinion.

TOBEY: Every time you say that you just indict yourself. . . . You certainly . . . look like a plugged nickel to me as superintendent of State Police.

GAFFNEY: Thank you very much. . . . I do not like to be abused. I am an honest man and I resent that. . . .

TOBEY: Well, you can resent it until that well-known place freezes over! The country will want to know what kind of a plugged nickel you are.

GAFFNEY: I am not a plugged nickel!

TOBEY: You are no good in my judgment, you are below par, and you are a counterfeit of what a good law enforcement officer should be. Just look at a picture of yourself, just look at yourself and search your own conscience.

GAFFNEY: I am an honest man. . . .

TOBEY: You are a passive man. . . . As a law enforcement officer you are no good.

GAFFNEY: That is an awful remark for you to make, Senator.

TOBEY: I am giving it to you straight with no compound interest. You indict yourself. "Out of their own mouths they indict themselves." . . . Of course you don't like it. No man likes to be found incompetent. That is what you have proved to me here today.

At one point Gaffney told us, "It wasn't my duty" to do anything about gambling in Saratoga and "I didn't think it was necessary" to transmit the gambling data to Governor Dewey. Then he admitted that if he had shown the governor the report he "would have been out on the sidewalk" for "falling down on the job I was supposed to be doing." At this, Senator Tobey let loose with an exclamation about "Janus facing both ways!"

One of the most damaging admissions made by Superintendent Gaffney, it seemed to the committee, was when Associate Counsel David Shivitz asked him:

Q. When you get to be the superintendent of the State Police, you are supposed to have enough savvy or understanding to leave it [the gambling at Saratoga] alone, unless you are told to go in; is that correct?

GAFFNEY: Well, probably, yes, it has been a policy over the years.

Senator Tobey's final shot was: "If I were the governor of this state, I would give you just five minutes to get out of this place, or I would kick you out." Gaffney replied, "I am glad you aren't the governor," and Tobey shot back: "I will bet you are. You have reason to be glad."

Behind the situation in Saratoga Springs, of course, was the official complacence of the small local Police Department. We interrogated an incredible local police chief, Patrick (Paddy) Rox, who admitted that he augumented his earnings as chief of police by collecting $10 a night for taking money from the bank to the Saratoga raceway.

There was one bit of dialogue between Counsel Halley and Chief Rox almost funny enough for a vaudeville skit. Halley had been attempting to get the chief to talk about "pressure" put upon him to protect the gambling casinos. The following exchange took place:

Rox: Mr. Halley, I am not looking for sympathy, but I have been sick for three years, almost, and I have been sick all fall, pressure and nerves.

HALLEY: Well, naturally there is pressure when anything like this is going on.

Rox: Pardon?

HALLEY: I say, naturally there is pressure when a thing like this is going on.

Rox: I have had this before, before this ever went on.

HALLEY: You have had what?

Rox: I have had this pressure before this.

HALLEY: What type of pressure are you referring to?

Rox: Blood pressure.

The final link in the disgraceful pattern was supplied by Detective Walter F. Ahearn, of the Saratoga Springs Police Department. Detective Ahearn was supposed to be in charge of suppressing any gambling he saw in the wide-open resort town. "There have been times where reports that gambling has been going on there has come to our attention," Ahearn cautiously admitted, ". . . but so far as I know, I have never seen it actually take place."

He told us he "never had no occasion" to go past the lobby of the gambling casinos. "The job of a detective is to detect, is it not?" Senator Tobey demanded. "Well," said Ahearn, "I still wanted to work."

Q. (*By Halley.*) In fact . . . you told our investigator . . . that the less you knew about it the better off you would be, is that right?

AHEARN: That is true, in this respect . . . I never tried to find out certain things, for the simple reason that if you don't know anything you can say truthfully and honestly that you don't know. I have always tried to go along and mind my own business.

SENATOR TOBEY: Have you ever seen those three monkeys, See No Evil, Hear No Evil, and Speak No Evil?

AHEARN: I have, yes, sir.

TOBEY: And you have certainly followed their example, haven't you?

AHEARN: To a certain extent. My father told me that a long, long time ago, sir. . . .

HALLEY: Now, what is your general information about what has to be done in order to operate a gambling place in Saratoga?

AHEARN: Well, if I was going to operate one . . . in order to get the real low-down, I would go to somebody who was operating one and see the right connections.

HALLEY: Who are the right connections, so far as common gossip is concerned, in Saratoga?

AHEARN: Well, your political leaders, I would say.

As we continued with the examination of Detective Ahearn we learned that he was not a complete stranger to the gambling casinos. He and his partner on the night shift, he testified, made a private deal with the Piping Rock casino to transport the bank roll and the gambling loot to and from the local bank every night. For this they were each paid $10 a night. The gamblers—though of course Ahearn "didn't know" they were gamblers—"were afraid of stick-ups more than anything else," he said. "We have just as many hoodlums in Saratoga as they have in Miami, during August," he added. When the gamblers needed them to transport the bank roll they would call the Police Department, which would put out a radio call for Ahearn and his partner, and the two officers would hurry along to the gambling casino in the city's police car, which was used for the job. "Just $10 a night for protecting all that swag?" Senator Tobey asked. "Well," Ahearn replied, "$70 a week is okay with me."

Ahearn also disclosed he had a similar arrangement with Arrowhead to haul its money, too, but Arrowhead only paid $50 a week for the services.

The committee had invited Governor Dewey to appear before us at the open hearings in New York. We would have welcomed his observations on crime and how it should be combated, based on his distinguished career as a prosecutor. We also wanted to hear his version of the Saratoga story and we further desired to talk with him about the circumstances which led to his parole of Lucky Luciano. In other states we had received extremely valuable testimony and suggestions from such crime-fighting governors as Stevenson of Illinois, Youngdahl of Minnesota, and Lausche of Ohio. We would not, of course, subpoena Governor Dewey, as we felt this would have been an affront. The governor countered our invitation by proposing that the Senate Committee—there were four senators sitting at the hearing, as well as a large staff of counsel, investigators, court stenographers, and so forth—come to Albany to see him. The senators could stay at the Executive Mansion, he said.

Obviously we could not accept this invitation to move our hearing to Albany. I felt it was both necessary and proper to read Governor Dewey's message into the record, and to repeat that the governor would be a most welcomed witness. Senator Tobey, a Republican, also urged him to come down; in a public statement Senator Tobey said: "If I were Governor Dewey, I'd come down here and sit down with the committee for a talk fest. It would be helpful all around."

Our next communication from Mr. Dewey was a telegram stating he was "surprised" that I had used his telegram "as an excuse . . . for discourteous personal remarks." If Mr. Dewey thought that the chairman or any member of the committee had been discourteous in inviting him a second time to appear before the committee he completely misconstrued our intentions. However, he still did not choose to accept our invitation, and all of us regretted his absence as we felt he could have shed considerable light on the purposes of our inquiry.

Some time after the committee's adjournment in New York, Governor Dewey issued a statement setting up a special grand jury investigation of the Saratoga situation. He also set up a State Crime Commission to conduct a state-wide inquiry similar to the investigation we were making on a national scale, a highly commendable project.

In the same statement, however, Governor Dewey exonerated Superintendent of Police Gaffney of any "impropriety." A companion statement by Governor Dewey's counsel complained that the Senate Committee failed to recognize an "interpretation of the undeviating State Police policy" not to act in areas that have uniformed police protection. "Policy" or not, the committee's position in New York—and I stand firm on it—was that, once having investigated and discovered gross violations of the law in Saratoga, the State Police had no justification for failing to take action. If the law is not to be laughed at in New York State the brazen and dangerous violations in Saratoga Springs certainly could not—and should not—be ignored. As I have pointed out many times, laws simply cannot be enforced for some and waived for others. That is not my idea of the way democracy should work.

CHAPTER 19

COSTELLO & CO.,
AND AN EMBATTLED AMBASSADOR

In eight days of public hearings in New York City during the month of March 1951 the Senate Crime Investigating Committee, then scheduled to go out of business in less than three weeks, became a national phenomenon. The hour-by-hour television coverage of the proceedings, relayed to other large cities, reached an estimated audience of between 20,000,000 and 30,000,000, and the effect was unbelievable. In New York City itself, some merchants wrote us, their businesses were paralyzed; many movie houses became "ghost" halls (some even installed television and invited the public to come in free and watch the crime hearings), and housewives did their ironing and mending in front of their TV sets. Throughout the country the Crime Committee became more than just a group of officials following the Senate's instructions to seek out certain information. We became a national crusade, a great debating forum, an arouser of public opinion on the state of the nation's morals.

For sheer drama, for wholesale peeling back of layers of

deceptive camouflage and perjury about the activities of criminals and certain politicians, the New York City open hearings
were the climax. In addition to the unfolding of the Saratoga
story, with its repercussions in the governor's office, we saw
and heard Frank Costello, described in testimony before us as
"the most influential underworld leader in America," do a
remarkable job of demolishing, through his own testimony, his
pose of present respectability and veracity. We witnessed a
truculent self-defense of his political and official conduct by
William O'Dwyer, former mayor of New York, and finally
we heard the ex-mayor and one of his chief political henchmen
accused by a witness, testifying under oath, of having received
large sums of cash from an organization interested in securing
their favors.

Naturally the handling of so much dynamite was not without its explosions. To me, the position of Mr. O'Dwyer was
particularly lamentable—a melancholy essay on political morality. It was not inspiring to see this man, who, at the moment
he was testifying, occupied the honored position of United
States Ambassador to Mexico, seek to defend his own conduct
by repeatedly shifting responsibilities to other officials. The
committee's final judgment on Mr. O'Dwyer's official conduct
as Kings County district attorney and mayor of New York,
was summed up in our report to the Senate as follows:

". . . Neither he [O'Dwyer] nor his appointees took any
effective action against the top echelons of the gambling, narcotics, waterfront, murder or bookmaking rackets. In fact, his
actions impeded promising investigations of such rackets. His
defense of public officials who were derelict in their duties,
and his actions in investigations of corruption, and his failure
to follow up concrete evidence of organized crime, particularly
in the case of Murder, Inc., and the waterfront, have contributed to the growth of organized crime, racketeering and gangsterism in New York City."

In everything I have said or written since the New York
hearings I have tried scrupulously to avoid prejudicing any
possible court actions by appearing to prejudge the factual is-

sues. At the same time, however, there has been no disposition on my part to side-step decisions and conclusions on the broader questions of propriety that are involved. At the time this was being written—possibly some positive action may have been taken by the time this appears in print—it was a matter of public record that a New York County grand jury was probing the truth or falsity of the charges by John P. Crane, then president of the New York City Uniformed Firemen's Association, affiliated with the American Federation of Labor. Crane, since forced to resign, testified that he had given $10,000 in cash to the then Mayor O'Dwyer and $55,000 to O'Dwyer's long-time confidant and the former first deputy fire commissioner, James. J. Moran. Since O'Dwyer and Moran swore before us they had received no such gifts—and Crane swore they had—the United States Attorney in Manhattan had been asked by our committee to determine, if possible, who had committed perjury and to take appropriate action, if any legal basis for prosecution could be found. U. S. Attorney Irving Saypol also was probing income tax returns of both O'Dwyer and Moran as result of the testimony concerning the alleged gifts.

An ambassador of the United States must be above suspicion —completely. I find it hard to believe that Mr. O'Dwyer will continue to occupy the critical post of ambassador to an important and friendly neighboring country. As a United States senator I could not vote again for Mr. O'Dwyer's confirmation.

The appearance of William O'Dwyer, the immigrant who rose from patrolman to mayor of a great city, was one of the dramatic highlights of our hearings. Ambassador O'Dwyer came up from Mexico at the committee's invitation to answer questions about a great many things—among them, his failure as district attorney to prosecute Albert Anastasia, one of the leading figures under suspicion in connection with the investigation of Murder, Inc., and a visit O'Dwyer paid to Frank Costello's apartment in December 1942. The visit, he maintained, occurred when he was serving the Air Force as a lieutenant colonel and was trying to track down Costello's alleged connection with a war racketeer. It was coincidence, he said, that other guests at Costello's apartment at the time included former Congressman Michael Kennedy, then leader of Tammany Hall; Bert Stand, Tammany secretary at that time; Surrogate Anthony P. Savarese, one of a number of judges with whom Costello enjoyed close friendship, and, to round out the incongruous assemblage, a man known as Irving Sherman, described to us as a close friend to both Costello and O'Dwyer. Despite O'Dwyer's contention that the presence of Kennedy and the other Tammany sachems was a coincidence, O'Dwyer's man Moran testified that he (Moran) had arranged the Costello appointment for his chief by requesting Tammany Leader Kennedy to set it up for O'Dwyer. O'Dwyer himself—and this was one of many inconsistencies in the record—testified it was his best recollection that he himself had arranged the meeting, not through Kennedy but through Irving Sherman. Sherman could not be found for questioning by the committee. A key to Sherman's reputation was the fact that a deputy chief inspector was retired from the New York City Police Department after FBI Director Hoover brought out before us that this inspector had a close relationship with Sherman.[1]

Even before Crane, self-styled "boss" of the firemen's union, testified, belligerent denials that they ever had taken money from him were entered by both O'Dwyer and his political friend, the red-faced, strapping, and occasionally vitriolic Moran, whom O'Dwyer, in one of his last acts as mayor, had appointed to a $15,000 "lifetime" job as a New York City Water Supply commissioner. This job was a political sinecure which an appointee could hold for life dependent on good conduct. The day after Crane's testimony Mayor O'Dwyer's successor, Mayor Impellitteri, immediately sent Moran an ultimatum to quit or be fired, and Moran resigned. Moran, who in an executive session had boasted that he had "a certain amount of gutter wisdom," had the gall to say in his letter of resignation that he was quitting "with a stomach that no longer can digest the

[1] Though Sherman has no record of convictions, the committee's report called him "a known gambler and intimate of racketeers."

hypocrisies of so-called 'politicians.'" The ways—and jargon —of politics sometimes is truly wonderful!

We got Crane's story only after obtaining a court order entitling us to use the minutes of testimony that the union official already had given to a grand jury conducted by District Attorney Hogan after having been promised immunity from prosecution. After we obtained this record Crane, abandoning his previous refusal to testify, told us of surreptitiously handing $55,000, in four installments, to Moran.

Without apparent shame Crane told us that he had "admired and liked" former Deputy Commissioner Moran and was "receiving assistance" from him. "I gave him the money," he said. ". . . In my experience, which is limited, when I find a man such as Mr. Moran, whose influence is such that a word from him can help or hurt us, I want him on my side." Senator Tobey asked the witness if it were not correct that the money "was the quid pro quo to get this good will and potential help from Moran whenever he could aid you?" Crane answered: "I was getting the help, and I wanted to keep getting it; let's put it that way."

Crane told how the Firemen's Association sought to defeat Mayor O'Dwyer in the 1949 election, after the mayor allegedly reneged on a promise to support legislation for a salary increase referendum. When it became obvious, however, that the opposition of the firemen's union was not going to have the slightest adverse effect on O'Dwyer's re-election, Crane coolly described how he went to the ever-friendly Moran and asked him to arrange a peace parley for him with the mayor.

"He [Moran] took me over," Crane said. "We straightened out our differences. He [O'Dwyer] committed himself to go along on our pension legislation then pending and we got on the band wagon."

A few weeks before Election Day, Crane said, he called on O'Dwyer at Gracie Mansion, the New York City mayoralty residence. Crane said the two of them were alone on the porch. (This, again, was a direct contradiction of testimony by

O'Dwyer, who swore Crane never visited him alone at Gracie Mansion.) The crowded hearing room was hushed, then an explosive gasp broke out as Crane stated:

"I told the mayor at that time that I had promised him the support of the firemen, and I offered him some evidence of that support on the occasion—in the form of $10,000."

The money, contained in a manila envelope, was in cash, as the gifts to Moran had been, Crane related.

"Did he say anything?" Halley asked.

"He thanked me," said Crane. "He didn't look in the envelope or anything else."

Crane also accounted for alleged expenditures of about $68,000 more of the union's funds on political and legislative purposes. Among the smaller items were a $2500 contribution which Crane said he made to the New York State Democratic Committee during the 1948 presidential campaign, and $3500 given to John Crews, Brooklyn Republican County Committee leader, which Crane said he believed "went to the Oregon primary campaign of Governor Dewey." Crane said he had gone to Crews seeking help in getting Governor Dewey to sign legislation benefiting firemen, and Crews told him of "the troubles the campaign committee was having in securing contributions to the Oregon primary campaign." One month after the first conversation Crane made the $3500 contribution to Crews. The bill was signed in the interim. Both the governor and Mr. Crews since have said that Mr. Dewey had no knowledge of the donation. As committee chairman, I remarked at the hearing that there was no evidence "that Mr. Dewey asked for or knew about the contribution."

As for Ambassador O'Dwyer's conduct in the witness chair, the committee thought it unfortunate that the angry ex-mayor at one point sought to divert the line of questioning by hurling an irrelevant and, as it developed, wholly unfounded insinuation against the personal integrity of Senator Tobey, Republican, of New Hampshire, one of the most honorable men in the United States Senate. In the midst of a verbal exchange O'Dwyer suddenly turned the discussion to the topic of alleged bookmaking in New Hampshire, then sneeringly said to Senator Tobey: "I can tell you that you don't know who supports you, because you sent here [to New York] for money to help you in your primaries and your election, and you got it, and you don't know where it came from." The inference was that Senator Tobey was mixed up with New York bookmakers, to which the senator shouted: "That is not true. . . . I will take the oath right now, if you will give it, Mr. Chairman. I hate a fourflusher!"

Next day I felt it my duty as chairman to require Mr. O'Dwyer to produce evidence, if he had it. All he had was a form letter written by Senator Tobey to a New Yorker—a stranger to the New Hampshire senator—thanking him for an unsolicited contribution which the New Yorker had made to Tobey's campaign through the National Committee for an Effective Congress, a reputable organization. O'Dwyer apologized "for the colloquy that started in the heat of passion." "There is nothing to it," he admitted.

The scene that followed was one of the most stirring of the entire hearings. Senator Tobey, who by then was wearing an old-fashioned green celluloid eyeshade, was deeply moved. His eyes moist and his voice trembling, he received a tremendous ovation from the spectators as he said: "Hate is a terrible thing. . . . I take my inspiration from a higher source and try to forget it. . . . I have lived long years and God has been good to me. I am a poor man, and always will be. . . . But there is one thing I am. I am a free man. And I am willing that anything I ever did or said or wrote should stand in the light of day to anybody, friend or foe alike. . . . Let's get on with the hearing."

O'Dwyer was questioned closely in connection with one phase of his handling, as district attorney, of the wholesale homicide ring known as Murder, Inc., an episode which Senator Tobey characterized as a "tawdry mess" which "smells under heaven." A former O'Dwyer appointee, Frank C. Bals, onetime chief investigator for District Attorney O'Dwyer and later the seventh deputy police commissioner when O'Dwyer was mayor, also was severely castigated by Senator Tobey. The

point of controversy was whether O'Dwyer and Bals had mis-
handled the case in such a manner as to permit Albert (Um-
berto) Anastasia, the alleged boss of the murder ring, to escape
prosecution.

Murder, Inc., which the gangsters themselves called "The
Combination," was a tightly run crime syndicate which police
investigators believe was responsible during the thirties for
the execution of between 120 and 130 persons throughout the
country. It has been charged publicly that Anastasia was in
direct charge of the execution branch of Murder, Inc., and
that no murder was permitted without Anastasia's authoriza-
tion. It also has been publicly charged that Joe Adonis was a
top leader of The Combination.

The operations of Murder, Inc., finally came to light when,
through confessions of underlings who operated as "troops"
in the homicide ring, police obtained ironclad evidence against
a gangster known as Abe (Kid Twist) Reles, who later admitted he actually carried out the murders under Anastasia's
orders. Losing his nerve when faced with the prospect of the
electric chair, Reles made a deal with O'Dwyer to turn informer in exchange for leniency. Information given by Reles
eventually sent eight men to the chair and some fifty others to
prison. But before the notorious Kid Twist could testify against
Anastasia, who was eluding arrest, the informer met a mysterious death. Reles was under protective custody, not, as would
be expected, in jail, but in the suite of a Coney Island hotel.
Early one morning while supposedly guarded by six policemen, Reles, fully clothed, went out of his hotel window and
was found dead five stories below. Out the window with him
went the case against Anastasia. Bals admitted that Reles was
frightened of gang reprisals and that it was unlikely he intended to escape; also that "he was too much of a coward to
commit suicide." When Senator Tobey, who later declared he
believed Reles must have been thrown from the window, demanded an explanation of what had happened, Bals finally
came up with the remarkable theory that the killer-informer
must have intended to climb down one floor on a knotted bed

sheet, come in a window, and then trot back up to "kid around" with his guards. Tobey angrily denounced this "peek-aboo" story, as he called it, and he also cried out: "Six policemen going to sleep at the same time, and you in charge of them! Why, it's ridiculous! O. Henry in all his wonderful moments never conceived of such a wonderful silly story as this!" Even O'Dwyer later said he could not go along with Bals on the "peekaboo" theory.

But the fact remained that somehow, whether through carelessness or design, not only was the star witness against Anastasia eliminated, but Anastasia himself never was apprehended, although the committee learned that he actually was serving in the United States Army—and the fact was no secret—during part of the time he was supposed to be a fugitive. Also there was another point of controversy in the fact that at one point O'Dwyer's appointee, James Moran, then serving as chief clerk of the Brooklyn district attorney's office, actually had caused withdrawal from the police files of the "wanted notice" cards for Anastasia and other fugitives in connection with the Murder, Inc., investigation.

The committee questioned Anastasia in executive session and learned that he now is a partner in a prosperous dress manufacturing business in Hazleton, Pennsylvania. Anastasia, who lives in a $65,000 home in New Jersey, replied, "I don't remember," when asked to name any occupation he had engaged in between 1919 and 1942. He refused to answer questions about his participation in the dress business today on the ground that "the government is investigating my income."

We further learned from Anastasia's brother Anthony, described by one witness as a waterfront "goon" and strikebreaker, that there are five Anastasia brothers in the United States and that all of them have entered this country by illegally jumping ship. Both Albert and Anthony were able to become naturalized citizens despite their illegal entries. Furthermore, only one month after the facts about how the Anastasia brothers sneaked into this country had been brought out in open hearing, still another brother, Gerardo, was admitted to citizenship by a United States judge in Brooklyn over the objections of U. S. Attorney Frank J. Parker. Collectively, the Anastasia brothers made out a pretty good case, I think, for the committee's contention that the naturalization laws of this country are drastically in need of overhauling.

As for Joe Adonis, born Joseph Doto, also known at various times as Arrosa, De Mio, and other aliases—"I have used so many names in those minor conflicts," he loftily told us at an early hearing—the committee found him one of the toughest, most determinedly contemptuous, and in some ways the most sinister of all the racketeers we questioned. Like others we examined, Adonis knew all the big boys of crime, and followed the gangster circuit of Miami in the winter; Hot Springs ("for d' bat's," he told us in his guttural voice) in the spring. To me, Adonis—that very name which he adopted for himself symbolizes his ego—was the evil personification of modern criminality. This man with bloodstained hands for years has set himself up as bigger than the law and unfortunately was able to get away with it until, in the wake of the committee hearings, he was sent to prison on the New Jersey gambling charges. Previously he had been arrested many times on charges ranging from grand larceny and felonious assault to kidnaping and extortion, but had paid only insignificant fines for disorderly conduct and prohibition violations.

Joe Adonis is slick, smooth; an expensively tailored figure with iron-gray hair pomaded into a Hollywood-style hair-do. His eyes are little and weak, and all during the hearing "Adonis," too vain apparently to wear glasses before the public, squinted at us—enmity and contempt plainly showing in his glance—as we questioned him. His voice, deep and gruff, was in character the conception of a gangster, but the words that came from his mouth were mostly windy legalistic phrases which sounded like the words of Counsel, adding up to the statement that Mr. Doto-Adonis refused to answer the proper questions of a committee of the United States Senate on the grounds that it would tend to incriminate him. He was cited for contempt of the Senate but went to jail on the New Jersey gambling charge before he could be tried in the contempt case.

One of the interesting avenues we explored in Adonis' thoroughly corrupt career was the period some years ago when he operated a speakeasy and restaurant in Brooklyn. Though the place was in a shoddy and inconvenient section, many New York City politicians, both Tammanyites and Republicans, beat a path to Adonis' door. They fawned on him and sought his help and money in elections. The arrogant Brooklyn gangster, we were told, poured many thousands of dollars and recruited scores of his "troops"—bums and strong-arm men—to "operate" at the polls.

We further learned that Adonis has sizable investments in a number of fields of legitimate enterprise which I, for one, do not like to see infiltrated by criminals. Most significant of Adonis' business activities was his connection with the Ford Motor Company, which I discussed in the Detroit chapter. When we were through questioning Joseph Doto-Adonis there was no doubt in the minds of the committee members that this gangster had achieved pre-eminence in all three fields that have become an unholy trinity in areas of the United States—crime, politics, and business.

Another of our star crimester witnesses—though, so far as giving us any information was concerned, he was a cipher—was Frank Erickson, the fallen big-time bookie of New York and New Jersey. Erickson is a bald, pudgy, loose-jowled man with the face of a sullen Cupid. He is a bitter man, and with good reason, for he has suffered the ignominy—something no successful crimester is supposed to do—of going to jail, and he keenly feels his loss of liberty and of "face." Back in the spring of 1950, Erickson had put in an arrogant appearance as a witness before the Senate Committee headed by Senator McFarland, which was gathering information on use of interstate communications facilities for gambling. In the course of his testimony Erickson made certain damaging admissions about his bookmaking activities, and New York District Attorney Hogan, who had been on his trail for some time, was able to secure an indictment and send him away for two years on sixty bookmaking counts. He also was fined $30,000. Since going to jail Erickson has suffered other blows, including his indictment by a Bergen County, New Jersey, grand jury for operating a huge telephone betting network, and a highly worrisome investigation of his federal income tax returns. He did not want to testify before us, and even attempted—unsuccessfully—to obtain a court order upholding his "right to privacy" in jail. We got him, but it was futile, necessitating, of course, the filing of a contempt citation against him for his stubborn refusal to answer most of our questions.

Well dressed and none the worse in appearance for his sojourn in jail, Erickson not only refused to answer legitimate questions but treated the committee to the additional contempt —I suspect it was deliberate—of refusing to raise his voice. We had to strain if we wanted to hear what he was mumbling. He was accompanied by the same attorney who came with Joe Adonis, but Erickson either was more ignorant than Adonis or didn't care, for he ludicrously garbled the stock reply by saying: "It may *in*tend to *criminate* me." Anxious to hear whatever it was the witness was whispering, Senator Tobey finally adjured him: "Mr. Erickson, just one question: if you were lost in the woods somewhere out in the country, and the shades of night were falling fast, and the owls began to hoot and the eerie shades of night gathered around you, and you wanted a helping hand, would you speak no louder than that, or would you holler as loud as you could?" The gambler looked quizzically at Senator Tobey, who had been on the McFarland Committee at the session which preceded Erickson's troubles, and replied: "The last time I spoke to you, Senator, I spoke too loud."

The silly, time-wasting exchange ended when Senator O'Conor broke in vigorously to accuse Erickson "of a direct and an outrageous affront to the United States Senate" and to move for his citation for contempt. Before Erickson filed out to return to his jail he hesitated a moment and said to me: "Thank you very much, Senator." So far as I could judge, there was no insolence in this remark. I think at that moment Frank

Erickson may have been repentant—even if only for a fleeting instant—for his misspent life. He must have wished that he could have faced up to us like a decent citizen.

Eighteen days later the jailed gambler had new troubles: the New York State Tax Department filed a $715,152 tax lien against him.

A fantastic picture of still another phase of underworld life was given the committee by one of the few women witnesses we heard anywhere. This was the former Virginia Hill, now Mrs. Hans Hauser, the once striking, erstwhile friend of the murdered Bugsy Siegel and other gangsters. The strain of the life she has led since she ran away to Chicago from her home in the little town of Bessemer, Alabama, at the age of seventeen has taken its toll of Miss Hill. Now thirty-five, she no longer is the captivating figure who once charmed such gangsters as Siegel, Adonis, and Frank Costello. The fading underworld queen now is a ravaged-looking woman with a mottled complexion and loose flesh that is beginning to wrinkle around the neck. I imagine Miss Hill would think hard today about whether the high life she led—while it lasted—was worth the price she has had to pay of having her name become nationally infamous.

We summoned Miss Hill, not to make a spectacle of her, but to see if she would help us with information about the operations of the interstate racketeers with whom she consorted. Actually the decision to call her as a witness was one which gave me considerable concern, for, despite the life she has led, I would have preferred to spare her the ordeal of telling her life's story in public. As it was, she told us little of value, except scraps of intelligence which fitted into the over-all picture we were gathering. However, Virginia Hill presented an interesting case study of what can happen to an attractive young girl who chooses to throw in her lot with criminals.

Miss Hill stormed almost hysterically into the hearing room. Swathed in silver-blue mink, she pulled a black picture hat over her eyes and shrieked that she would "throw something" if "those bums" (the press photographers) didn't stop taking her picture. Soon, however, her tension seemed to disappear, and she seemed quite self-possessed, almost as if she were enjoying her role. She told a fantastic story of how, without working, she collected an annual income that ran into thousands of dollars from "the men I was around"—only, she indignantly insisted, they "were not gangsters or racketeers." "The only time I ever got anything from them was going out and having fun, and maybe a few presents," she explained. Down in Mexico, too, where she waˢ a great favorite, she met fellows who "bought me everything I want." When she began living with Ben Siegel—her eyes flashed indignantly when Counsel Halley referred to him as "Bugsy"—the gifts ran into big money and even "a house in Florida" costing $49,000.

It is hard to capture in words the impression this woman gave. Her speech was ungrammatical, her voice a curious mixture of her Southern origin and Chicago gangsterese. You felt she wanted to give the impression of being very, very dumb; instead she made you feel she was very much the opposite. When Halley talked with her about the fabulous parties she used to give as hostess for the gangsters, Miss Hill petulantly and ingenuously protested: "I didn't pay for it. If I was paying for it, I wouldn't have gone in the first place." She gave Counsel Halley and all of us a challenging look and said: "After all, I didn't have to give my own parties, I don't think."

Halley questioned Miss Hill about a famous six weeks she spent at Sun Valley, where, incidentally, she met her latest husband, a skiing instructor. In six weeks she squandered $12,000 —all but $1500 of it paid in cash. Most of the money came from some Mexican gentlemen whose names she refused to reveal—as Halley suggested, "out of chivalry."

Fantastic and unlucky things were always happening to Miss Hill. When a friend mailed her $5000 in cash to Mexico, somebody stole it. When Bugsy Siegel borrowed a fine roadster from gangster Mickey Cohen for her to drive in Hollywood, she parked it one night and, again, somebody stole it. Coming back from Paris, all broken up after Bugsy had been murdered by a shotgun blast in the living room of the California home he had rented for her, she was going through customs examination at the airport when a plane crashed right outside. Everybody rushed over to see the accident, and when she came back somebody had swiped one of her rings. She didn't complain, however, it was just a plain little trinket—"some gold with little diamonds," not "worth more than $500."

Miss Hill now has bought a new little home in Spokane, Washington, for $31,500 (with a $16,000 down payment) in which she lives with her new husband, and she thought she still had about $15,000 tucked away with a Chicago friend who keeps her money and bonds for her. She is living modestly, spending not more than $15,000 or $20,000 a year. "I haven't been going any place," she said in explanation of her reduced expenditures over the past year. "I only had a baby, and that didn't cost too much."

Her income tax returns show that she used to report large winnings from betting on the horses, anywhere from $15,000 to $24,000. Usually she would just report an even $16,000 winnings in a return which was made out and signed for her by another Chicago friend. "I didn't keep any books or accounts or anything, but I paid what I thought was right," she explained. When Halley suggested that this sort of tax reporting system might seem a little irregular to Uncle Sam, she peevishly snapped: "Well, then, he'll have to take care of that, won't he?" "Uncle Sam? Maybe he will, Mrs. Hauser," Halley said. "Well," she retorted in her tough little voice, "that's all right, sure. I don't blame him."

I inquired how she was able to win $15,000 to $24,000 a year on the horses. "I knew what I was betting on before I'd bet," she replied. People would give her "good tips," and she would put up anywhere from $100 to $500 on these tips; the amount, she said, "would depend on the horse."

I asked her how her friends got such good inside information. "Never asked them," she crisply replied.

In fact Miss Hill was a girl who apparently never asked anybody anything. If Bugsy or Joe Adonis or any of her friends started to talk business around her, she testified, she would just get up and walk away. "Whether you believe it or not," she flared at Halley, "I don't know anything about their business. . . . I didn't want to know." Even when she lived with Bugsy at his gambling headquarters, the Flamingo Hotel in Las Vegas, she never knew a single person who visited him there because she stayed in her room and "didn't even go out." "In the first place," she said, "I had hay fever. I was allergic to the cactus. . . ." Bugsy encouraged this know-nothing attitude, she went on. Once when she picked up a news magazine and started to read an article that explained how Bugsy was one of the kingpins of the West Coast wire service he snatched it away from her and told her, "Don't read that baloney." "He didn't want me evidently to know about anything," Miss Hill said.

Mr. Siegel, she summed up, was just a congenial soul who never told her anything except that "he liked to travel and that's why I should go with him, because we would go to Europe and all this stuff—and he knew all the pretty places. He used to go with me to little resorts, and he liked to ride horses like I did, and swim, and all that stuff. I never knew these other things."

When the examination was over and we told Miss Hill she could go, she apparently was astonished that it hadn't been worse. "Is that all?" she inquired in obvious amazement. She paused a moment, took a sip of water, smiled for once at the photographers—looking almost pretty in the process—and got up and left. Once out in the corridor, something threw her in a tantrum again, and in a matter of a few minutes she had punched a woman reporter in the face, calling her a foul name, it was reported, in the process, and had kicked one gentleman of the press in the shins.

Of all the witnesses from the crime world summoned before us in New York, Frank Costello was the focal point of interest. The remarkable thing about his appearance before us is that Costello, the vaunted "prime minister" of the underworld, made himself out—and needlessly so—to be unintelligent. This in itself is a paradox, for it is hard for anyone who has studied Costello's persistent criminal activities, his influence in criminal and political circles, and the skill with which he has covered up the tracks of some of his operations, to believe the man really is a fool. In this case it is obvious that he was the victim of outraged personal vanity; the "elder statesman" of crime probably has come to believe the picture he has painted of himself as an important character. Possibly, too, he and his legal counsel had some misguided ideas on what they thought Costello might be able to get away with before a committee of the United States Senate.

But Costello's strategy didn't work. He trapped himself in what the record shows are a certain number of outright lies, and in other "evasions" almost too numerous to count. The stupidity of it all is that the truth came out anyhow, and that in most of the instances Costello could have admitted the truth in the first place without exposing himself to any prosecution. The principal effect of his tactics was to prolong what must have been an ordeal for him; he made it necessary for us to continue his examination over a period of seven days, when we could have finished up with him in a day.

He also exposed himself as a whiner and something of a crybaby; he did not even display particular courage, for, after threatening twice to walk out on the committee, he lost his nerve, came back, and abjectly answered most of our questions in a manner that indicated his defiance was gone. I do not pretend to understand how the minds of mobsters work, but I should think that Frank Costello, by his senseless performance before us, would forfeit the respect of even the hoodlums to whom he has given orders. In fact his pal Joe Adonis, watching Costello's squirming exhibition via television, was quoted by *Life* magazine as having muttered, "What a sucker!"

Costello—born Francesco Castiglia in Italy sixty years ago— was brought to the United States at the age of two. Early in life, as a young tough, he adopted the name by which he since has been known—Frank Costello. However, when he was arrested and convicted in 1915 for carrying a pistol—the only time in

his life he ever served a jail term—he used his mother's maiden
name, Severio, as an alias.

Costello, nee Castiglia, didn't like jail. It didn't reform him
but, on being released, he patterned his career shrewdly toward
becoming a big shot—a white-collar criminal instead of a gun-
carrying hoodlum. He mixed legitimate and quasi-legitimate
enterprises with gambling and bootlegging activities, at the
same time meddling heavily in politics. One of his early quasi-
legitimate activities—spectators in the hearing room tittered
when he told it to us in his hoarse, quavering voice—was a
partnership "in a business of manufacturing Kewpie dolls."
Further questions revealed that even Kewpie dolls, when manufactured by a Costello, have a shady angle: Costello's Kewpies
were used "as prizes for punchboards."

As he appeared before us, Costello was an impeccably and
expensively groomed figure. None of the tailor's or barber's
arts had been spared in perfecting his appearance. He dressed
conservatively; the only flamboyant touch was the white hand-
kerchief he wore in his breast pocket one day: embroidered on
it in large red script was his full name—"FRANK COSTELLO." The
nails of his nervously writhing fingers on the hairy-wristed
hands were freshly manicured. When he approached or left
the witness stand he walked slowly and ponderously in a sort
of stiff-shouldered gait. He was suffering, as was widely advertised by his counsel, from a sore throat, which accentuated the
gravelly quality of his normally thin voice. At the outset he
looked younger than his sixty years; his hard, sallow face was
set in impassive lines and he obviously sought to control both
his facial expressions and his language. Under the relentless
questioning of Counsel Halley, Costello broke, and became an
old, beaten man. He grimaced, scowled, showed his teeth,
mopped his face, and stared at the ceiling in anguish. His
grammar failed him, and he garbled his words—"I gotta re-
freshen my mem'ry about dese t'ings" and such and such was
like "a moom pitcha set!" he would exclaim.

In addition to being a confessed ex-bootlegger, the Costello who appeared before us was—or had been—a slot-machine king in New York and New Orleans; a partner in swank gambling casinos in New Orleans and Saratoga; president of a real estate corporation; partner in a wildcat oil prospecting company, chronic horseplayer, and investor in enterprises manufacturing such diverse products as electric broilers, television sets for barrooms, and chocolate-covered ice cream sticks. His advice, he said, was sought at one time by the late Senator Huey Long of Louisiana, who wanted him to "survey" the possibilities of raising state revenue through legalized slot-machine operations. In Manhattan, Costello was a man whose favor was curried by Tammany leaders, would-be magistrates, and district attorneys. People were impressed as he drifted around town, holding court in various expensive bars and barbershops, or in his lavish apartment, where he kept between $40,000 and $50,000 cash in a wall safe.

Before we encountered Costello at the public hearings the committee had questioned him privately and had heard a great deal about his activities from other sources—enough to convince us he was one of the heads of the New York crime syndicate, which has roots and working arrangements with mobs in other cities. We said as much in an interim report we had been required to submit to the Senate. This piqued the "prime minister," and he decided to censure us by withholding his "cooperation."

Costello's opening gambit was in the form of a pontifical statement, read for him by his diligent attorney, George Wolf, a man with a sonorous and never tiring voice. The statement told of Costello's "shock" when he discovered the committee had labeled him as a bad man in its interim report. "You have prejudged me without a bit of respectable proof to support your judgment," we were told. ". . . I am willing to assume the burden of proving my innocence to you and to the world. Give me—I ask you—this last opportunity of proving that your charges against me are unjustified and that they should be retracted. . . . I am begging you to treat me as a human being."

Then began the inexorable process—protracted over seven days because of his resistance—of proving that Frank Costello's pose was a fake. The committee even ordered television cameras kept off Costello's face while he was testifying; we did not want to provide him with an excuse to walk out. Bit by bit questions by Counsel and committee members broke down his pretensions. When it was finished these points, among others, had been scored against Costello:

THE ROOSEVELT RACEWAY DEAL. A lawyer named George Morton Levy, engaged in running a harness track at Roosevelt Raceway, Westbury, Long Island, admitted paying his good friend Costello $60,000—at the rate of $15,000 per annum for four years—to keep "bookies" away from his track. Levy insisted that there really weren't many bookies at the track; that it was a "phobia" on the part of an elderly chairman —now deceased—of the racing commission, and that he turned to Costello, the one man he knew who had "a reputation of having influence with gamblers," purely to "appease" the old commissioner. The commissioner's complaints did not cease immediately, however, Levy testified. Costello protested, "I didn't do a damn thing" to earn the $60,000; "I just spread a little propaganda in bars and restaurants." He really didn't want any money for it, he said, but Levy "insisted" on paying him.

Both Levy and Costello swore they never had any business conversations about operating the track and that Costello had no interest in it. Then we sprang a transcription of a telephone conversation between Levy and Costello—obtained through a court-authorized wire tap—in which the lawyer, talking about track problems, cryptically said to Costello, "You're the boss," and Costello spoke of coming out to Levy's home to "sit on your front lawn and cut up your business." Levy subsequently denied he had meant Costello was the boss, and Costello told Senator Tobey that the "cut up your business" reference was "just slang." "Maybe," Costello suggested, "I wanted to cut up a piece of his steak."

THE SLOT MACHINES. Costello admitted that he and his lieutenant, Dandy Phil Kastel, ran a slot-machine racket in New York City until the late Mayor LaGuardia ran them out. Then, after the conversation with Huey ˸ong, Costello sent Dandy Phil to New Orleans. Louisiana never quite got around to legalizing one-armed bandits, but Costello and Kastel set up an illegal slot-machine business anyhow under the name of Louisiana Mint Company. "You got mints" when you put in your nickel, Costello ingenuously explained. Again, Costello elucidated in injured tones, he really had nothing to do with operating the company; he just took his share of the profits—in 1944, for instance, it was $70,685.33. But once again we produced tapped phone conversations between Costello and Kastel which proved that Costello arbitrarily dictated even such small details as to what prices should be paid for the slot machines, and that Dandy Phil had little to say except "Okay." Costello also had to admit he was a party to a lawsuit against New Orleans city officials to recover damages for some 600 slot machines which the city finally confiscated. But Costello insisted that he, personally, "don't care if they chop them up and they throw them in the Mississippi River . . . if it was up to me, I would run away from it."

THE GAMBLING CASINOS. Sure, he was a partner in the Beverly Country Club, New Orleans gambling casino, along with Dandy Phil and Carlos Marcello, a vicious Louisiana criminal, Costello said. The Beverly Club paid him a monthly salary of $1000 (raised to $1500 in 1950) to act as "good-will man"—"if someone was going to Louisiana, I would recommend the place"—and to "recommend" acts for its floor show. As for Piping Rock Casino in Saratoga, in which the partners included two notorious gamblers, Jake Lansky and Joe Adonis, Costello maintained he really had no interest in it. "Gimme a chance to explain," he said, and went on to enlighten us as to how a pal named Joe Stein, known to Costello as a square guy, was short of cash one season and asked Costello if he'd buy into Piping Rock with him. Costello didn't want to buy in, so all he did was lend Stein the money and "go fifty-fifty" on Stein's profits. At this *Alice in Wonderland* twist, Senator Tobey, exclaimed, "We are getting a lesson in economics and high finance!"

THE SCOTCH WHISKY DEAL. Costello maintained repeatedly its was "absolutely nothing; pure friendship" that induced him in 1937 to guarantee a $325,000 note for Phil Kastel, who was attempting to buy into a distillery in Scotland that produced two famous brands of scotch whisky. Then we literally dragged out of Costello that, in addition to the "pure friendship," there was a side deal whereby Costello was to receive $25,000 a year from the British company to "promote" the sales of these particular brands of scotch, plus a bonus of five shillings—approximately one dollar at that time—for every case above a certain number sold in America. This deal aborted, apparently because of objections to Costello's reputation. Asked at this point if he couldn't begin to see "a certain pattern" in his activities of "wandering around bars," giving orders to bookies and "suggesting" the use of certain whiskies, that might make the committee suspicious, Costello shakily replied: "Well, I don't know what your impression can be." He further protested: "They weren't cutting me in. They were giving me a job!"

THE POLITICAL RACKET. "No, Mr. Halley," Costello said toward the end of his long examination when Counsel asked him if he had supported a certain judge's candidacy. "Since the Aurelio case I burned my fingers once and I never participated in any candidates [sic]." This was a reference to the 1943 scandal in which it was learned, through a tapped telephone conversation, that Costello had shoved Magistrate Thomas A. Aurelio's nomination to the New York Supreme Court down Tammany Hall's throat, even saying to the then Tammany leader, the late Michael Kennedy, "Are you a man or a mouse?" Painfully we extracted from Costello admission of friendships and favors granted and sought between him and

Tammany district leaders, and of cocktail parties in his home for the Tammany elite. It was not a convincing picture that Costello sought to paint of his lack of political influence. "There can be no question," the committee concluded, "that Frank Costello has exercised a major influence upon the New York County Democratic organization, Tammany Hall, because of his personal friendships and working relationships with its officers, and with Democratic district leaders in ten of the sixteen Manhattan districts. Costello also had relationships with some Republican political leaders." In this connection the committee also found that Mayor O'Dwyer had "appointed friends of both Costello and Adonis to high public office."

In addition to the damaging admissions that shook his claim to veracity Costello exposed himself to possible serious consequences on three points. We developed that Costello, when he answered questions in 1925 in connection with his citizenship application, failed to note, as required, that he had used the alias of Severio when convicted of the pistol-carrying charge in 1915. We also established a conflict as to whether Costello had engaged in bootlegging only "after 1927," as he claimed to us, or whether he was in it prior to 1925, as he previously had admitted to other investigating bodies. These irregularities, which might affect the validity of his naturalization papers, caused the committee to recommend that the Justice Department promptly investigate the possibility of denaturalizing and deporting this undesirable racketeer. Attorney General McGrath advised us in public hearings that there might be a chance of denaturalizing Costello, but because of red tape in the laws governing deportation he thought it would be impossible to send him back to Italy. This strengthened the committee's determination to put teeth in the immigration laws; at the same time I personally urged upon the Immigration Department that, regardless of difficulties, every avenue be explored for a means to take action against Costello.

Second, Costello's prosecution for contempt of Congress has been voted by the Senate because of his stubborn refusal to keep his word, given to us in our executive session, that he would submit a statement of his financial net worth. If convicted, he can be sentenced to one year in jail.

Finally, a possible case of perjury was established when Costello flatly denied paying money to James Francis McLaughlin, a former telephone company employee, to check his telephone to see whether it was tapped. He said he had no recollection of knowing McLaughlin and was certain that he "never give anybody a contract to check my wires." McLaughlin took the witness chair and testified that he was introduced to Costello by Irving Sherman; that Costello paid him to make periodical wire checks; and that he checked other wires for friends of Sherman. McLaughlin even made arrangements to have Mayor O'Dwyer's phone checked at Sherman's behest, he said.

It was after the McLaughlin testimony, with the threat of a perjury indictment looming, that Costello attempted to stage his first walkout on the grounds that he was sick and "confused." "He has reached the end," Costello's lawyer dramatically intoned. "He cannot go on." But he did go on, after the committee proved there was no medical basis for his claims of serious discomfort.

Costello pretty much wrote his own epitaph toward the end of his examination. Senator Tobey asked him why he became an American citizen. "Why?" croaked Costello. "Because I love this country." The senator beseeched him eloquently to look back over the past twenty years and think of one thing he could speak of "to [his] credit as an American citizen." Costello sat stunned while the seconds ticked by; then finally he blurted:

"Paid my tax."

At that moment the whole courtroom laughed at the man who calls himself Costello. His self-deflation was complete.

As we closed our excursion into the bailiwick of Costello, Adonis, Anastasia, et al., and of the equally culpable politicians who have made it possible for them to exist, my personal feelings were at a pitch of high moral indignation. I would like to close this chapter on the same note: why, I ask, in the name of everything sacred to our democratic civilization, should these killers and extortionists—the master racketeers and the erstwhile bosses of Murder, Inc., be permitted to get away with it? Even assuming that the gangsters have forsaken crime as they claim—and of course they lie in their teeth when they say it, for all of them are still up to their armpits in crime—why should they have been permitted to slide into legitimate fields and escape unpunished?

I know it is hard to pin anything on the Costellos, Adonises, Anastasias, Zwillmans, Lanskys, and all the rest of that dirty crew. That is no excuse. Cities, counties, states, and the federal government should turn loose everything they have on these rotters. If it takes years or even decades we should get them. We should put them where they belong and in so doing let the decent citizens and the young people who are growing up in our wonderful country know, once and for all, that America is *not* a land where crime rules.

CHAPTER 20

HOW THE NATIONAL CRIME SYNDI-
CATE CAN BE SMASHED

A T THE conclusion of the New York hearings most of us, committee members and staff alike, were physically exhausted. We had intended originally to conclude the New York sessions in one week, but the tremendous struggle involved in unfolding the stories of Costello, O'Dwyer, et al. forced us to continue for three days into the second week so that we did not wind up in New York until March 21. We already had a series of crowded final hearings scheduled to begin in Washington the very next day, with important witnesses from the government and odds and ends from the underworld due to appear. Also, since the life of the committee as of that time was scheduled to expire on March 31, we had ten days—really nine days, as the last day of the month fell on a Sunday—in which to complete the job of reviewing the millions of words of testimony and writing our recommendations and a final report to the Senate.

Obviously, after Frank Costello, Virginia Hill, Ambassador O'Dwyer, and the startling disclosures of the firemen's lobbyist, Crane, anything was bound to be anticlimactic. Some of the anticlimax, however, was engrossing drama. Hoarse-voiced Greasy Thumb Guzik, the flabby master mind of the Chicago-Capone Syndicate, was brought in by the Senate sergeant at arms to play out his strange drama of refusing to answer any questions. Mr. Carroll, the hypocritical big-time gambler from St. Louis, came down to get himself off the contempt hook. Moe Kleinman and Lou Rothkopf, the ignoble pair of ex-convicts from Cleveland, who had ducked the committee for months, staged their big defiance act in front of the television cameras. Longie Zwillman, the millionaire racketeer from Newark, New Jersey, made his delayed appearance. We also had a long session with an evasive witness, Lew Farrell, alias Fratto, who, despite a criminal record and admitted connections with the notorious Gargotta brothers of Kansas City, has managed to operate on a large scale as a licensed beer distributor in Des Moines, Iowa.

We also cleaned up loose ends, gathered in many places, on the workings of a vast bootleg liquor ring operating out of Cairo, Illinois, which is running whisky illegally into dry Southern states. This operation was reminiscent of the bloody twenties, when trucks were highjacked, liquor shipments were disguised as legal merchandise, and public officials were corrupted on a wholesale scale; an up-to-date wrinkle was the use of counterfeit federal and state liquor stamps by the new-style rumrunners. Some of the wholesalers involved in this racket, we discovered, had been connected with a huge black market liquor operation in World War II. Leading distillers have been appealed to both by a conference of Southern state revenue and alcohol commissioners and by the Senate Crime Committee to take steps to remedy this situation. James C. Evans, commissioner of finance and taxation in Tennessee, assisted the Crime Committee in organizing the conference of Southern officials, which specifically requested the distillers to cancel franchises of distributors involved in the bootlegging ring. The distillers agreed to do this, but so far have failed to take action.

Our own investigation established that all the major distillers and certain large breweries have granted franchises to hoodlums—"including some in the top ranks of organized crime." One such wholesaler, for instance, was the notorious Joseph Di Giovanni of Kansas City. We noted with regret that "while these distillers and brewers state that they did not know of the criminal associations at the time they granted the franchises, they were almost all vague on the question of whether they would fire a distributor upon finding he had criminal associations."

The committee felt that federal and state units, by granting licenses to undesirable characters with criminal records, had been regrettably lax. It is my personal feeling that the whisky industry is shortsighted in thus failing to keep its house clean. Such abuses provide powerful ammunition to the advocates of the return of prohibition.

We also examined in Washington a new type of witness from the gambling world—forty-two-year-old Sydney Brodson, of Milwaukee, Wisconsin, who told us he is licensed to practice law in two states. The committee was indebted to Police Chief John W. Polcyn of Milwaukee for assistance in the investigation of this unique gambler.

Brodson, polite and soft-spoken though almost unbearably cocky at times, is a graduate of two colleges. Some years ago when his law business was poor he found he had a talent for picking winners in football and basketball pools. Letting his law practice slide, Brodson set up a small office in Milwaukee, describing himself fictitiously as a "food broker," and went into the full-time business of scientifically analyzing nationwide football and basketball games and wagering on his conclusions. With the help of trained assistants, he combed as many as a hundred newspapers a day for helpful information. To secure the necessary number of telephones for this operation, he set up a "Get the Vote Committee," but he affably conceded to us that "get the vote" really meant "get the bets." He estimated that he placed bets with bookies and other gamblers in about twenty states and that his wagers amounted to a gross of $1,000,000 per year. He used the telephones almost exclusively in placing bets, and his annual long-distance telephone bill was approximately $15,000. His net profit, Brodson testified, is approximately $80,000 a year, and in seven uninterrupted years of this operation, he said, he has amassed a net worth of approximately $250,000, some of which he has invested in legitimate business ventures.

Brodson, who was not distinguished for his modesty, insisted he paid no commissions to the gamblers with whom he placed his bets. The reason for this, he explained, "is because Sydney Brodson—I do not mean to be egotistical—has a pretty good opinion and is known to win more than he loses"; therefore, the gamblers, he claimed, were willing to handle his bets free in order to ride the same wagers. Brodson further said he did all his business outside the state of Wisconsin in order to avoid local or state prosecution.

The smart young man, however, was smart enough to know what a degrading game he was playing. His attractive, modest-looking wife sat behind him in the hearing room; her face was plainly visible to the millions of television viewers. Abandoning his attitude of self-enjoyment for a moment, Brodson soberly said: "My wife has always brought pressure on me to get out of this thing and perhaps I should have abided by her advice." Perhaps he should have, for, on the heels of Brodson's testimony before the committee, the state assessor of income in the Milwaukee area announced that the income Brodson had reported over recent years simply did not add up to what he told the committee he was worth, and that a thorough investigation would be undertaken.

Certain of the bookmakers who handled Brodson's bets also must have wished he had talked less, for law enforcement officers in various cities, watching or listening to our proceedings by television and radio, jotted down the names, addresses, and telephone numbers of the various individuals with whom he said he placed bets. As our report noted: "They immediately visited the addresses mentioned and, before Brodson had left the stand, they had located and arrested his betting associates in cities separated by thousands of miles." This probably marked the first time in history that police were apprised of law violations by means of television.

At one point in Brodson's interrogation the questioning got off the subject of Brodson's own activities and the witness attempted, with what seemed to me an air of unconscionable arrogance, to advise the committee on the hopelessness of controlling gambling in America—a line that is popular with professional gamblers. At this point I felt it necessary to remark: "I personally do not think that this witness or anybody whose profession is that of a gambler is a very good witness to ask . . . whether legalized gambling is a good or a bad thing. I do not think he is in a position to advise the American people." Judge Samuel S. Leibowitz, the vastly experienced Brooklyn jurist, who later appeared before the committee as an expert witness on crime, had some eloquent words to say on this subject. "I think something should be said to the people of America about Brodson," the jurist stated. "Here you had a man who was a graduate of two universities . . . a lawyer, a handsome man, a man of nice presence, an articulate man and a man of quite some charm. . . . It is really shocking that the youth of our country might get the impression that this is the proper way to live; that a university man, a college graduate, need not go to work, need not practice his profession, but should hire an office somewhere in some city, with some gangster at his elbow, and live the life of Riley on the fruits of gambling and associate with the most venal characters. . . .

"I wish that I could take these youngsters into my courtroom when I sit on the bench," the judge continued, "to see some of the people that I sentence to the electric chair, the state's prison, the penitentiary; to see some of the human wrecks that come into that courtroom, people that have frequented the gambling places, have been caused to rob their employers, and in many instances have gone out with a gun and stuck up a haberdashery man or a taxicab chauffeur, and have resorted to the use of dope . . . [and] to all sorts of crimes and venality in order to get the funds with which to go out and gamble. . . .

Then they would see a true picture of what gambling means. . . .

"It is a pity that a man like Brodson should be permitted, without a challenge, to show off before this committee, and I am happy that Senator Tobey brought out that he was a criminal; I am happy that your chairman, Senator Kefauver, called out to him that this Senate Committee is not going to take advice from a character of that kind."

In addition to the characters from the underworld and the gambling world, the committee, in its final days of hearings under my chairmanship, heard valuable expert testimony from a number of important federal and state officials, whose opinions on the serious business of what to do about curbing the illegal practices which we had exposed were extremely important. These witnesses included the Attorney General of the United States, J. Howard McGrath, and several of his top assistants; the director of the Federal Bureau of Investigation, J. Edgar Hoover; Edward H. Foley, Under Secretary of the United States Treasury; George J. Schoeneman, commissioner of the Bureau of Internal Revenue; Commissioner Harry J. Anslinger of the Bureau of Narcotics; and a number of others. Throughout the hearings, wherever we visited, we had similarly helpful testimony from state and local officials concerning their particular problems and how the federal government might help without encroaching on local sovereignty.

Toward the end of the hearings under my chairmanship, the twentieth-century phenomenon of television became a major factor in our operations. At some of the early public hearings local television stations presented programs pieced together from newsreel shots. In New Orleans permission was granted to Station WNOE to bring its cameras into the hearing room and telecast the actual proceedings. The station took the bold step of shelving its scheduled commercial programs while we were in session and telecasting the entire proceedings—morning, afternoon, and night. Public response in New Orleans was tremendous. After that, wherever we held open hearings, our proceedings were fully televised. In New York and in the last few days in Washington the programs joined the network and were seen by an audience estimated at between 20,000,000 and 30,000,000 persons.

Admittedly the question of "live" telecasting of congressional committee inquiries has both good and bad features, but in my opinion the benefits tremendously outweigh the drawbacks. I liked the ring of a letter—and it was typical of thousands received—from a St. Louis man who wrote: "I think that television has contributed greatly as the means whereby the people can see the brazen arrogance of these carrion and through their testimony note their entire disregard for all law and decency."

Furthermore, to my mind, there is ample precedent for our decision to permit television, the latest media of public information, to join its sister media, the press, radio, and newsreels, at our public hearings. A public hearing is a public hearing, and to me it makes no sense to say that certain types of information-gathering agencies may be admitted but that television may not, simply because it lifts the voices and faces of the witnesses from the hearing rooms to the living rooms of the people of America. I recognize the right of the individual not to be unduly held up to ridicule, but I cannot see where testifying before a television camera violates that right. After all, the question of whether a person exposes himself to ridicule depends on the demeanor, candor, and basic honesty of the witness himself—not on whether he is being televised. In my opinion the Constitution is a living, growing organism which must keep abreast and take cognizance of all new technological developments that operate for the benefit of the country of which the same Constitution is our proudest document.

I might point out that not all of my fellow senators agree with me on the subject of televising hearings. I stand, however, on my conviction that it is a tremendously healthy thing to give an opportunity to millions of American citizens to witness important public affairs at first hand, instead of confining the privilege to a few dozen who can crowd into a hearing room. Important public addresses before joint sessions of Congress, such as addresses by the President and the historic appearance by General Douglas MacArthur, now are being televised. I for one would give serious consideration to breaking a hoary and outmoded tradition and permitting "live" television and radio to pick up special events in both houses of Congress. For instance, if Congress ever adopts a suggestion I have been urging for years, to have periodic personal reports to Congress by cabinet officers and other administration officials, in which direct and impromptu questions would be asked and answered, such sessions certainly ought to be carried to the American public. Televising congressional sessions certainly would keep us senators on our toes, and I predict that on these occasions there would be less inattention on the floor and fewer instances when as few as five or six senators are present to hear an address by some member—or even to vote on a measure involving public interest.

On the subject of televising witnesses at a public hearing, I would protect their rights and well-being by making this reservation, which should be subject to the discretion of the chairman presiding over the hearing. If it can be established that the television lights actually cause the witness physical discomfort and distract him from giving fair and intelligent responses to the questions, some modification should be made. Our committee solved this, after we made the decision in New Orleans for the first time to permit "live" telecasting, by requiring that the lights be kept out of the eyes of the witnesses and that the number of lights be limited so that the heat would not be oppressive. Actually and sincerely, I do not believe that testifying under television lights and cameras is any great ordeal, except for witnesses who want to be troublesome. There is no great heat generated from the lights, and the cameras are noiseless, unlike those used for newsreels, which have been permitted for years to operate at most important hearings.

I do favor a thorough study and adoption of a general code of conduct governing all phases of congressional committee hearings, including telecasting. For one thing, if a witness' appearance is to be televised, the whole thing should be recorded and telecast, so that the passages will not be taken out of context and left unexplained. It also would be desirable if physical facilities could be set up so the cameras and crews are behind glass—such as is the case when United Nations sessions are telecast—to reduce any possibility of disturbance or distraction.

On the general subject of protecting the rights of witnesses, the committee was proud of its record. I personally have always been opposed to hearings which degenerated into "smear" sessions or witch hunts, and I am not proud of some of the things that occasionally are done along this line by certain congressional committees. All of us on the Crime Committee were determined from the outset to do our best to prevent this sort of thing from occurring. Probably some of the crooks, hoodlums, and shady politicians who received thorough goings-over from counsel and committee members will not agree with us, but I think our record was fair. We established a few rules that might well be adopted by future committees. One was the practice of affording any person who was accused of some reprehensible act by another witness and who desired to make an explanation the opportunity either to be heard or to file a communication with us on the subject. We further attempted to safeguard against possible unjust smearing by conducting closed sessions wherever we could, in order to sift the evidence before hearing witnesses in public.

A second wholesome rule we followed was to permit witnesses to be accompanied by counsel and to allow their counsel considerable latitude in protecting the interests of the witnesses. As congressional committee hearings are not court proceedings, it is a matter for each committee's discretion as to whether counsel shall be permitted to participate. Some congressional committees do not allow counsel for witnesses to participate at all; others allow counsel to ask questions in behalf of their clients only if they write them out and submit them to the committee chairman, who then exercises his discretion as to whether the question may be asked. We felt the fair thing to do, particularly in an inquiry such as ours, was to permit counsel for witnesses wide compass. In the majority of cases counsel respected this privilege; however, some attorneys for embattled and evasive gangsters and other satellites of the crime world took advantage of the courtesy we extended them. Even though our courtesy was occasionally abused, I still think our decision was fair and judicious, and I feel it is a precedent that can be followed to advantage by other committees in the future.

As a side light, one facet of the committee's operation which pleased all of us was the fact that the initial appropriation voted for the Senate Crime Committee's work was only $150,000, and that, even with additional appropriations, the total amount voted for our operations during the twelve months of my chairmanship came to only $265,000. When the state of New York set up its state-wide crime probe it started off with an initial budget of $250,000.

In addition to the impetus given the work of the committee by the telecasting of the hearings and the further dissemination of information by radio and newsreels, the practical assistance which we received from the press of America was enormous. As I pointed out at the final session over which I presided in Washington, part of the inspiration for the birth of the Crime Committee stemmed from the example of sixteen aggressive newspapers throughout the nation which joined forces to pool information in a crusade against interstate crime. The newspapers turned up much concrete evidence which aided us in establishing the fact that there was a national crime syndicate, linked by operations of local mobs. Not only the sixteen papers in this anti-crime pool but newspapers everywhere gave us valuable assistance. Wherever the committee went we could count on the help of veteran local crime reporters and their fact-laden personal files. In Washington, the committee's base of operation, Philip Graham, publisher, and J. Russell Wiggins, managing editor of the Washington *Post,* had been among the first to urge me personally to undertake the crime investigation.

Even before our hearings were concluded certain members of the staff had been assigned to work on preparation of our report to the Senate, and a great deal of ground had been covered. The majority of the committee felt, however, that it would be impossible to prepare an adequate report and consider recommendations carefully, while attempting at the same time to wind up our hearings, which actually did not end until March 29. Therefore an extension of one month was obtained from the Senate in order to give proper attention to what I had hoped would be the committee's final report but which emerged as our third interim report.

In the meantime, tremendous pressure for continuing the committee had built up. There were various proposals, some to keep it in operation until 1952 and some even to make it permanent.

I opposed further continuance. I realized, of course, that there were facets of interstate crime which could have been explored further. I felt, however, that we had done the basic job of exposing the framework of nationwide criminal operations and of arousing the country to a feeling of high moral indignation; in short, an atmosphere in which it might have been possible to secure immediate passage of some of the desired legislation necessary to cure the evils we exposed. As a practical matter, there is such a thing, to employ an old cliché, as "striking while the iron is hot." The iron was awfully hot when we submitted what would have been our final report to the Senate on May 1, 1951.

I also felt—and I regret to say it, for the committee itself had worked hard and successfully to keep any partisan tinge out of our proceedings—that there was a certain aura of politics, emanating from the other side of the aisle, enveloping the proposals to keep the Crime Committee going. This became so obvious that virtually every seasoned political commentator took note of the fact that the Republican party felt that continuance of the committee would provide good ammunition for the 1952 campaign. So far as I personally was concerned, I tried to do the job without concerning myself with whether Democrats or Republicans were hurt or helped by our exposures—and I believe this feeling is shared by thoughtful members of both parties. If, in my opinion, the basic work of the committee had not been completed, I would have favored proceeding with it on the same non-partisan basis. I did not like to see the future of the Crime Committee being linked even by discussion with a political campaign.

As it so happened, I had traveled more than any of my colleagues and, as a matter of fact, had operated as a subcommittee of one in conducting a majority of the hearings. I knew what it meant to devote practically one's full time to the business of ferreting out crime. To do it properly, it had to be virtually a full-time job. I did not feel it was the proper function of a United States senator to continue to neglect his other duties and spend his days and nights running down additional details on the broad pattern of a situation the existence of which we had already established.

I felt the job should be continued, but through establishment of a permanent federal crime commission, rather than by a committee of the Senate.

But the pressure for continuance was overwhelming, the letters were pouring in by the thousands, and I was overruled. A compromise was effected whereby the committee would continue for another four months until September 1, 1951, and then turn over its functions to the standing Senate Committee on Interstate and Foreign Commerce, on which the Crime Committee was represented by three of its members—Senators O'Conor, Hunt, and Tobey.

Feeling as I did that it was a mistake to continue the work of the committee, and that we should be pressing instead for passage of legislation while we still had an aroused public opinion behind us, I felt I should not remain on the committee. However, I was prevailed upon by the Democratic Policy Committee—I believe Majority Leader McFarland was quoted as saying that "Kefauver was a hard man to persuade!"—to stay with the committee for a limited time, but I insisted that the committee should have a new chairman. Senator O'Conor of Maryland was chosen to succeed me. I was confident that, under the chairmanship of this distinguished senator, former governor, and outstanding prosecuting attorney, the committee would continue to exclude irrelevant matters from its considerations and that useful avenues of investigation, such as the probe which has been undertaken into further aspects of the narcotics traffic, would be pursued. I am certain that the committee's investigations under its new chairman will lead to recommendations for additional useful legislation.

Meanwhile, a new chief counsel, Richard Moser, able member of the New York bar, was chosen. Rudolph Halley, who had gone to the hospital almost immediately after the grueling New York hearings, also felt it was time to step down.

The committee, under my chairmanship, made twenty-two specific recommendations to the Senate. All but one had the unanimous backing of every member of the committee. That exception was our Recommendation III, proposing establishment of an independent federal crime commission in the executive branch of the government, from which Senator Wiley dissented. It was an interesting side light on the unanimity with which our committee operated that, though we had our differences in discussions of various plans, this was the only dissent by any member on any major point of policy that remained on the record.

Concerning the federal crime commission, the committee majority recommended that it be composed of three members, "all of whom are prominent citizens and not otherwise members or employees of the federal government," and that it should be organized promptly and be ready to function on September 1, 1951, the date currently set for final expiration of the Crime Committee's authority.

The federal crime commission would be empowered to hear witnesses and conduct hearings but would lack the subpoena power which the Senate Committee has had. When it found it necessary to subpoena witnesses or take testimony under oath, the commission would apply either to the Senate Committee on Interstate and Foreign Commerce or to any other congressional committee with jurisdiction over the subject matter under investigation.

Among the aims of the three-man crime commission would be keeping alive a continuing study of the activities of the national crime syndicate; doing the vital job of maintaining proper liaison among federal, state, and local law enforcement agencies and crime commissions; and recommending legislation and other corrective policies. Also it would undertake the all-important and needed work of maintaining files and records "as a national clearing house of information respecting criminal activities in interstate commerce, to be made available to properly authorized individuals and groups, subject to suitable security measures. . . ." This last provision would eliminate the condition of which some law enforcement officers, who testified before us, complained—namely, that exchange of information with the FBI is "a one-way street." There are twenty-four federal investigative agencies, including the FBI, whose information would be correlated by the proposed commission.

Attorney General McGrath and FBI Director Hoover, in their statements to our committee, opposed creation of a federal crime commission. They felt—and in my opinion it was unfortunate that we could not convince them otherwise—that creation of such a commission might lead to establishment of a so-called national-type police force. I respect their judgment and sincerity—also that of Senator Wiley, who concurred with them—but I strongly feel that nothing could be further from the mark. There is no connection between a federal crime commission and a national police force. Every senator I know —myself included—would stand up and fight to the last breath any suggestion that we create anything resembling an American Gestapo. Nor does Recommendation III contemplate any infringement on the authority and jurisdiction of the justly applauded FBI.

My own original ideas for a federal crime commission went even further, but I modified them in the interests of harmony and in the hope of getting the recommendation, as agreed to by four of the five members of the committee, enacted into law. I wanted to see a representative of the Justice Department —preferably the head of the FBI—and some high-ranking official from the Treasury Department on the commission along with the three non-governmental members. For workability, I also favored granting the commission the power to subpoena witnesses upon a showing to a federal judge that each subpoena requested was necessary for the furtherance of the commission's operations.

Our full list of twenty-two recommendations was as follows:

I. Congress should continue the Crime Committee for a limited period. The primary purpose of the committee would be to observe what the federal agencies are doing to suppress interstate criminal operations, and to follow up on our legislative recommendations, rather than to continue with "the exposition of situations which can only give cumulative support to the now overwhelming evidence that there is a serious organized crime problem which must be met." This recommendation, as I stated above, is being carried out.

II. The committee favored and approved the organization of a racket squad in the Justice Department to go after gangsters, racketeers, and organized criminal mobs, using any lawful weapon to smash them. This work is an extension of the special grand jury investigations conducted in Kansas City and Philadelphia by Special Assistant Attorney General Max Goldschein. Attorney General McGrath already has put into effect plans for stepping up employment of the racket squad blitz technique against organized criminal syndicates. He has also proposed to the ninety-three United States attorneys throughout the nation that on-the-spot rackets investigations be conducted by federal grand juries in each judicial district at least once a year. The committee was in full accord with this plan.

III. This recommendation concerned creation of a federal crime commission, which I have discussed.

IV. The committee endorsed the setting up by the Internal Revenue Bureau of special fraud squads in each of the fourteen field divisions of its intelligence unit. This step was taken by the Treasury Department after the committee, in its second interim report, had noted that organized crimesters were defrauding the government of tax revenue possibly running into hundreds of millions of dollars. The new special fraud section will be staffed by selected experts who will concentrate their attention on tax accounts of gamblers and other racketeers. The committee applauded this step by the department and recommended that it be backed up by Congress with the necessary appropriations of operating funds. We noted that it was "absolutely vital" for the government to streamline its legislation and for both the Internal Revenue Bureau and the Justice Department to cut away the red tape which now constricts the war on tax evasion by criminals. "Money is the key to power in the underworld," we observed. "It buys protection for illegitimate enterprises and enables underworld characters to buy up legitimate business and to claim respectability by contributions to worthy causes. The large financial resources at the disposal of criminal gangs and syndicates make such gangs and syndicates a serious menace to our institutions.

"It is obvious to anyone familiar with income tax prosecutions that the procedures presently employed by the Department of Justice and the Bureau of Internal Revenue are entirely too laborious and time-consuming. . . . The committee urges the Bureau of Internal Revenue to make a study with a view to simplifying its procedures for income tax fraud. Swift prosecution and punishment are deterrents to crime in the tax field as much as anywhere else."

V. The Internal Revenue Bureau should take effective action to stop the continual violation by gamblers, gangsters, and racketeers of regulations which require taxpayers to keep adequate books and records of their income and expenses. Honest taxpayers go to a great deal of trouble to obey the law and keep these records, while many criminals make a mockery of the procedure. All too often we encountered big-time gamblers who told us they kept a "running balance" of their gambling profits and losses in their heads, or wrote down the figures on a "slip of paper," which they promptly tore up as soon as their tax returns were submitted. We found that the Bureau "had not utilized this regulation to its full potentialities." To stiffen enforcement of the law, the committee has introduced a bill which would make it a felony to violate this regulation, which currently is a misdemeanor. The Treasury Department itself approved and joined in this proposal.

VI. Gambling casinos, which also outrageously flout internal revenue requirements by their so-called "bookkeeping" methods, should be required to maintain daily records of moneys won and lost and to file these records with the Bureau. The Bureau should have authority to demand additional data as it saw fit, and internal revenue agents should have unrestricted access to the premises of gambling casinos and to their books and records at all times. We noted: "The committee is well aware that these provisions may well put illegal gambling casinos out of business."

VII. The biggest farce and effrontery, in so far as the application of internal revenue regulations to illegal gamblers is concerned, is the fact that the present law permits gamblers to deduct wagering losses and overhead costs as "business expenses." Such deductions often include the hidden bribes paid to law enforcement officials. The committee felt this latitude in deductions for illegal enterprises is "not only incongruous but highly undesirable," and we recommended an amendment in the law that would prohibit any sort of deduction—including salaries, rent, protection money, and so forth—for tax purposes. Our proposal specifically is designed as a blow against the big-time professional gambler.

VIII. The Crime Committee has recommended passage of a bill completely outlawing interstate transmission of gambling information, by means of telegraph, telephone, radio, television, or other communication facilities, by any individual, service, or organization *"devoted to a substantial extent to providing information used in illegal gambling."* Our recommendation is in harmony with a previous bill introduced by the McFarland Committee, passage of which unfortunately has been delayed. The general purpose of the recommendation also has been endorsed by the Attorney General's Conference on Organized Crime. The bill is aimed not at legitimate media of information such as newspapers, etc., but is directly intended to smash the operation of the so-called Continental Press Service, which keeps alive a multimillion-dollar industry for the underworld by feeding race news wire service throughout the country. We gave consideration to the proposal that all dissemination of betting information across state lines be declared illegal, but we rejected this proposal for the time being, at least, in the hope that the measure we proposed would secure the desired result with a minimum disruption of legitimate news-dissemination activities.

IX. Another amendment to the internal revenue laws was proposed which would require any person engaged for the past five years in illegitimate activities, netting him more than $2500 a year, to file a net-worth statement of all his assets, along with his income tax returns. It is difficult to pin income tax evasions on lawbreakers without some starting point to show that they have concealed their gains. As Assistant Attorney General Lamar Caudle pointed out, proof of a lawbreaker's net worth usually is the best point from which to begin to prove he has lied in reporting his income.

X. It should be illegal to use the telegraph, telephone, or any other interstate communications facilities, including the United States mails, for transmission across state lines of bets; also of currency, checks, money orders, or other means of payment of such wagers. This bill is aimed squarely at the big-time gamblers and gambling syndicates who, in connection with their illegal operations, keep millions of dollars moving constantly throughout the country.

XI. The present law against interstate transportation of slot machines should be extended to include the other gambling devices on which individual racketeers and organized crime syndicates thrive, such as punchboards, roulette wheels, and so forth. We noted that "the lowly punchboard has attained the proportion of a major racketeering enterprise in many sections of the country."

XII. Penalties against the illegal sale, distribution, and smuggling of narcotic drugs should be increased substantially. There is an alarming rise in the use of narcotics, particularly among teen-agers, who begin with marijuana and gradually become hopeless addicts to heroin and cocaine. The average prison sentence meted out to narcotics traffickers is eighteen months, and, as Narcotics Commissioner Anslinger told us, "short sentences do not deter." The committee endorsed the commissioner's recommendation that the law be amended to fix a mandatory penalty of at least five years' imprisonment for dope peddlers and others engaged in commercial aspects of the narcotics traffic, on conviction for a second offense. Passage of such a bill has been recommended by the House Ways and Means Committee.

XIII. Immigration laws should be amended to facilitate deportation of undesirable aliens, including criminals. Earlier in these pages I expressed myself fully on the need for putting teeth in the denaturalization and deportation laws. The committee endorsed a legislative proposal to this effect, which has been recommended by the immigration commissioner and was under study, as this was written, by the Senate Judiciary Committee.

XIV. Likewise the Immigration Act of February 5, 1917, should be amended to provide punishment for smuggling, concealing, or harboring aliens who are not entitled by law to enter or reside in the United States. We endorsed legislation on this point which has been recommended by the Justice Department. The proposed amendment would correct a Supreme Court decision which holds there is no provision under present law by which a person may be punished for smuggling or otherwise assisting an illegal alien.

XV. The Attorney General should be empowered to revoke suspensions of deportations and to make such revocations grounds for canceling naturalization certificates granted to aliens who were able to become citizens by taking advantage of various loopholes in the present law.

XVI. The committee went on record as favoring in general increases in personnel of seriously understaffed federal law enforcement agencies and elimination of inequities in the salaries of these federal law enforcement officers, many of whom, we noted, "are woefully underpaid" for the difficult and dangerous duties they perform. The committee commented:

"It should be borne in mind that higher salaries for persons engaged in law enforcement will not necessarily result in a drain on the Treasury. Better law enforcement will bring increased revenues to the government through collection of taxes which undoubtedly are now being avoided by the underworld. Spending of more money to compensate enforcement employees adequately will mean that reduced tribute will be paid to racketeers and gangsters by persons who unknowingly depend on gangster-infiltrated businesses for the purchase of commodities or services in their own communities. It is indeed a fact, well established by testimony before this committee, that where crime has enabled the gangster to infiltrate into legitimate business, the average consumer has to pay increased costs, as witness the waterfront rackets, through which millions of dollars in tribute are exacted by the racketeer—all of which ultimately comes out of the pocket of the consumer."

XVII. The committee had plenty of experience with witnesses who obviously were committing perjury. Present federal laws defining the rules for convictions in perjury cases are so stringent that many of those who lied under oath before the Crime Committee could not be punished. The committee favored a bill backed by the Attorney General, tightening up the perjury laws and cutting some of the red tape that presently is a bar to effective prosecution.

XVIII. One of the weaknesses in the proceedings of the Crime Committee was the fact that we had no power, such as can be exercised by some state grand juries, to grant witnesses immunity from prosecution. The Fifth Amendment to the federal Constitution provides that no person "shall be compelled in any criminal case to be a witness against himself." This gave many witnesses an excuse to defy us by claiming that their constitutional rights would be violated if they answered our questions. In many cases, quite obviously, these claims were completely without merit, and the committee was forced to recommend contempt citations which subsequently were voted by the Senate against some thirty-three recalcitrant witnesses.

The committee recommended that the Attorney General of the United States should be given authority to grant immunity from prosecution on federal charges to witnesses whose testimony is essential to an inquiry conducted by a congressional committee or by a federal grand jury. If we could have granted such immunity to certain witnesses we would undoubtedly have received much more information—though I have no illusions that some of the hoodlums before us would have refused to testify under any circumstances. In the latter cases, where witnesses remained defiant even though granted immunity, prosecution for contempt would be enormously simplified. We advised, however, that "this power . . . should be exercised only with the greatest caution, and only upon the written permission of the Attorney General after he has cleared the granting of immunity with other federal agencies which might have an interest in the matter." We would not want the immunity clause to be exploited by lawbreakers into an instrument for escaping prosecution.

XIX. The committee had repeated experiences with witnesses who evaded service of subpoenas "with obvious intent to hinder and delay the committee's investigation." Therefore we recommended that congressional committees be given the same right permitted federal courts to secure service of a subpoena on a witness who could not be found otherwise by legal publication of the fact that he is wanted and by leaving a copy of the subpoena at his home or place of business. With this provision, a witness who evaded personal service of a subpoena, once arrested, could be punished for contempt. Under present rules such a witness may be arrested but not punished for contempt.

XX. The committee has introduced a bill, recommended by the Treasury's Alcohol Tax Unit, designed to prevent racketeering elements from entering the wholesale liquor industry and to eliminate such elements now entrenched in it. On this line, previously introduced bills, which would require liquor distributors to secure yearly renewals of their federal licenses, are pending in Congress. At present no periodic renewal is required. Feeling that annual renewal might place too much of a burden on both the liquor industry and, from an enforcement standpoint, on the ATU—also "that such a bill would seriously impair the industry's ability to obtain credit"—the committee recommended that renewal be required every two years, instead of annually. We already have introduced such a bill in the Senate. However, we stated our belief "that the industry is overfearful" of the effect that such a bill would have on its ability to obtain financial credit. We felt strongly that many racketeering elements now are so firmly entrenched in the liquor distributing business under the original post-repeal legislation that the only effective means of eliminating them would be such a bill, requiring biennial scrutiny of who's who in the liquor business.

We also took note of the extremely serious problem of bootlegging liquor into dry and local option states. Such a racket has been set up by a number of old-time prohibition era hoodlums. To provide a weapon against this new post-repeal racket, we recommended that the Bureau of Internal Revenue take steps to require careful identification of applicants who come in to buy the special tax stamps required of retail and wholesale liquor dealers.

XXI. As a further weapon in the needed drive to purge the liquor industry of its racketeering elements, we recommended that a present federal regulation requiring a listing only of individual owners, partners, and holders of ATU permits be amended so as to require, in addition, the listing of names of all persons who benefit financially from the business. We also recommended that application forms for such permits require disclosure under oath of any arrests and convictions by any of the parties whose names would appear. To this proposed reform we secured the acquiescence of representatives of the liquor industry.

XXII. Finally there was the recommendation which I outlined in Chapter 14, dealing with the infiltration of Joe Adonis and other notorious criminal characters into the interstate trucking business. The Interstate Commerce Commission would be required to consider the "moral fitness" of applicants for the necessary operating certificates in the interstate transportation industry, before such licenses were issued by the ICC. As in the case of liquor distributors, we also proposed that all officers, directors, and principal stockholders of interstate trucking and transit companies be listed under oath in connection with the application for permits.

While it was outside our jurisdiction to make recommendations for actions on state and local levels, the committee, with the help of state and municipal authorities, learned of numerous serious defects in non-federal laws which make easier the operations of the national crime syndicate. We made several suggestions for corrective action that might be considered on state and local levels. I shall not review all of them here, but some of the suggestions included creation of more state and local crime commissions (which, in general, where they are set up, have achieved effective results); more local rackets investigations by unhampered grand juries; and the clearing up of jurisdictional arguments between local law enforcement officers, which usually result in the lawbreaker escaping all punishment.

I have come now to the end of my story.

It is not the end, however, but only the beginning for the cause to which we of the Crime Committee dedicated ourselves in May 1950.

We uncovered the ugly, dirty truth about the infection of politico-criminal corruption that is eating away at the strong, healthy tissues of our nation.

We shall not stop battling against the politico-criminal alliance. I want to battle it with effective, concrete action.

That is why, on the day that the last report of the Crime Committee under my chairmanship was submitted to the United States Senate, I took the floor to urge:

"I trust that members of the Congress and the public will not feel, since the life of the committee has been extended for four months, that there should be a letup in the vigorous presentation of the legislative recommendations which are contained in the report. We feel that these recommendations, if enacted into law, virtually will bring to an end the big-time racketeering in interstate commerce, which is the basis of a great deal of the criminality in the country today. . . . The time is at hand for an all-out effort against these criminal activities at all levels of government—federal, state, and local. . . ."

Earlier in these pages I expressed my concern over the terrible power and ruthlessness of the enemy we are fighting in the national crime syndicate. This concern does not spell defeatism. To the contrary, the more I learned about the nature of the evil thing with which we are confronted, the more determined I became that the American people, sufficiently aroused, *can* and *must* strangle the national crime syndicate and put the syndicate's foul leaders where they belong.

I look about the country and see the continuing and expanding results of what our committee has started: numerous states are setting up their own legislative committees to dig into intrastate crime along the pattern which our committee developed on a national scale. Local grand juries are joining the anti-crime crusade with zeal. Towns once wide open to vice and gambling are cleaning up, and the crooked officeholders who fattened on the bribes of the lawbreakers they protected are crawling for cover. The new racket and fraud squads of the Justice Department and Internal Revenue Bureau are going into action, and some stirrings are evident from other agencies which have been half asleep for generations. Criminals of the lowest order, who for years have sneered at the law and successfully evaded payment of any penalty for their illegal acts, are going to jail.

All these things are tremendously heartening, and when I see them I am confident that, if we keep it up and do not relax our vigor, we can put the Frank Costellos, the Joe Adonises (already in jail), the Zwillmans, the Anastasias, the Marcellos, the Guziks and Accardos, the Tony Gizzos, the Mickey Cohens, the smug Jimmy Carrolls and Kleinmans and Rothkopfs—and all the rest—out of business.

However, I have a message for all the tens of thousands of American citizens who, when the activity of the committee was at fever pitch, took the trouble to write and tell us they were behind us. I address myself to Mr. and Mrs. Clarence Ernst, of Fort Loramie, Ohio, who wrote: "Yes, get these rats out that are robbing the small people of all rights"; to the woman in Bradford, Ohio, who signed herself "One who is hot under the collar" and who told us: "Surely the American people never have taken such an interest in our country as in the last few months"; to Erskine H. Early, of Spring Hill, Tennessee, who said: "No matter what groups may oppose you, keep up your work and efforts because the folks at the crossroads, the plowhandle and the drill presses are behind you. They don't forget— God bless you"; to Paul Harber, of the Chamber of Commerce in Cartersville, Georgia, who wrote: "John Doe on Main Street, U.S.A., Henry Roe on Broad Street, U.S.A., and all their cousins in Hickory Hollow have been shocked to learn of the conditions your Committee brought to light"; and to Robert Bekeart, of Honolulu, who asked, simply, "Is there any way a citizen can assist you in your tasks?"

Yes, Robert Bekeart, and all the thousands like you who asked, "Is there any way we can help?"—there is a way. In your local communities and your state legislatures there is much to be done in the way of beneficial legislation, in arousing public opinion against the local hoodlums, and in strengthening the hands of your honest local and state officials. Then study our list of twenty-two recommendations to the Congress and to the law enforcement agencies of the country. Read them slowly and carefully, for, in cold print, they are not nearly as exciting as the live drama of seeing Rudy Halley on the television screen, coldly dissecting a Costello, or Charles Tobey venting his righteous wrath on a crooked sheriff.

But the broad answer to the Costellos and the crooked officers and officials lies in those recommendations. Get behind us and help us get those laws passed. There is going to be powerful opposition, not only from the national crime syndicate, whose influence, as we have shown you, is strong and whose financial and political resources are powerful. There will be passive opposition, too, from the natural inertia that operates against any far-reaching program of social reform. But, I repeat, get behind us; help us pass those bills which will provide the ammunition for the war against organized crime in America.

It is in the hope that you—all the people of America who want this wonderful land of ours to be a decent, honorable place for us, our children, and the generations to come—will help us that I have written this book.